T0401326

Heritage and Its Missions

Heritage and Its Missions

CONTESTED MEANINGS AND CONSTRUCTIVE APPROPRIATIONS

Cristóbal Gnecco and Adriana Schmidt Dias, Editors

FORDHAM UNIVERSITY PRESS
New York 2025

Visit us online at www.fordhampress.com.

Library of Congress Cataloging-in-Publication Data available online at https://catalog.loc.gov.

Printed in the United States of America

27 26 25   5 4 3 2 1

First edition

Contents

Heritage and Its Missions

Introduction

CRISTÓBAL GNECCO AND
ADRIANA SCHMIDT DIAS

Investigations on heritage, ranging from the empirical to the theoretical, from the local to the global, have flourished in the last two decades. While many studies try to understand just what heritage is about (highlighting its function alongside collective histories, such as that of the nation) and provide arguments for its promotion and protection, others have adopted a critical stance for examining its entanglement with politics, identity, and knowledge. As a result, the focus on empirical, technical, and legal concerns—research, protection, and exhibition of objects and sites—has shifted to issues of narratives, publics, and even performances. Interdisciplinary in scope and classed under the name "critical heritage studies," these investigations make extensive use of ethnographic perspectives to examine heritage not as a collection of inert things (or intangibles, to use more recent parlance) upon which a general historical interest is centered, but as a series of active meanings that have consequences in the social, political, and economic arenas. An ethnographic approach to the matter—that is, a preoccupation with the effects of heritage-related activities (excavation, exhibition, curation, dissemination) upon local publics and, conversely, with the way local publics engage them—consider the places of interaction between heritage discourses and local publics (sites, museums, books, videos, booklets) as constructed spaces where the very materiality of the social and the political unfolds.

Such critical, relational approaches are beginning to have a bearing in studies of the heritage meanings accorded to the standing remains and the legacy of the pre-Republican Catholic missions in the old Spanish realm in the Americas, most notably in California, the Sonoran Desert (southwestern United States and northern Mexico), and the Southern Cone. The missions have attracted the attention of several stakeholders since the nineteenth century, but only in the last two decades have they begun to be seen seriously as heritage object-signs by scholars and Indigenous activists. Yet, no academic event had been devoted to engaging those meanings in comparative terms, exploring issues that are important for a number of actors/collectives, not just those related to the states and the disciplines. This book, conceived precisely in that spirit, brings together the presentations made at a symposium we organized in Dumbarton Oaks at the end of 2020. It summoned researchers from several countries interested in the missions as heritage.

The essays in this book aim to discuss past and current heritage meanings accorded to the missions by national and multicultural states, local communities (especially, but not exclusively, Indigenous ones), international heritage institutions, and scholars (historians, archaeologists, anthropologists, heritage experts, and the like). Around and through those meanings struggles of various kinds and intensities, some of which are decisively counter-hegemonic, have been taking place. The understanding of such struggles show how global policies on heritage are performed locally, even if the purported heritage is of colonial origin, such as that of the Catholic missions. The papers address: (a) how heritage actors produce knowledge from their positioned perspectives; (b) how different actors, collectives, communities, and publics relate to them; (c) how heritage representations are deployed (and many times countered) as social facts; and (d) how different conceptions of "heritage" collide, collaborate, and intersperse in order to produce the meanings around which heritage struggles unfold.

The mission legacy, which is way more comprehensive and far-reaching than the (codified) heritage meanings accorded to the individual missions, is still paramount in the Americas, where the civilization / savagery dichotomy is not a thing of the past but a living monster of the present. The civilizational spirit of the missions not only survives in the heritage celebration; it is also alive in the way it haunts national and post-national histories and projections. Since the mid-nineteenth century and then from the 1950s onward, the discourse on progress and development, respectively, took over the civilizational role left by the dwindling missions: a secular discourse complemented, more than replaced, a centuries-old religious narrative. In this regard, the importance of the missions cannot be underestimated. They started the ignominious path of modern-colonial interventions on Indigenous societies that continues to this date.

The Missions in the Americas

The rapid expansion of the Spanish colonial frontier in the Americas was accompanied by the decisive participation of the Catholic Church. As Herbert Bolton (1917, 42–43) pointed out in an essay published over a century ago:

> In the Spanish colonies the men to whom fell the task of extending and holding the frontiers were the conquistador, the presidial soldier, and the missionary. All of these agents were important; but in my study of frontier institutions in general, and in my endeavor in particular to understand the methods and forces by which Spain's frontiers were extended, held, and developed, I have been more and more impressed with the importance of the mission as a pioneering agency.

As Bolton abundantly noted in his prolific work, the missions were frontier institutions. Ever since the beginning of the Spanish conquest in what would become Mexico, the role of the Catholic Church in the subjection of Indigenous societies was paramount, from the creation of *colegios* to convert the young elite to the construction and functioning of monasteries and churches for the population at large and to the teaching of doctrine in native languages. Catholicism meant civilization. Only ten years elapsed from the conquest of Tenochtitlán (1521) to the appearance of the virgin in the Tepeyac (1531), an astonishingly rapid tour de force with few parallels in world history. Several orders were involved in the feat, especially Franciscans and Jesuits, following a rigid script in which the salvation of the savages had the leading role. The Mexican experience was soon replicated elsewhere, most notably in the Central Andes.

The missions were an important part of the overall project of the Catholic Church in the Americas, one of the three projects that coexisted during colonial times in the region and that more often than not were at odds regarding their ultimate goals—the two others being that of the Spanish and Portuguese crowns, mostly preoccupied with the existence and protection of potential tribute-payers, and that of the settlers, eager to have cheap (if not free) labor, no matter if their practices led to an acute demographic collapse of the Indigenous population. The church wanted souls, newborns in the faith it represented, portrayed as the only legitimate one amid a plethora of savage idolatries. To pursue this goal the church countered the crowns and the settlers whenever necessary;

this also meant that the Indians felt relatively protected in the missions (to a certain extent) from the settlers' greed. Protection ran parallel with conversion, however, giving to the missions a capital role in the destruction of Native cultures. Their function was not only religious, but also civil and political, adding to their importance.

Throughout the three long centuries that preceded the wars of independence there were missions in every conceivable frontier and biome—desserts, forests, savannas—all over the continent, wherever the savages were to be found. Although there were missions all over the Americas, this is not tantamount to saying that they all were of the same importance. Three regions stand out as emblems of what Catholicism achieved in civilizational terms: California, the Sonoran Desert, and the Southern Cone. Their success was undeniable: they reduced immense populations to village life; taught them the arts of civilization (literacy, doctrine, music, advanced craftsmanship, rudimentary science, animal husbandry); established the canon of a historical narrative (baptism as birth in civilization; culture as reigning over nature; evolution as an unavoidable leap forward) crucial to national and regional identities (that is, to white and mestizo identities); and set the model of what a pious, non-savage life could mean (discipline, obedience, temperance, containment). In doing so, they paved the road for other forms of modern-colonial occupation, still extant. Yet, the relevance of these three areas must also be assessed in temporal terms beyond their functioning existence, given that missions in other areas also succeeded: the physical survival of some of the mission buildings adds to their eventual significance; their ruins or their later recast, some quite impressive, were to be a fundamental contribution to their imprint and importance. Yet, another argument accrues to their current significance: as in the case of slavery—whose contemporary, contentious presence in specific countries, as Trouillot (1995) argued, was not based on its past imprint as much as in its current role in racial tensions—the extant (and even augmented) relevance of the missions is tied to their later part (even when they had already ceased to exist as functioning entities) in those national histories where the civilization/savagery dichotomy was (and still is) of the utmost importance—Unites States, Mexico, Brazil, Argentina, Paraguay.

The missions constituted a relatively autonomous civilizing project that had a strong and lasting influence on the lives of the Indigenous societies they contributed to subdue; they were also a reference to how the policy of nucleation and conversion promoted by Spain (and Portugal, to a lesser extent) should, or should not, be carried out. Indeed, the mission's legacy still appears as a notable example, whether as idealized and bucolic, purely utopian model of coexistence, or as a peaceful way of inserting the Indians into modernity—getting around the fact that it happened through religious violence. It was, say, a civilized way of civilizing, the realization of the Lascasian dream. Later on, in the twentieth century, that way was iterated by indigenism, a secular heir of the missions.

Although the missions in the Americas played a similar pivotal role, that of being a beachhead of civilization, their historical trajectory was far from being uniform, as the essays in this book testify. They fit differently in the historical puzzle according to the conditions adopted by the colonial order in specific areas—a puzzle mostly composed of the importance of Catholicism before other projects, of the strength of regional and panregional identities, and of the characteristics of the regimes of otherness. In this regard, the missions were a rhetoric battleground where clashing views of the Hispanic-white legacy in the Americas were deployed: while Bolton (1933) stressed its uniformity, O'Gorman (1942) highlighted its differences. Referring to Bolton's argument, O'Gorman (1942, 225) noted:

> Two capital errors were thus made: believing that a total structure of continental history can only be conceived based on similarities between the histories of the two Americas, and believing that true knowledge of those histories consists, precisely, in discovering those similarities. But among the most different things it is always possible to find similarities; however, this says nothing; the important thing is to stand out the differences that reveal to us the individuality and peculiarity of what is compared. Only in this way we can distinguish them, that is, know them.

This clash is important for the comparative perspective of this book, for it brings to the fore fundamental differences in the missionary project in the three areas it deals with. Those differences are not restricted to the past but, importantly, have a bearing in the present and what can be glimpsed of the future.

California

The Franciscans accompanied the Spanish expansion into the unknown and unconquered northern frontier of the New Spain late in the eighteenth century, eventually establishing twenty-one missions in Alta California from 1769 to 1823 (Haas 2014; Hackel 2005; Sandos 2004). At their peak, they "had over thirty thousand Indians under instruction" (Bolton 1917, 45) (Figure 1). They were secularized in 1834 but given back to the Catholic Church in 1865, becoming centers of a civil-religious devotion fundamental for the white-civilization narrative. The missions not only converted to the Catholic faith a wealth of Native peoples—among them Chumash, Tongva, Salinan, Ohlone, and Kumeyaay, some of them no-madic hunter-gatherers at the time, but also reduced them and used their labor for mission and extra-mission purposes (Silliman 2001).

The ruins of the missions, the majority fully restored to their original grandeur (unlike most of the missions in the other two areas this book deals with) and acting centers of worship again, became heritage targets since at least the 1930s, symbolic anchors of what it meant (and still means) to be civilized. Not surprisingly, it was the legacy of the padres that was

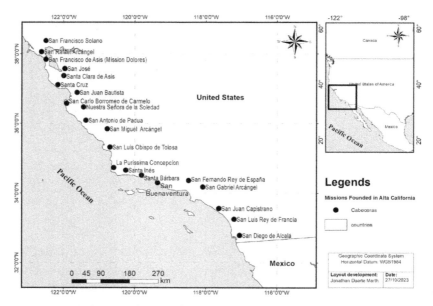

FIGURE 1. Map locating the sites of the twenty-one missions in California. (Drawn by Jonathan Duarte Marth, 2023)

exalted, leaving no voice to the subjected populations. Even though that narrative has been revised to a large extent, especially in the last two decades, thanks to Indigenous activism, the missions still gather quite a lot of attention and are superstars in the market of things historical in California (leaving their mark in architecture, literature, art, and other various cultural products), a market that not only commodifies but also supports a one-sided story, that of the triumph of civilization over savagery.

In 2015, the canonization of Junípero Serra, the main actor in the California missions (he founded nine of them and presided over another fifteen), adds to the glorification of the missions and their purposes. Serra has also been consecrated at the national level in civil temples—like the Capitol building in Washington, where he was honored with a statue in the National Statuary Hall "devoted to sculptures of prominent Americans," even though Serra was Spanish, an irrelevant fact, given his paramount contribution to the American civilizational crusade—and in civil milieu, such as the postal service, which issued a stamp honoring him as late as 1986. At the regional level, Serra (embodying in his name the whole of the Franciscan's achievements) is one of the most prominent and revered historical figures (Hackel 2013).

The missions are important pedagogical players. In California the drive toward incorporating the civilizational narrative of the missions in the school curricula was forceful, especially from 1920 to 1965, with the instillment of state pride—that is to say, of the legacy of the white pioneers—among which Serra ranks high (Gutfreund 2010; Kryder-Reid 2016). That means that most Californians were raised, from elementary years, with the idea that the missions were something good that happened to the Indians; that they bestowed upon them the blessings of civilization and gave them the unique opportunity to shed away their retrograde savagery. Until recent years, no counterpart—a balanced story showing the darker side of the missionary project or the Indigenous views on the missions, for instance—was offered. Two large projects—the "California Indian History Curriculum Coalition (CIHCC), a confluence of California Indians, activists, educators, allies, and policy makers who are working to teach a history that incorporates Native California perspectives" (Schneider et al. 2019, 59), and the UCLA-led grant program Critical Mission Studies—are designed to help achieve that turning point. The prominent role in educational matters they have enjoyed for several decades marks an important difference of the California missions with the missions' legacy and imprint in the Sonoran Desert and the Southern Cone. Notwithstanding its importance, or perhaps because of it, this battlefield occupied most of the Indigenous contest against the missions and left other spaces relatively empty until recently.

The heritage meaning of the missions also interested other stakeholders, not just white Anglos and Indigenes. Mexican Americans felt that their claim to the official heritage meaning of the missions "forged ties to white privilege" (Gutfreund 2010, 180–81). The Chicano movement, however, took a different path: "Rather than appealing to a wider Anglo audience . . . Chicano youths angrily rejected the Spanish fantasy past. Turning to their Indian heritage as a marker of minority status, Chicano radicals rode the wave of protests that swept into cities across the country in 1968" (184).

Sonoran Desert

The Jesuits established twenty missions in a part of the Sonoran Desert (known as Pimería Alta), in the southern United States and northern Mexico, between 1647 and 1704 (Figure 2), although the missions were besieged by instability (triggered, as it seems, by the opposition of the local tribes) since the 1680s (Almada et al. 2007). Some missions languished after the expulsion of the Jesuits, while others boomed under different orders; at any rate, their nucleation effect remained. The Native peoples reduced at those missions were, above all, O'odham (*pima* and *pápagos*) and Comcaac (*seris*). As in California, the missions were civilizing centers.

These missions also had a central protagonist, Eusebio Kino, around whom their civilizing role is still articulated (Polzer 1998). He founded twenty missions and wrote a report to the Spanish king in 1710 (Bolton 1919) detailing a process that cannot be labeled but as a conquest, albeit religious . . . with military assistance—in which repression and sheer violence played a pivotal role (Hausberger 1993)—no wonder, given the fierce opposition presented by the Indigenous nations amid which the missions were established (Mirafuentes 1993). The link between the religious project of the missions and the political project of the sovereignty of the nation-states in the Americas lingered until the twentieth century. Colombian

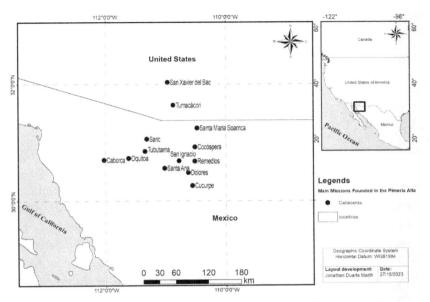

FIGURE 2. Map locating the sites of some of the missions in the Sonoran Desert in southern United States and northern Mexico. (Drawn by Jonathan Duarte Marth, 2023)

politician Rafael Uribe (1907) outlined at the onset of that century his project for dealing with frontier Indians, in which his "savages reduction machine" was paramount; as in California and the Sonoran Desert, the three sprockets in the machine were the soldier, the professor, and the missionary.

Not unlike with California and the Southern Cone, the historiography of the missions in the Sonoran Desert was dominated by an ardent defense and eulogy of the missionaries—Kino was also enshrined, as was Serra, with a statue in the United States Statuary Hall as one of the two representatives of Arizona—to the detriment of Indigenous agency. Yet, and also as in the other two regions, the situation has notably changed to acknowledge not only the effects of the missions over the lives of the Indigenous populations (showing how the missionary project meant a profound cultural, social, economic, and political transformation), but also the active role of the latter (Reff 1991; Spicer 1994; Radding 1997; Almada et al. 2007; Hausberger 2015).

Perhaps because the Sonoran Desert does not epitomize the civilizational dream embodied in California—it is a non-glamorous desert with few economic attractions, relatively unimportant for the white gaze, save that of the hippies, but even that as late as the 1960s, its missions have not received the same heritage attention, and only a handful of them has been restored through the years.

Southern Cone

In the seventeenth century the Jesuits created thirty missions in the territory of the Guarani, one of the largest Indigenous groups at the time, in what are now southwestern Brazil, southeastern Paraguay, and northeastern Argentina—a region known in colonial times as the "Jesuit Province of Paraguay" or "Paracuaria" (Figure 3). The missions established by the Jesuits in Guarani territory between 1632 and 1767 (which subsisted, albeit diminished, till the early nineteenth century) organized communal life, built temples and houses, tilled the land (especially with mate and cotton), established ranches, and created a centralized, large-scale trade. The missions were true towns (some with up to 6,000 inhabitants) grouped around imposing stone churches and other buildings. The Indians were drawn to the missions and settled in or around them, though not without a great deal of resistance to colonial imposition, not just religious. There they were instructed in religion, literacy, weaving, wood carving, iron works, stonework, agriculture, and music. At the height of its power (around 1730), the thirty missions gathered some 130,000 Indians (Maeder and Bolsi 1980). One of the main features of the missions was their relative autonomy—religious, of course, but also political, administrative, and economic. That virtue was their doom: by the mid-eighteenth century the missionary project clashed with the Spanish and Portuguese crowns because it had become a loose wheel with its own purpose (the conversion of souls), at times quite apart from imperial policies, economic and otherwise (e.g., Becker 1982). This clash and several others in the metropolitan and colonial realms ended with the expulsion of the Jesuits from the Portuguese (1759) and Spanish (1767) empires. Although other religious orders, especially the Franciscans, took over after the expulsion of the Jesuits, the remaining missions were abandoned or closed by force in the first decades of the nineteenth century, which resulted in the dispersion and fragmentation of the Guarani that had been nucleated. The Guarani population in the missions was dispersed, resettled, or "liberated" (Wilde 2001).

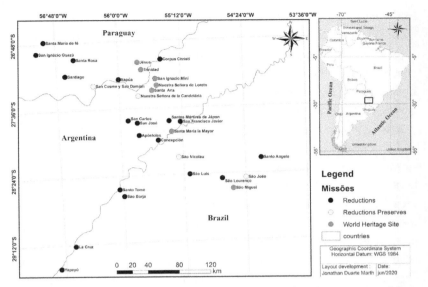

FIGURE 3. Map locating the sites of the thirty missions in colonial Paracuaria and their current locations in Paraguay, Argentina, and Brazil. (Drawn by Jonathan Duarte Marth, 2020)

The constructions of most of the missions soon turned into ruins, some of which became a part of the daily landscape of the new settlers of the region, mostly European immigrants. Yet, the civilizational imprint of the missions survived, albeit differently, in the national histories of the three countries created in the region after 1810. Heritage concerns started in the region in different moments and for apparently different, yet similar reasons. The missions, in particular, came to regional attention in Argentina late in the nineteenth century, when the northern frontier had no place in the nation. Later on, the nation itself became interested. In Brazil, the elevation of the ruins of the missions to heritage started in the 1930s, in close association with the nationalism of the New State (Estado Novo). How those colonial ruins with a Spanish imprint became icons of things Brazilian in a modern guise could be intriguing, but it is not. It was their civilizational aura that won their respect, as in Argentina a few decades earlier. In Paraguay, after the War of the Triple Alliance (1864–70), the process of national construction was exacerbated. The place of the Jesuits (and their missions) in the nation was bitterly discussed, but not that of the Indians, who had (and still have) no place in the national scene. These considerations—a mix of nationalism, regional pride, and civilization—explain a curious and tragic oxymoron: a colonial legacy becoming heritage for all in young nation-states that were striving to become modern by leaving behind their colonial pasts—this in spite of the fact that the historical role of the missions and the Jesuits was not consensual and that some thought that theirs was not a legacy worth remembering but a part of the heinous colonial epoch: backward and obscurantist.

More recently, the inclusion of the ruins of seven missions in the world heritage list of UNESCO in 1984 and 1993 has placed their renewed heritage meaning in a formerly inexistent global discourse—that of a humanistic/mercantile heritage—that is currently challenged by Indigenous peoples, eager to claim the historical/mythical meaning of the missions as their own and from their own particular ontologies; indeed, the mission experience also lingers in ethnic (non-national) memories, such as in the oral (and nowadays even written and visual) traditions of the Guarani currently inhabiting the area (de Souza 1998; Garlet and Assis 2002; Ladeira 2007; de Souza et al. 2012). The missions also have heritage importance for the descendants of European immigrants who settled in the region from the 1850s onward. A curious *missionary culture* (given that the relationship of the new settlers to missions who had disappeared as functioning institutions decades before is exclusively tied to their religious and civilizational deeds, not to the existence of historical ties) has been crafted and is periodically reinforced in ceremonies, gatherings, and merchandising (see Wilde 2003).

The Essays in This Book

We have allotted the chapters into two parts. The first one, "Alternative Readings of Heritage: Subjects, Alterization, and the Different Meanings of the Past," groups five essays that present how heritage meanings (mostly, but not exclusively, linked to ethnic agendas) that depart from the official script are constructed and deployed.

Guillermo Wilde considers that the heritage meaning of the South American Jesuitic missions are a symbolic construction, the product of long-term history in continuous transformation. In the chapter "Crisis of the 'Heritage Order': Disputed Representations of the Jesuit Missions'

Past," Wilde shows how over the last two centuries the Jesuit missionary past was the subject of disputes in the countries of the Southern Cone. In the second half of the eighteenth century, the missions had an important place in the Enlightenment. In that same century, an ideological polarization emerged between apologetics and detractors of the Jesuits' project that culminated with their expulsion. In the second half of the nineteenth century, the erratic efforts of nation-states in the Southern Cone accelerated the destruction of the structures of the ancient missions. Only since the late 1930s have the missions been the subject of official heritage policies in Brazil and Argentina, with a strong technical approach focused on the restauration of the ruins, which emphasized the monumental and artistic dimension of the sites following international legislation. In Paraguay this process was only initiated in the 1970s from an initiative of the Catholic Church interested in revitalizing the myth of the civilizing missionary, soon entering in conflict with the secular gaze of international heritage policies that culminated with the UNESCO declaration of seven mission ruins as world heritage. In the last twenty years, the inclusion of new perspectives has contributed to a renovated understanding of the mission's past as an inherently fragmentary and disputed phenomenon. The current moment is characterized by the growing participation of local communities in (re)defining conservation policies in order to include traditionally relegated actors and perspectives, such as the Mbyá-Guarani communities that live in the old territory of the missions and the current inhabitants of the towns where the mission sites are located, for the most part a migrant population of European origin that settled in the region at the end of the nineteenth century and beginnings of the twentieth century.

Some 20,000 Mbyá-Guarani currently live in the former mission's area, of which more than half are in Paraguay. The expansion of soybean agriculture in the 1970s spread the Mbyá-Guarani over a large territory extending from the Argentine forests, between the Paraná and Uruguay rivers, to the Atlantic coast of southern and southeastern Brazil. The relationship of the Mbyá and the missions varies according to the indigenist and heritage policies of each country. In the chapter "Semiotic Policies in Conflict at São Miguel Arcanjo Mission (Brazil)," Adriana Schmidt Dias analyzes a project led by the Brazilian heritage agency between 2004 and 2014 to document Mbyá-Guarani appropriation of the ruins as an intangible asset. During this process the official civilizing discourse did not disappear, and the missions became a place of performance for distinct and conflicting notions of "being in time": the Western historicity and its notion of heritage as opposed to the Mbyá-Guarani historicity and its notion of belonging. To the Mbyá-Guarani the ruins of the missions are not a monument of their defeat in the past but a place that gives visibility to their struggles for the right to a transnational Indigenous territory in the present. The struggle of the Mbyá-Guarani to defend their historical meaning of the missions is, therefore, a political act to avoid submission to official heritage discourses that, in the name of diversity, depoliticize other symbolic fields and, ultimately, attempts to appropriate the Indigenous cultural capital to increase the symbolic value of heritage assets under UNESCO custody as a touristic commodity.

In the chapter "Teaching Missions, Training Citizens: The California Missions as Curriculum," Elizabeth Kryder-Reid explores the ideological implications of the missions as pedagogical instruments in formal and informal learning experiences that have the potential to shape public understanding of the past and of its ongoing role in the present. For Kryder-Reid, analyzing the construction of the Franciscan missions' experience in California's fourth-grade social studies curriculum is a productive entry into a critical examination of heritage meanings in the United States. The California missions have played a well-documented role in the construction of what has been called the "Spanish fantasy past," an imagined version of colonial history that celebrates a romanticized Mediterranean aesthetic and presents the past as a white-centered triumphalist narrative. While erasing the oppression implied in the colonial project, this settler colonial narrative elevates the padres as civilizing heroes. In the past decades, educators, tribal scholars, and Native activists have advocated for a curricular reform that includes Indigenous voices and challenges racist practices that perpetuated the violence of settler colonialism. As a result of these efforts to decolonize both education and heritage fields, the current history–social science framework in California explores the role of the missions in public memory and the ways in which official narratives and dissident counternarratives expose religious and heritage tensions. The ultimate question highlighted by Kryder-Reid is whether the educational apparatus has the courage to acknowledge the painful injustices of the past and to create the space to include all voices and experiences.

An important initiative to oppose "the politics of erasure" that serves to limit Indigenous sovereignty across California is presented by Lee Panich and Charlene Nijmeh in their chapter, "Native Heritage and the California Missions: A Collaborative Approach at Mission Santa Clara." For the authors, the physical attributes of mission sites have shaped the different ways in which Native peoples, scholars, and the general public have engaged them. Their standing architecture, the romanticized recreations of buildings and landscapes, and what has survived below ground in the archaeological record are significant elements in the general notion of the missions as heritage. Some 11,000 individuals were baptized at mission Santa Clara de Asís until the 1840s, most of them belonging to Ohlone tribes. After that, Indigenous peoples were alienated from the mission lands when the territory was claimed by Mexican elites and by settlers from the United States. The Jesuits founded Santa Clara College at the site of mission Santa Clara in 1851, but the residents only assigned significant Euro-American heritage value to the campus; in the early twentieth century the United States government declared the Ohlone to be extinct. Only in the 1980s and 1990s were the questions about the Indigenous heritage brought to light by a project of archaeological mitigation at Santa Clara University Campus that affected the mission's cemetery. Federal and state laws governing cultural resources require varying levels of consultation with tribal groups, particularly when human remains are encountered. Given the fact that some 7,500 Native individuals are buried at mission Santa Clara, CRM projects on the SCU campus provided an opportunity for Ohlone communities to propose a counternarrative to the official heritage discourse from a collaborative and interdisciplinary perspective.

The heritagization of the missionary past associated with the demands of contemporary cultural tourism tend to value positive and passive representations about Indigenous history, often erasing the memories of violence. In the chapter "Heritage at Stake: The Contemporary Guarani and the Missions," Cristóbal Gnecco asks why the historical relation of the current Guarani people with the missions is highly contested in the heritage field. Disciplinary arguments usually exclude the political context in which they unfold and to which they contribute, while political arguments ignore the academic context. The civilizing deed of the missions was resignified since their ruins were elevated to world heritage and the creation of the Common Market of the Southern Cone started a search for a common history and, above all, for common commodities. This new context has placed the missions' ruins in a formerly inexistent global and multicultural discourse focused on cultural tourism, currently challenged by Indigenous peoples from their ethnic and non-national ontologies. The civilizational imprint of the missions still lingers, and the current academic traditions and heritage interventions are additional layers of coloniality that deny that the Mbyá-Guarani struggle to survive in the present post-national societies are a consequence of the utopian mission experience inherited, mythologized, and still sensed as violent and catastrophic.

The second part of the book, "Local Appropriations of the Historical Meanings of the Missions," is composed of four essays that present how local publics engage with heritage, not just with the official meaning but with other meanings that have been put forward in the last decades and that have a crucial role in the political and the social.

In the chapter "Uses and Meanings of the Jesuit Missions of Paraguay," Maximiliano von Thüngen presents the perspective of peasant populations who remain in everyday contact with the missions, an important element in the shaping of their social identities. The economic activity connected to tourism has transformed the uses the locals make of the missions in their day-to-day life, with deep cultural and socioeconomic consequences. In the last fifty years museums of sacred art were inaugurated in the small towns that originated in the missions; further, several projects of restauration took place instigated by national and international heritage agencies, but also involving the Catholic Church (both of Paraguay and of Germany) that defended the notion that the Jesuit heritage ought to contribute to developing Native populations according to the theological climate prevailing after the Second Vatican Council (1965). After the nomination of two Paraguay missions for the UNESCO World Heritage List in the 1990s, the transformation of the missions into tourist sites has taken place in an economic setting marked by the lack of productive activities and by structural unemployment. The prevailing practices and heritage-related discourses are controlled by the state through the actions of institutions, tourist agencies, and NGOs. The Jesuit reductions stand in the local imaginaries as a promise of work and economic development.

In her chapter "Claiming the Missions as Indigenous Spaces," Lisbeth Haas understands the missions as colonial and tribal places. When the Franciscans arrived on the coast of California, it was one of the most highly populated and diverse Indigenous territories outside of central Mexico. California's Indigenous geography connected resources, religious sites, and trade routes through tribal territories. However, the official narrative that created the myth of the church as promoter of civilization has a long legacy of absent stories about Indigenous people's resistance to the colonial project in California in the eighteenth and nineteenth centuries and how the mission violence devastated their communities. After the 1850s violent dispossession became the norm as American settlers arrived in California in huge numbers; the lingering consequence is that many tribes whose ancestors formed part of the missions are not officially recognized by the government and have continued to wrestle with the denial of their heritage rights to the mission history. Junipero Serra's canonization in 2015 triggered Indigenous critiques demanding their historic rights to the missions. Though embedded in an Indigenous geography, the missionary story presents the missions as if connected to each other along a romanticized Camino Real instead of showing the contentious boundaries, geographical and otherwise, between missions and tribes. It underlines how the civilizing myth of the missions continues to produce deep cultural wounds and traumatic memories of violence.

An important example of an Indigenous heritage program is presented by Deana Dartt in the chapter "Reclaiming Cha'alayash through Applied Decolonization: Intervening and Indigenizing the Narrative in, around, and about California's Sites of Conscience." As Dartt shows, California's Native history is of the utmost complexity, yet it is routinely portrayed in the official heritage script as uncomplicated and stereotypical, sequestered in a romantic past, far from the difficult reality of over 100,000 people living today in California who identify themselves as American Indians. This omission is directly linked to their current disenfranchisement in terms of federal acknowledgment. Discontinuities in heritage narratives between the dominant discourse of Indian-ness and the alternative histories and experiences put forward by those peoples cause new forms of trauma. As an alternative, Dartt proposes a decolonial methodology through a project designed to create a collaborative digital data base for allowing Native communities of California to express their histories on their own terms and to honor their ancestral connections through Cha'alayash, "the road that connects our people."

In the chapter "Violence, Destruction, and Patrimonialization of the Missionary Past: The Tohono O'Odham Memory, the Silenced Voice of the

Magical Town Magdalena de Kino," Edith Llamas analyzes how the colonial discourse is articulated when the town of Magdalena de Kino, in the Sonoran Desert, is placed in the category "Pueblo mágico," a Mexican government project designed to stimulate cultural tourism by offering intercultural experiences associated with local living traditions, particularly Indigenous ones. The "magical" properties of the town are tied to the Jesuit Eusebio Kino and his missionary deeds in the seventeenth century among the O'odham people. The narrative of "Pueblo mágico" not only erases the long history of resistance and rebellion of the O'odham to the forced conversion, but also ignores the Native appropriation of Christianism in contemporary religious practices never labeled as heritage. The annual pilgrimage to Magdalena de Kino allows one to go beyond the discourse that preserves, reproduces, and justifies the colonizing narrative, centered on the imposition of the Catholic faith as a civilizing action that silences Indigenous voices.

All in all, the essays in this book denaturalize and pluralize heritage. The first strategy is pretty clear: heritage is not something immanent or transcendental, but a social creation and, thus, nested in historical circumstances. Denaturalizing heritage implies its critical reading, showing that it has created conflicts everywhere: dispossession (territorial, it is true, but also in other areas of culture); breakdown of social fabrics; complicity with the modern-colonial (onto)logic. Those conflicts have been framed (and sought to be resolved) within modern-colonial boundaries: better regulations; democratization of nomination and management processes; guarantee of access to markets; broader, although controlled, participation in decision-making about what is patrimonialized, how it is protected, how it is exhibited. But the problems created by heritage are modern, and their solution, as Santos (2011) already noted, cannot be modern. To modern problems, not (so) modern solutions. Placing these problems on the ontological terrain is one of those solutions—not the end of the conflict, though, but rather its confrontation—and one of the main tasks of pluralizing heritage. That is why the second strategy taken by the essays in this book is creative and, above all, ontological. The suspension of the naturalization of heritage, of its ontological hardness, is carried out by other memories, other forms of corporeality, other forms of relationship with time (in plural, times) and with the beings, ghosts, and haunted materialities that populate it: it is about the rebellion of memories formerly suppressed by heritage and its discourse of sovereignty.

References

Almada, Ignacio, José Marcos Medina, and María del Valle Borrero. 2007. "Hacia una nueva interpretación del régimen colonial en Sonora: Descubriendo a los indios y redimensionando a los misioneros, 1681–1821." *Región y Sociedad* 19: 237–66.

Becker, Félix. 1982. "La guerra guaranítica desde una nueva perspectiva: Historia, ficción e historiografía." *Boletín Americanista* 32: 7–37.

Bolton, Herbert. 1917. "The Mission as a Frontier Institution in the Spanish-American Colonies." *American Historical Review* 23 (1): 42–61.

———. 1919. *Kino's Historical Memoir of Pimería Alta*. Cleveland: Arthur H. Clark Company.

———. 1933. "The Epic of Greater America." *American Historical Review* 38 (3): 448–74.

de Souza, José Otávio Catafesto. 1998. "Aos fantasmas das brenhas: Etnografia, invisibilidade e etnicidade de alteridades originárias no sul do Brasil." PhD diss. Porto Alegre: UFRGS.

de Souza, José Otávio Catafesto, Mónica Arnt, Carlos Eduardo de Moraes, Daniele Pires, and Rita Lewkowicz. 2012. "Dimensões imateriais da Tava mirí São Miguel no discurso Mbyá-Guarani contemporâneo." In *Missões, militância indigenista e protagonismo indígena*, edited by Protasio Langer and Gabriela Chamorro, 135–51. São Bernardo do Campo: Nhanduti Editora.

Garlet, Ivori, and Valéria Assis. 2002. "A imagem do Kechuíta no universo mitológico dos Mbyá." *Revista de História Regional* 7 (2): 99–114.

Gutfreund, Zevi. 2010. "Standing Up to Sugar Cubes: The Contest over Ethnic Identity in California's Fourth-Grade Mission Curriculum." *Southern California Quarterly* 92 (2): 161–97.

Haas, Lisbeth. 2014. *Saints and Citizens: Indigenous Histories of Colonial Missions and Mexican California*. Berkeley: University of California Press.

Hackel, Steven. 2005. *Children of the Coyote, Missionaries of Saint Francis: Indian–Spanish Relations in Colonial California, 1769–1850*. Chapel Hill: University of North Carolina Press.

———. 2013. *Junípero Serra: California's Founding Father*. New York: Hill and Wang.

Hausberger, Bernd. 1993. "La violencia en la conquista spiritual: Las misiones jesuitas de Sonora." *Anuario de Historia de América Latina* 30: 27–54.

———. 2015. *Miradas a la misión jesuita en la Nueva España*. Mexico: Colegio de México.

Kryder-Reid, Elizabeth. 2016. *California Mission Landscapes: Race, Memory, and the Politics of Heritage*. Minneapolis: University of Minnesota Press.

Ladeira, Maria Inês. 2007. *O caminhar sob a luz: Território mbya a beira do oceano*. São Paulo: UNESP.

Maeder, Ernesto, and Alfredo Bolsi. 1980. *La población guaraní de las misiones jesuíticas: Evolución y características, 1671–1767*. Corrientes: Instituto de Investigaciones Geohistóricas.

Mirafuentes, José Luis. 1993. Estructuras de poder político, fuerzas sociales y rebeliones indígenas en Sonora (siglo XVIII). *Estudios de Historia Novohispana* 14 (2): 117–43.

O'Gorman, Edmundo. 1942. "¿Tienen las Américas una historia común?" *Filosofía y Letras* 3 (6): 215–35.

Polzer, Charles. 1998. *Kino: A Legacy*. Tucson: Jesuit Fathers of Southern Arizona.

Radding, Cynthia. 1997. *Wandering Peoples: Colonialism, Ethnic Spaces, and Ecological Frontiers in Northwestern Mexico, 1700–1850*. Durham, NC: Duke University Press.

Reff, Daniel. 1991. *Disease, Depopulation, and Cultural Change in Northwestern New Spain, 1518–1764*. Salt Lake City: University of Utah Press.

Sandos, James. 2004.   *Converting California: Indians and Franciscans in the Missions*. New Haven: Yale University Press.

Santos, Boaventura de Sousa. 2011. "Epistemologías del sur." *Revista Internacional de Filosofía Iberoamericana y Teoría Social* 54: 17–39.

Schneider, Khal, Dale Allender, Margarita Berta-Ávila, Rose Borunda, Gregg Castro, Amy Murray, and Jenna Porter. 2019. "More Than Missions: Native Californians and Allies Changing the Story of California History. *Journal of American Indian Education* 58 (3): 58–77.

Silliman, Stephen. 2001. "Theoretical Perspectives on Labor and Colonialism: Reconsidering the California Missions. *Journal of Anthropological Archaeology* 20 (4): 379–407.

Spicer, Edward. 1994. *Los Yaquis: Historia de una cultura*. Mexico: Universidad Nacional Autónoma de México.

Trouillot, Michel-Rolph. 1995. *Silencing the Past: Power and the Production of History*. Boston: Beacon Press.

Uribe, Rafael. 1907. *Reducción de salvajes*. Cúcuta: Imprenta de El Trabajo.

Wilde, Guillermo. 2001. "Los guaraníes después de la expulsión de los jesuitas: Dinámicas políticas y transacciones simbólicas." *Revista Complutense de Historia de América* 27: 69–106.

———. 2003. "Imaginarios oficiales y evocaciones locales: Los usos del pasado jesuíticoguaraní." *Avá* 4: 53–72.

Part I: Alternative Readings of Heritage

Subjects, Alterization, and the Different Meanings of the Past

Crisis of the "Heritage Order"

Disputed Representations of the Jesuit Missions' Past

GUILLERMO WILDE

The past is not an objective fact that can be read in material remains or texts. As Jacques Le Goff has pointed out, vestiges are "monuments," traces of the past that do not speak for themselves. It is through the gaze (or the voice) that gives them meaning that "monuments" become "documents" (Le Goff 1991). The past is then a subjective, historical, and symbolic construction, conditioned by a conceptual context and disputes of meaning. These premises apply to the history of the Jesuit missions and the heritage policies associated with them. Both Jesuit missions' history and their vestiges adopt and transform their meanings over time, involving cultural representations and interests of different kinds (political-ideological, economic, scientific). A Jesuit mission's past does not exist in itself but as the result of a long-term historical process and interpretation, which needs to be studied in its successive transformations, its social inscriptions, and its political disputes. The history of the missions can be divided into different *periods* in which views of the Jesuit's past at the local, regional, and global scale and national and international heritage policies change. While expressing latent tensions, these periods are characterized by some stability and consensus around a given idea of that past. They shape what François Hartog (2003, 15) has called "regimes of historicity"—that is, ways "to engage past, present and future or to compose a mix of the three categories." These regimes also experience crises that mark transitions in ideas about the past (or the perceptions of time in general) and consequently those around the policy that should be addressed to preserve it (or not)—material objects, sites, and texts understood as indexes of the past that may be conserved, concealed, filed, or even destroyed.

Periods also define what I call "heritage order," a consensus around policies aimed at the vestiges of the Jesuit past, informed in certain ideas (interpretations) about the historical and cultural value of that past (understood as a whole) and its cultural, political, and economic functionality. Transitions between periods are marked by crisis in that "heritage order." A long-term historical analysis of this process is particularly relevant today, when both the Jesuit past and Jesuit missions' heritage policies experience deep fissures—a true crisis driven by both a turn in the historiographic paradigms and the explosion of social events that impose a revision of heritage values. The current context of pandemics is perhaps a decisive fact in that evolution.

I would like to identify three periods in the construction of the Jesuit past as a "heritage order" in the last two centuries. The first corresponds to the second half of the eighteenth century, the last phase of presence of the Jesuits in Latin America before their expulsion from the Hispanic domains in 1767–68. In this period takes shape a confrontation between pro-Jesuit and anti-Jesuit positions around the missions' contribution to Western civilization. The second period coincides with the formation of national states in the Southern Cone (mainly Brazil, Argentina, and Paraguay) and the disputes over the historical value of both the Jesuit past and vestiges in the construction of national histories. This dispute was immediately translated, as we will see, into the design of the first official heritage policies of nation-states. The third period corresponds to the situation of the last twenty years, characterized by two important facts and trends: (a) the growing participation of local communities in (re)defining heritage policies of and in Jesuit missions sites (the "ruins") leading to an expansion of policies and concepts at the regional and global level; and (b) the revision of the history and the very conception of the use of space in the Jesuit missions influenced by new approaches of the social sciences and humanities. These facts and trends clearly point to a displacement in the definition of the past and the heritage policies and the role of specific actors: from state agents to Indigenous actors, from experts in conservation to social theorists. The current moment faces the challenge of redesigning display and conservation policies to include the new actors and perspectives. Inclusion of new perspectives (and the revision of coherent classical views) will contribute to a renovated understanding of the mission's past as an inherently fragmentary, disputed, and materially distributed phenomenon.

Pro-Jesuit and Anti-Jesuit Factions

Although the Jesuit missions had been founded in the early seventeenth century, it was not until the following century that letters and chronicles of these spaces began to be widely disseminated. An ideological polarization rapidly emerged between those who saw the missions as a utopian experiment aimed at ensuring the salvation of Indigenous peoples and spreading Western civilization and those who regarded them as a reprehensible political venture designed to oppress Indigenous peoples. These antinomic gazes formed a radical division between apologetics and detractors of the order that culminated in one of the most significant events of the eighteenth century: the expulsion of the Jesuits from all the Hispanic domains (1767). The missions had an important place in the intellectual reflection developed in Europe's enlightenment movement, involving such important figures as Montesquieu and Voltaire, who devoted several pages of their works to the government of the Jesuits in Paraguay. The anti-clerical position of these authors did not inhibit favorable opinion about the missions on their part. In a paragraph of his treatise *De l'esprit de lois*, Montesquieu praised the Society of Jesus, stating that the Jesuit missions were a model of civilization that managed to combine religion and humanity in the diffusion of a good government, thus repairing the devastation caused by the Spanish conquerors (Montesquieu 2016 [1748]). At the same time, Jesuit letters selectively published and pro-Jesuit treatises of wide circulation such as that of Ludovico Antonio Muratori, *Il cristianesimo felice* (1752), managed to install an extremely positive view of the missions in the European lettered circles and the public opinion.

This positive view was confronted with allegations about Jesuits' projects of independence of and conspiracy against the European monarchies. Several fables and rumors around the Jesuit order circulated at the time. One of great effect on both sides of the Atlantic spoke about a kingdom in the distant lands of South America that the Jesuits had built. In the 1750s, in the Río de la Plata, in the context of the conflict that confronted the Guarani Indians against the crowns of Portugal and Spain for control of Paraguay's missions, a *History of Nicolas I, Emperor of Paraguay*, circulated in several languages. The story refers to the coronation of a king in the missions whose effigy coins were supposed to be circulating in the region. Some years before the Jesuit's expulsion appeared the work *El*

Reino Jesuítico, by Bernardo Ibáñez de Echavarri, a Jesuit expelled from the school of Buenos Aires who sought to inform about the characteristics of the Jesuit government of the missions and how it evaded the subjection to the Iberian authorities by various obscure and secret means (Furlong 1933). The idea that the Jesuits hid riches and treasures in their missions circulated from early times, largely inspired by the economic growth and prosperity of missions.[1] Since the seventeenth century, it was suspected that the Jesuits concealed gold mines somewhere in the territory of the missions. In 1656, an Indian named Domingo came to indicate in a drawing the precise location of those mines and how the missions were assembled to defend them.[2] The Spanish authorities ordered investigations into the veracity of those informations by sending officials to the region who had not been able to prove them. However, the Jesuit missions would continue to be shrouded in mysteries for many decades.

The existence of gold mines in the missions' surroundings would be the object of well-documented investigations, visits, complaints, and even legal processes against the Jesuits, against which they would defend themselves in comprehensive documents.[3] More than a century after the history of the Indian Domingo, and in the context of the expulsion of the Jesuits and the confiscation of their properties by the Bourbon administration, the central authorities ordered local officials to find out the whereabouts of a golden image that was supposed to exist in one of the mission towns. According to a file, it was an image of Our Lady of Good Counsel, "all of it made of solid gold with the child, little angels and other ornaments of the same metal."[4] The governor of the towns of Misiones, Francisco Bruno de Zavala, requested in a letter to the priest of one of the towns to recognize "with particular examination and sight of the eyes" if an image of the virgin in his town, "with four little angels, a golden arch, and in the doors some small reliquaries inlaid with relics of saints," was effectively made of solid gold or if it was only made of gilt wood, which he ought to certify under oath. Undoubtedly, the anecdote was part of the countless stories that circulated for more than a century about the wealth and splendor of the missions.

In 1792, the Spanish authorities of the Río de la Plata investigated, by order of the king, an information according to which in the vicinity of the mission town of San Carlos there was a Jesuit priest who lived with a dozen women and many children, hidden in the forest. Although the information was not verified, the history of a long-lived Jesuit living in the Paraguayan lands would continue to circulate. In those years the explorer Félix de Azara explained in his book *Geografía Física y Esférica* that one Jesuit had stayed in Paraguay after the expulsion, dying in one of the mission towns when he was more than a hundred years old (Azara 1904). Even though we know that a Jesuit named Segismundo Aperger stayed in Paraguay after the Jesuits' expulsion and that it is very likely that he had inspired the rumor, he indisputably died before he was a hundred years old. This kind of story was common and was considered truthful at the time, which explains the king's worry on the matter. The stories nurtured the imagination and collective memory around two myths widespread at the time: that of hidden riches and that of the despotic or benevolent government of the Jesuits. The riddles and secrets prevailing in the opinion related to Jesuits' internal organization and their usual procedures regarding moral issues immediately made the Jesuits suspected of instigating conspiracies, intrigues, and destabilizing riots. In any case, anecdotes support historian Jerry Cooney's claim that "the Jesuits may have been officially 'dead'; [but] they were certainly not forgotten" (Cooney 1984, 558).

With the expulsion of the Jesuits, the missions passed to the secular administration of the Spanish crown and suffered a rapid process of deterioration. During this period there was an abrupt decline in the Indigenous population caused by epidemics and flights. After the collapse of the Spanish monarchy in 1810 began a dramatic period of civil wars in the Río de la Plata region that caused the destruction of most of the missions founded in the Argentine territory. A Guarani diaspora contributed to an accelerated process of cultural and political *mestizaje* (Maeder and Bolsi 1980). The missions founded in the territory of what is currently Paraguay and Brazil survived or experienced a less dramatic situation. Several foreign travelers that explored those regions in the first half of the nineteenth century reported the state of deep deterioration of the mission towns.[5]

Disputing the Nation's Past

In the second half of the nineteenth century, the remnants of the ancient missions remained forgotten except for sporadic mentions made by travelers exploring the region. This situation began to change in the last decades of that century, when the national states designed policies of territorial colonization with the aim of expanding their economies. During and after the War of the Triple Alliance (1865–70), a conflict in which Brazil, Argentina, and Uruguay defeated Paraguay, some of the mission towns located in the Paraguayan territory were looted and their objects transferred to Argentina and Brazil by members of the triumphant armies. At the end of the war, public institutions such as the Museum of Natural Sciences of the city of La Plata, in Buenos Aires, organized expeditions to gather vestiges from the region for their future collections. The French expert Adolfo Bourgoing gives details about the expedition to Paraguay and Misiones in 1894 and the tense dealings with the locals as expedition members attempted to obtain cult objects that were still in use and to which the locals were very attached (Bollini and Levinton 2018; De Barrio 1932).

In this period, national heritage policy was taking shape in an erratic and contradictory way. While certain officials thought that the vestiges of Jesuit missions should be preserved, others thought that preservation was not essential to a region that instead needed economic development. Ana Gorosito has lucidly identified these two attitudes toward the remains of the Jesuit missions with an arrow of time that alternatively pointed back and forth (Gorosito 2000). The prospects of travelers and officials clearly put into tension visions of the value of Jesuit vestiges, which were conceived as either historical witnesses of the nation's past or productive resources for the nation's progress. These visions are represented respectively by the archaeologist Juan Bautista Ambrosetti, who made three trips to Misiones in the last decade of the nineteenth century to collect information and pieces for the collections of nascent scientific institutions, and the surveyor Rafael Hernández (brother of the author of the famous poem *El Martín Fierro*), who made a trip to project the installation of agricultural colonies of European migrants in the region (Ambrosetti 1894, 1896, 1983).

While Ambrosetti was an active advocate of preservation, Hernandez prioritized the full development of the region's economy at the expense of the ruins' sites. Moreover, Hernandez's view of the Jesuit past was extremely negative, as his writings reveal. He believes that the despotic domination of the Jesuits had left only a lethargic and apathetic population in the region that resisted progress.[6] As Gorosito noted, both positions were aimed at the urgency of a particular action to be carried out by the national state: one inspired in instrumental reason accelerating the destruction of the ancient structures and allowing the construction of roads, bridges, and public buildings for the state administration, education, and public policies in a new territory (time arrow to the future), and another inspired in cultural reason preserving vestiges of the past (both natural and cultural) as part of the construction of a metaphoric and symbolic sense, a historical bedrock of the nation (time arrow to the past).

Before the evidence of the natural deterioration of the sites, both intellectuals recognized the imminent disappearance of the ancient structures, but they had totally confronted positions regarding the decision to make: either accelerating the process of destruction or preserving the vestiges as ruins. Yet neither Hernández nor Ambrosetti was considering in his projects the opinions or real practices of the local populations inhabiting the concrete places of the region. As Gordillo pointed out for a different region, the ruin was conceived as a sort of abstraction that did not "correspond with the texture and the great diversity of places and objects to which alluded the term" (Gordillo 2019). While the locals represented those places as an intrinsic part of the flux of their daily life, Hernandez and Ambrosetti, even representing opposed positions, abstracted the Jesuit past of its context "of use." As members of the metropolitan elite involved in the construction of the Argentine nation's state ideology, they presented the ruins as an object separated from the present and oriented their aims at replacing what they conceived as an actual and growing decadence by a certain idea of transcendence, that of the technological progress or of the glorious past. Both presented the ruins as objects without life or a chance for survival *in the place*, in the best case—relics of the past to be preserved and contemplated in a museum.

Shortly after Hernández and Ambrosetti's visits, another surveyor, Juan Queirel, prospected the region of the ruins and provided systematic information about their situation, drawing up-to-date plans of some sites. In an excerpt from his book devoted to the ruins, he took a stand in the debate:

> If it were up to me, those ruins, those carved and sculpted stones that represent the art of the Jesuits and the attention, perseverance, sweat of thousands of Guarani; those stones that have heard so many chants,

so many Christian prayers uttered in a primitive language; that have
attended so many scenes of a unique civilization in history; if it were
up to me, I repeat, those ruins would be respected, cared for, preserved
so that they would be, as Ambrosetti says, one more attraction of Misiones (the Argentinian province), and not the least, a future touristic
interest. (Queirel 1901, 18)

Although there were no official institutions for the preservation of Jesuit
heritage, the preservationist position would eventually gain ground among
Argentina's national elites, attracting the attention of the press. In the context of these disputes, it was debated whether the portico of the Church
of San Ignacio Miní should be moved to Buenos Aires to be exhibited in
a public park for the entertainment of passers-by or be kept at its place of
origin, the province of Misiones (Petrosini 2018). As noted in Queirel's
quotation and the metropolitan debate, a certain concern about tourism
was already present when reflecting on preservation.

The framework of these anecdotes and opinions was certainly broader:
they put forward a debate on the historical value of the Jesuits' past in
the construction of the Argentine nation. Writers and public intellectuals
confront pro- and anti-Jesuit positions over the decades. One of them was
the conspicuous Argentine writer Leopoldo Lugones, who in 1901 published the book *El Imperio Jesuítico*, in which he provides a negative view
of the Jesuits and the aesthetic quality of the architectural structures of
the mission buildings, which he himself had visited in the preparation of
the book. Lugones anticipates the imminent disappearance of the remnants of the Jesuit past and the relentless advancement of Argentinian
progress linked to European migration (Lugones 1985 [1904]). On the
other side of the Paraná River, the Paraguayan intellectual Blas Garay
had published a small booklet entitled *El comunismo en las misiones Jesuíticas* (1897) as a preliminary study to the modern translation of the
first chronicle of Paraguay by Jesuit Nicolás del Techo. Garay offered an
opaque vision of the Society of Jesus as a despotic organization characterized by its rigid verticalism and centralization, denying any influence
of the Jesuit tradition in Paraguayan national identity (Garay 1897; Telesca 2014; Couchonnal, Telesca, and Wilde 2015).[7]

Disputes over the historical value of the Jesuit past would continue in
the first half of the twentieth century in professional historiography. In

the first decades of that century, certain prominent figures of the Jesuit order would raise and mark a new era of debate around the missions. One of them is the Spanish Jesuit Pablo Hernández, author of a two-volume work entitled *Organización Social de las Doctrinas Guaranies* (1913), which includes a thick documentary appendix including transcriptions of several sources unknown at the time. Its final chapters provide photographs of the ruins visited by the author in the three countries and an inventory of the pieces kept at La Plata Natural History Museum (Hernández 1913). Hernandez's book is highly apologetic, but it is also an excellently documented work that brings to light several unknown sources from the archives of the Jesuits in Rome. The other figure is the Argentine Jesuit Guillermo Furlong Cardiff, a true militant of the Jesuit cause who published hundreds of pages devoted to the history of the missions and the Jesuits' contribution to the formation of the Argentine nation (Furlong 1946, 1962). Furlong not only highlights the role of the Jesuits in the cultural development of the region, but also defends their role as forerunners of independence in Latin America (Furlong 1960).[8] Furlong's apologetic position would prevail throughout most of the twentieth century and would decisively influence the national heritage policies from the outset.

Origins of the Heritage Policy

Since the late 1930s, the missions' sites have been the subject of official heritage policies of the states of the region. These policies were foundational to the extent that they were the basis for the creation of national institutions for the protection of heritage and historical sites, such as the National Commission of Museums and Historical Monuments (1940), in the case of Argentina, or the National Service for the Protection of Heritage in Brazil (1937). The whole movement was fostered and controlled by architects who developed policies for the recovery and material valorization of Jesuit sites in general (Ribeiro 2017). For around half a century the national heritage institution consolidated, restored, and protected sites according to international legislation. The process gained new impetus with the inclusion of Jesuit sites of San Ignacio (Argentina) and São Miguel (Brazil) on the UNESCO Heritage list in 1984. In 1972, the OEA sent an architect to Paraguay to study the situation of Jesuit sites and work on a coordinated policy of restoration. In 1994, Trinidad and Jesus (both in

Paraguay) entered the UNESCO list (von Thüngen 2021). This initiated a real boom in ad hoc publications and programs developed in the three countries and subsequently the development of integration projects such as the Jesuit missions corridor within the framework of cultural Mercosur.

We still need comparative research of heritage policies in the countries of the region. However, it is clear that their general orientation privileged (it still does) an eminently technical approach that emphasized almost exclusively the monumental (architectural) dimension of the sites, represented by urban centers and churches, transformed into fetishes of both the official heritage policy and the regional tourist circuits. The ruins of San Ignacio Miní in Argentina and São Miguel in Brazil became stages for light and sound shows recreating the mission's history. Apart from the evidence of a process of commodification of the past that can also be observed in other similar places in the world, it is worthwhile noting that the narrative conveyed in the official heritage policy emphasizes an apologetic bias. It favored a historical narrative that emulates in many respects the famous film *The Mission*, in which the missionary experience is seen as an initiative of inclusion of the Indigenous peoples in modern civility, guided by the Jesuit priests.

In Paraguay, the contemporary church played a highly active role in revitalizing the myth of the civilizing missionary. As shown by Maximiliano von Thüngen, the Paraguayan church got involved in the preservation and restoration of the Jesuit historical sites. In 1977 the Paracuaria Foundation, an initiative of the German Jesuits with the purpose of "preserving religious and cultural values," was created. The foundation funded and coordinated the works of restoration in Trinidad with the collaboration of UNESCO and the Paraguayan national state (von Thüngen 2021, 56). In this particular view, religious action and cultural preservation were seen as two sides of the same coin. This conception was rooted in an ancient apologetic view of the missions as an initiative that saved the Indigenous people from colonial oppression and that could be taken as a humanistic example in the contemporary policies of development. Such a view soon entered in conflict with the modern secular gaze of national and international officials and technicians who understood that the sites represented cultural and artistic value from the past, stripped of religious connotations.[9]

Also in Argentina, the church developed strategies to recreate the missionary past among contemporary Indigenous communities of the region, the Mbyá Guarani. In the late 1970s, a group of Guarani families were resettled in lands owned by the Diocese of Misiones (Argentina), where the relics of Jesuit martyr Roque González de Santa Cruz were presented in a grand ceremony where the church high authorities attended. It is known that the Mbyá Guarani communities resisted the missionary project for many centuries and that they kept distant to official intents of colonial and republican states to integrate them into broader society. These communities are also known for preserving their traditional religious values, keeping them inaccessible to the whites (jurua). However, in this "experiment" by the diocese we see a deliberate attempt to equate the ancient Guarani of the missions, who accepted conversion to Christianity and who mostly disappeared decades after the Jesuit's expulsion as a result of demographic collapse and violence, with the current Guarani populations who always resisted the missionary project (Abou and Micolis 2013).

While aiming at revitalizing a past that is supposed to be authentic, the heritage policy ironically reproduces simplistic views of the past, in this case those identified with the apologetic position and the goodness of missionary action. The mission towns of Chiquitos, in present-day Bolivia, represent a paradigm in this sense. Even though these missions were not part of the Guarani system, they also depended administratively on the Jesuit Province of Paraguay and followed the same model. This missionary region was fundamental in successfully reproducing one of the most pregnant myths of the Jesuit missions past: that of music as an instrument of civilization. In 1980, while developing an architectural restoration project in Chiquitos, Swiss architect Hans Roth found hundreds of abandoned and forgotten musical scores from the Jesuit era, with which was formed the musical archive of Concepción. This discovery immediately unleashed a wave of research projects and a movement of orchestras, recordings, and periodic festivals mobilized in the interest of recovering authentic expressions of the missionary musical past.[10]

In the center of the town square of Concepción de Chiquitos was erected a monument (Figure 4) reifying the ancient orphic narrative of music as a civilizing tool.[11] The monument portrays three hierarchical representations of the Indian as imagined in Western "civilization" since colonial

FIGURE 4. Monument in Concepción de Chiquitos, Bolivia. (Photo by Guillermo Wilde, 2004)

times: that of the nomadic hunter located in the lowest stage of the scale, that of the Indian who knows the rudiments of work and sedentary life in an intermediate stage, and that of the Native turned to the spiritual life and the arts, under the leadership of the missionaries, in the highest stage of civility. Music appears as a means par excellence to tame the Indigenous "wild soul."

This hierarchy echoes that disseminated by Jesuit José de Acosta in his *Historia natural y moral de las Indias*, from the end of the sixteenth century. Resorting to a classic trichotomy, Acosta divided the peoples of the world according to their degrees of civilization, the highest being the consolidated kingdoms and empires, followed by the *behetrías* or peoples governed by "councils," although not hierarchical. Finally, there were those groups with a government "totally barbarous," "without law, neither king nor seat" (del Pino and Lázaro 1995, 70). In Acosta's vision, only the most civilized peoples were capable of adopting the Christian religion, since the highest degree of civilization corresponded to this religion, hence the first task with the barbarian Indians should be to educate them in the values of civility before transmitting the Christian faith to them. The monument of Concepción de Chiquitos synthesizes this path from a low stage represented by nature to a higher one identified with culture or civilization. The lowest stage combines a contradictory perception of the state of nature in between innocence, embodied in a half-naked mother with her child, and war, portrayed as a brave hunter shooting an arrow into the sky.

The emerging heritage discourse in this second period ended up building an image that elicits all kinds of conflict around the meanings and appropriations of the past and the use of Jesuit sites. It was oriented in three ways that currently need a revision: (a) an eminently technical view, represented by architects, which excluded critical reflection of humanistic and social disciplines; (b) a narrative of the past that reduced complexity to a vision highlighting either civilizing paternalism of the missionaries or, sometimes, Indigenous libertarian heroism; and (c) a devaluation of local cultural and material appropriations and uses. The sites were gradually separated from the flow of social life, in line with a conception of the past marked by the temporal cut (before and after the Jesuits) and the necessity of showing the ruins as relics, sacred objects, as a kind of authentic window to the past.

The Return of Indigenous Agency

The twentieth century witnesses the acceleration of a general process of "patrimonialization" in which "diverse spaces, practices and goods are withdrawn from the flow of daily life." [Jesuit sites] participate in the specific dynamics that public policies create and recreate over the long term. Once they become heritage, the processes involved in their "selection and interpretation remain hidden" (Rosas 1998, 5). In a way, heritage becomes a commodity for sale in the tourist market (Harvey 2005). But, as Cruces remarked, the process is double: it first separates the objects, places, and expressions from the flux of ordinary social life to then return them to that flux "in a codified, normalized and interpretated way through the work of mediation" (Cruces 1998, 76). As a part of this evolution, official heritage policy, established from above down in the global multicultural context, seeks for the resolution of contradictions by the inclusion of local voices, the absorption of differences and contradictions in a coherent discourse about the past. This discourse is now in crisis because of a number of factors or emerging movements of the last two decades. I will focus on two that fall within the broader context of the current sociocultural and intellectual shift of paradigm.

The first factor or movement is the contemporary revalorization of the subaltern agency in historical processes that has led to a recovery of the role of Indigenous subjects in the construction of past and to a growing participation of local communities in the design of public policies. The multicultural redesign of hegemonic heritage policies seeks to include traditionally relegated actors. This is the case of the Guarani Mbyá communities near the sites of the ruins. São Miguel das Missões, in Brazil, illustrates very well this process of inclusion. In the framework of the recognition by national states of territorial rights and ancestral occupation of space, the Mbyá communities have begun to intervene gradually and directly in defining the history of the spaces of the ruins as places of memory and economic activity. With the technical support of universities and experts, this history displays in the most diverse media, challenging the Western text-centered perspective. The production of materials such as records, films, catalogues, and maps (for example, the Guarani retä project), gives visibility and permanence to communities with the official recognition of heritage institutions such as the IPHAN.[12]

The dispute over the "ownership" of ruins is also involved in alternative narratives of the past that Indigenous peoples propose about the presence of the Jesuits and of white people in the region. In spite of having been registered in the work of ethnographers since at least half a century ago, these alternative narratives have been generally neglected in the official historical discourse. Egon Schaden and León Cadogan reported in the '60s and '70s about the presence of a figure called "kechuita" in the cosmological accounts of the Mbyá Guarani of Paraguay and Brazil (Melià 2004). This figure falls within the set of "hybrid" entities recognized by the Guarani of the different regions (Hesu, Tupasy, Tani, Andejara, Noendasu, Añang) as an integral part of the cosmos. Although from a Western point of view these entities make clear reference to the external introduction, even ephemeral, of elements of Christianity since colonial times, the significance they acquire in the Indigenous tradition is completely different (Mordo 2000, 53). The members of the communities conceived these figures as wholly belonging to the Native cosmology. The same can be said of European objects, such as musical instruments, that became an integral part of Indigenous ritual culture (Chamorro 2004; Ruíz 1996). These forms of "appropriation" and "resignification" of objects do not have a very defined place in heritage policy so far, but they challenge a static conception of history, materiality, and identity, which have been a mark of hegemonic heritage policies in modernity. Indigenous conceptions defy that static conception and propose different "regimes of historicity" where the figures of the past and the objects of the present acquire alternative meanings.[13]

This is not to say that states lose their monopoly on the construction of the past, but they become clearly contested in their perspective, also becoming sensitive to other regards and realities, and seek to include them in some way, as the case of São Miguel das Missões shows. In my opinion, the orientation of the new hegemonic heritage discourse must be monitored to enable the inclusion of new (still contradictory) voices and in this way bring greater complexity to the understanding of the past. This has not been the general orientation of the heritage discourse of the Jesuit ruins, which on one level has tended to install an exclusively technical look based on the preservation of the walls and, on another level, has tended to reproduce ancient dichotomies of the Jesuit past.

Challenges to the hegemonic construction of the past manifest in at least three different situations in the regions of former Jesuit missionary presence, defining not only particular types of appropriations but also unique forms of construction of memory: (a) current Mbyá Guarani communities who live in the old territory of the missions and the Paraná jungle that resisted to evangelization; (b) the current inhabitants of the towns where the mission sites are located, for the most part a creole or migrant population settled in the region during the nineteenth and twentieth centuries; and (c) communities directly descending from the missionary Indigenous populations, originated in the process of missionary ethnogenesis during the seventeenth and eighteenth centuries. While the two first situations are typical of the region of the Guarani missions (in Argentina, Brazil, and Paraguay), the last one is characteristic of the region of the old missions of Chiquitos and Moxos (current Bolivia), which claim a direct continuity with the missionary culture, expressing what is called "living cultures" in heritage discourse.

In all three situations, and for reasons that must be studied in context, local populations strategically appropriated the instruments provided by official heritage policies in their struggles for recognition. The attraction of programs to strengthen tourism activity has been particularly present, in many cases as a way to combat situations of extreme poverty. This is the case of Mbyá Guarani communities in Paraguay that have claimed participation in the regional tourist circuits.[14]

In the Moxos and Chiquitos regions there has been a fairly empathetic confluence between the heritage policy of preservation of Jesuit sites and the so-called living culture. In contrast with the Guarani region, an uninterrupted continuity between present reality and Jesuit past is revendicated. The very language spoken by the settlers is a result of the process of missionary ethnogenesis. As this is not a closed process, the heritage discourse now occupies a central place in the construction of identities in these regions. Identity is reaffirmed, transformed, commercialized through the symbols introduced in the process of patrimonialization. The case of music is exalted in this region as an element of continuity reified in imagery and monuments. It is observed, however, that in that region a vision of missionary history as a civilizing process has tended to predominate.

Villagers that currently inhabit the towns surrounding the mission sites historically maintained a fluid relationship with those places. However, they have been generally neglected from heritage and historical research as elements of disturbance and agents of destruction. Few recent studies have highlighted their daily practices and circulations as relevant dimensions in the configuration of missions' landscape and their surroundings, as well as alternative and little-known devices of memory construction (Wilde 2003; Marchi and Ferreira 2015; Brum 2007). Locals developed creative ways of relating themselves with mission remains as places of social activities: activities that literally traverse the mission sites, distribute their pieces, and develop beyond the protective fence of the ruin over the long term (from the use of cemeteries and churches for feasts or social gatherings to the building of houses with ruin materials). These uses have a forgotten history that need to be included in the current construction of heritage and narration of history. The recent renewal of social theory can help in this regard.

This leads us to a second factor or movement in the current interest in highlighting that has to do with the reconceptualization of the missionary Jesuit past and the space of the missions. On the one hand, ethnohistorical, linguistic, and musicological studies have emphasized, from the discovery of new sources, Indigenous prominence in the history of missions. Studies on the figure of Indigenous elite, as a producer of political and religious writings, have brought some of the most important advances in recent years. The recent discovery of hundreds of handwritten documents in Indigenous languages of the missionary regions has shifted the focus of attention from Jesuit missionaries' culture and action to Indigenous mechanisms of memory construction and sui generis modes of transmission (Neumann 2015; Wilde and Vega 2019; Saito 2005). Simultaneously, the discovery of a cartographic corpus showing traces of Indigenous intervention contributes to a new understanding of missions' spatiality.

Some cartographic examples are especially eloquent in showing that the missionary space was conceived by Indigenous actors as a large network of places significant for daily social life. These included the urban centers and the entire region with its rivers, streams, and mountains, including connecting paths, bridges, hospitals, water sources, ports, ranches, chapels, *yerbales*, warehouses, etc. In the context of land disputes during the eighteenth century, some maps provide indications of a unique vision of the territory and the history in which Indian cartographers may have been involved. Its iconic style highlights the utilitarian dimension of the territory, oversizing, for example, river courses and roads. They also point to historical contingencies of the territorial colonization process, such as the creation of *vaquerías*, the presence of specific chiefdoms (*cacicazgos*), and the martyrdom of certain Jesuits. In a complementary way, the Indigenous *cabildos* kept detailed written records of the territorial history of each mission town and its region, in the form of *memoriales* that were kept in the archives of the mission towns, with the aim of preserving legal evidence of the possession and use of lands (Wilde and Takeda 2021; Wilde and Vega 2019).

Based on this corpus, recent archaeological literature has revised the conception of missionary space dominated by urban structures to include a network of sites and places beyond those urban structures. Missionary space is now conceived as a crosslinking of places, where the urban core is a node within a larger network made up of a variety of places (Barcelos 2000). This spatial conception leads to observing both distributions and internal hierarchies within urban centers as political spaces of surveillance, as well as gaps for certain emerging Indigenous expressions that give away the articulation of nonregulated, playful, and peripheral spaces. The study of Indigenous visual, written, and spatial expressions reveals this aspect normally relegated to the background (Wilde 2019a, 2019b).

These findings and advances in research make it necessary to rethink the treatment of Jesuit heritage, the approach and dissemination of missionary history, and the design of conservation and exhibition policies.

Conclusion

I have tried to show how over time the reconstruction of the Jesuit missional past was the subject of disputes in the countries of the Southern Cone. The value of its remains (sites, urban structures, buildings, objects) caused conflicts and guided national public policies in the last two centuries. I have synthesized this long process in three periods that coincide chronologically with the end of the colonial era, the formation of nation states, and the current processes of redefinition of heritage. If in the early days the valuations of the Jesuit past and its vestiges are ambivalent, the need to preserve the sites, objects, and practices ends, in the twentieth century, by favoring an apologetic vision of missionary action, conceived as a civilizing enterprise and an eminently technical gaze that fetishizes heritage and expropriates it from the continuous flow of social life to, ultimately, transform it into merchandise. This patrimonial order is witnessing a crisis, perhaps terminal, in the present time, when the silenced voices of the past (in Indigenous sources and actors) return to reconfigure the missionary landscape and to appropriate space and objects.

The current crisis of the heritage order consists of the rupture of univocal (or dichotomous) narratives of the past that have dominated for almost two centuries. Socially, the consolidation of multiculturalism and the processes of ethnic and territorial vindication and, intellectually, the material and spatial transformation of theory have a decisive impact on the ways we conceive the past, social life, and objects. Both factors shape a new look at heritage, which corresponds to the beginnings of the third (and contemporary) period in which the past becomes a conflictive and fragmentary field of dispute.

References

Abou, Sélim, and Marisa Micolis. 2013. *Los Mbyas Guaraníes: El tiempo del reconocimiento*. Beirut–Buenos Aires Presses de l'universitè Saint-Joseph-Editorial de Arte.

Albert, Bruce, and Alcida Rita Ramos, eds. 2002. *Pacificando o branco: Cosmologias do contato no norte amazônico*. São Paulo: Editora UNESP.

Ambrosetti, Juan Bautista. 1894. *Segundo viaje a Misiones por el Alto Paraná e Iguazú*. Buenos Aires: J. Carbone.

———. 1896. *Tercer viaje a Misiones*. Buenos Aires: J. Carbone.

———. 1983. *Dos estudios sobre Misiones: Viaje a las misiones argentinas y brasileras por el Alto Uruguay. Rápida ojeada sobre el territorio de Misiones*. Resistencia: IIGH-CONICET-FUNDANORD.

Azara, Félix de. 1904. *Geografía física y esférica de las provincias del Paraguay y misiones Guaranies*. Montevideo: Anales del Museo Nacional.

Barcelos, Artur. 2000. *Espaço & arqueologia nas missões Jesuíticas: O caso de São João Batista*. Porto Alegre: EDIPUCRS.

Bollini, Horacio, and Norberto Levinton. 2018. *Iconicidad Jesuítico-Guarani (1609–1768)*. Buenos Aires: Editorial Las Cuarenta.

Brum, Ceres Karam. 2007. "Narrativas cruzadas: Turismo, arqueologia e literatura." *Revista Estudos Históricos* 2 (40): 71–90.

Carbonell de Masy, Rafael. 1992. *Estrategias de desarrollo rural en los pueblos Guaranies (1609–1767)*. Barcelona: Instituto de Estudios Fiscales.

Chamorro, Graciela. 2004. "La buena palabra: Experiencias y reflexiones religosas de los grupos Guaranies." *Revista de Indias* 69 (230): 117–40.

Cooney, Jerry. 1984. "Paranoia and Paraguay, or "Catch that Jesuit!!" *Americas* 40 (4): 555–58.

Couchonnal, Ana, Ignacio Telesca, and Guillermo Wilde. 2015. "Paraguay: La mémoire des missions Jésuites dans la fondation de la Nation." *Raison Présente* 193: 19–31.

Cruces, Francisco. 1998. "Problemas en torno a la restitución del patrimonio: Una visión desde la antropología." *Alteridades* 8 (16): 75–84.

Cushner, Nicholas P. 1983. *Jesuit Ranches and the Agrarian Development of Colonial Argentina, 1650–1767*. Albany: State University of New York Press.

Custódio, Luiz Antônio. 2018. "Lucas Mayerhofer: A reconstituição do povo de São Miguel das Missões." In *La primera generación de historiadores laicos de la Compañía de Jesús en Iberoamérica*, edited by Carlos Page, 53–81. Córdoba: Baez Ediciones.

D'Orbigny, Alcides. 1834. *Voyage dans l'Amérique meridionale (Le Brésil, la Republique Orientale de l'Uruguay, la Patagonie, la Republique Du Chili, la Republique du Perou, la Republique de Bolivia) executé pendat les années 1826 à 1833*. Paris: P. Bertrand.

de Barrio, Maximino. 1932. "Las colecciones de las misiones jesuíticas del Paraguay existentes en el Museo de La Plata." *Revista del Museo de La Plata* 33: 195–205.

del Pino, Fermín, and Carlos Lázaro. 1995. *Visión de los otros y visión de sí mismos: ¿Descubrimiento o invención entre el Nuevo Mundo y el viejo?* Madrid: CSIC.

de Moraes, Carlos Eduardo, Daniele Pires, José Otávio de Souza, and Mônica Arnt. 2009. "Os Mbyá-Guarani e as missões Jesuíticas no Brasil: Outra história." Paper presented in the VIII Reunião de Antropologia do Mercosul, Buenos Aires.

Demersay, Alfred. 1864. *Histoire physique, économique et politique du Paraguay et des établissements des jésuites*. Paris: Hachette.

de Souza, José Otávio, Daniele Pires, Cristian Ávil, Carlos Eduardo de Moraes, and Beatriz Freire. 2005. "Refletindo sobre o registro do patrimônio imaterial Mbyá-Guarani de São Miguel das Missões." Paper presented in the VI Reunión de Antropología del Mercosur, Montevideo.

de Souza, José Otávio, Carlos Eduardo Moraes, Daniele Pires, José Cirilo Morinoco, and Mônica Arnt. 2007. *Tava miri São Miguel Arcanjo, sagrada aldeia de pedra: Os Mbyá-Guarani nas missões*. Porto Alegre: IPHAN.

de Souza, José Otávio, and Vera Taddeu. 2005. "Pesquisa arqueológica e políticas federais de patrimônio cultural dos guaranis no noroeste do Rio Grande Do Sul." Paper presented in the VI Reunión de Antropología del Mercosur, Montevideo.

Fausto, Carlos, and Michael Heckenberger. 2007. *Time and Memory in Indigenous Amazonia: Anthropological Perspectives*. Gainesville: University Press of Florida.

Furlong, Guillermo. 1933. "El expulso Bernardo Ybañez de Echavarri y sus obras sobre las misiones Del Paraguay." *Archivum Historicum Societas Iesu* 2: 25–35.

———. 1946. *Los jesuitas y la cultura rioplatense*. Buenos Aires: Editorial Huarpes.

———. 1960. *Los jesuitas y la escisión del Reino de Indias*. Buenos Aires: Amorrortu.

———. 1962. *Misiones y sus pueblos Guaranies*. Buenos Aires: Balmes.

Garavaglia, Juan Carlos. 1987. *Economía, sociedad y regiones*. Buenos Aires: Ediciones de la Flor.

Garay, Blas. 1897. *El comunismo de las misiones de la Compañía de Jesús en el Paraguay*. Madrid: Viuda e hijos de M. Tello.

Gordillo, Gastón. 2019. *Los escombros del progreso: Ciudades perdidas, estaciones abandonadas y deforestación sojera en el norte argentino*. Buenos Aires: Siglo XXI.

Gorosito, Ana María. 2000. "Monumentos Jesuíticos de Misiones (Argentina): Disputas sobre el patrimonio." Segundo Congreso Virtual de Antropología y Arqueología. https://equiponaya.com.ar/congreso2000/ponencias/Ana_Gorosito.htm.

Groussac, Paul. 1918. *Estudios de historia argentina*. Buenos Aires: Coni.

Hartog, François. 2003. *Regímenes de historicidad: Presentismo y experiencias del tiempo*. México: Universidad Iberoamericana.

Harvey, David. 2005. *Espacios de esperanza*. Madrid: AKAL.

Hernández, Pablo. 1913. *Organización social de las doctrinas Guaranies de la Compañía de Jesús*. Vol. 1. Barcelona: Gustavo Gilli.

Imolesi, María Elena. 2014. "De la utopía a la historia: La reinvención del pasado en los textos de Guillermo Furlong." *Mélanges de l'École française de Rome* 126 (1).

Le Goff, Jacques. 1991. *El orden de la historia: El tiempo como imaginario*. Barcelona: Paidós.

Leite, Serafim. 1938a. *História da Companhia de Jesus no Brasil*. Lisbon: Livraria Portugalia.

———. 1938b. *Os missionários da Companhia de Jesus no Brasil e a sua contribuição para as ciências médicas*. Lisbon: Casa Holandesa.

Lugones, Leopoldo. 1985 [1904]. *El imperio Jesuítico*. Buenos Aires: Hyspamérica.

Maeder, Ernesto, and Alfredo Bolsi. 1980. *La población Guarani de las misiones jesuíticas: Evolución y características, 1671–1767*. Corrientes: Instituto de Investigaciones Geohistóricas.

Marchi, Darlan de Mamann, and Maria Leticia Ferreira. 2015. "Paisagem e patrimônio cultural em imagens: Um estudo sobre São Miguel Das Missões, Brasil." *Territorios* 33: 103–22.

Melià, Bartomeu. 2004. "La novedad Guarani (viejas cuestiones y nuevas preguntas)." *Revista de Indias* 64 (230): 175–226.

Monod-Becquelin, Aurore, and Antoinette Molinié. 1993. *Mémoire de la tradition*. Paris: Societé d'Ethnologie.

Montesquieu, Charles Louis de Secondat. 2016 [1748]. *De l'esprit des lois*. Paris: Flammarion.

Mordo, Carlos. 2000. *El cesto y el arco: Metáforas de la estética Mbyá-Guarani*. Asunción: CEADUC.

Mörner, Magnus. 1953. *The Political and Economic Activities of the Jesuits in the La Plata Region: The Hapsburg Era*. Stockholm: Library and Institute of Ibero-American Studies.

Moussy, Martin de. 1864. *Mémorie historique sur la décadence et la ruine des missions des Jesuites dans le bassin de La Plata: L'eur état actuel*. Paris: Librairie de Carles Douniol.

Neumann, Eduardo. 2015. *Letra de indio: Cultura escrita, comunicação e memória indígena nas reduções do Paraguai*. São Bernardo do Campo: Nhanduti.

Petrosini, Alejo Ricardo. 2018. "Reensamblar el patrimonio Jesuítico-Guarani: El debate en Argentina a principios del siglo XX." *Anais Do Museu Paulista: História e Cultura Material* 26: 1–34.

Queirel, Juan. 1901. *Las ruinas de Misiones*. Buenos Aires: Imprenta de la Nación.

Ribeiro, David. 2017. "Da redução jesuítica à sagrada aldeia de pedra Mbyá-Guarani: Uma reflexão sobre as políticas patrimoniais no Brasil a partir do caso do sítio arqueológico de São Miguel Arcanjo." Paper presented at the XXIX Congreso Nacional de História, Brasilia.

Rosas, Ana. 1998. "Presentación: El patrimonio cultural." *Alteridades* 16: 3–9.

Ruíz, Irma. 1996. "Acerca de la sustitución de un idiófono indígena por un cordófono europeo: Los mbaraká de los Mbyá-Guarani." *Revista Argentina de Musicología* 1: 81–92.

Saint Hilaire, Auguste. 1820. *Viaje ao Rio Grande do Sul (1820–1821)*. São Paulo: Companhia Editora Nacional.

Saito, Akira. 2005. "Las misiones y la administración del documento: El caso de Mojos, siglos XVIII–XX." *Senri Ethnological Studies* 68: 27–72.

Santos-Granero, Fernando. 2009. *The Occult Life of Things: Native Amazonian Theories of Materiality and Personhood*. Tucson: University of Arizona Press.

Sarreal, Julia. 2014. *The Guarani and Their Missions: A Socioeconomic History*. Stanford, CA: Stanford University Press.

Telesca, Ignacio. 2014. "La reinvención del Paraguay: La operación historiográfica de Blas Garay sobre las misiones Jesuíticas." *Revista Paraguay desde las Ciencias Sociales* 5 (12): 1–17.

von Thüngen, Maximiliano. 2021. *Ruinas jesuíticas, paisajes de la memoria: El patrimonio cultural de los antiguos pueblos de Guaranies*. Buenos Aires: Editorial SB.

Wilde, Guillermo. 2003. "Imaginarios oficiales y evocaciones locales: Los usos del pasado jesuítico-Guarani." *Avá* 4: 53–72.

———. 2019a. "Frontier Missions in South America: Impositions, Adaptations and Appropriations." In *The Oxford Handbook of Borderlands of the Iberian world*, edited by Danna Rojo and Cynthia Radding, 545–67. Oxford: Oxford University Press.

———. 2019b. "Regímenes de Memoria Misional: Formas visuales emergentes en las Reducciones Jesuíticas de América Del Sur." *Colonial Latin American Review* 28 (1): 10–36.

Wilde, Guillermo, and Kazuhisa Takeda. 2021. "Tecnologías de la memoria: Mapas y padrones en la configuración del territorio Guarani de las misiones." *Hispanic American Historical Review* 101 (4): 597–627.

Wilde, Guillermo, Fernando Torre-Londoño, and Franz Obermeier. 2018. "Jesuits in Portuguese-Speaking America: A Historiographic Vacuum in Post-Restoration Period." *Jesuit Historiography Online*. ri.conicet.gov.ar /handle/11336/177895.

Wilde, Guillermo, and Fabián Vega. 2019. "De la indiferencia entre lo temporal y lo eterno: Élites indígenas, cultura textual y memoria en las fronteras de América del Sur." *Varia Historia* 35 (68): 461–506.

Notes

1. For a long-term economic history of the missions, several works can be consulted: Mörner 1953; Garavaglia 1987; Cushner 1983; Sarreal 2014.

2. Archivo General de Indias, MP-BUENOS_AIRES, 19BIS. Consultado en el Portal de Archivos Españoles (PARES). En mismo legajo existen dos copias de este documento.

3. It is the case of a document at the Archive of the Jesuits in Rome, in the context of research made by the official Blazquez de Valderde, "para poder imprimir los testimonios que presentan sobre la calumnia que dizen padecieron en las Provincias del Paraguay, sobre las minas del oro, que en dichas Provincias afirmaron muchas personas, ocultauan"; Archivum Historicum Societatis Iesu, Paraq 11, f. 341.

4. Expediente sobre imagen de la virgen en oro, 1771; Archivo General de la Nación (Buenos Aires), IX.17.3.6.

5. Among the most important were the French voyagers Martin de Moussy, Alfred Demersay, Auguste Saint-Hilaire, Aimé Bonpland, and Alcides D'Orbigny. Most of them left detailed descriptions of the state of the missions (Moussy 1864; Demersay 1864; Saint Hilaire 1820; D'Orbigny 1834).

6. The extremely negative vision of Hernández is clearly expressed in the following paragraph: "Hombres en cuyas fibras no se encuentre la herencia de la semilla de plomo sembrada por los jesuitas, hombres que sacudan la inercia y la apatía que inculcaron con su dominación despótica de 100 años. Ese es el

defecto y la desgracia de toda la región misionera que por un hombre inteli-gente, despreocupado y activo que se encuentra, uno tropieza con 200 negligentes, apáticos y llenos de ridículas preocupaciones" (Gorosito 2000).

7. In 1918, Paul Groussac, then director of the Argentinian National Library, publishes in a book devoted to the Argentine History an essay about the work of the last Jesuit chronicler of Paraguay in the eighteenth century, José Guevara. He remarks that the National Library holds a Jesuit "Libro de consultas" of "inappreciable" value for the understanding of the Jesuit history of Paraguay (Groussac 1918).

8. The Jesuit Serafim Leite had a similar role to that of Furlong in Brazil, where he revindicated the role of the Jesuits in the formation of the nation (Imolesi 2014; Leite 1938a, 1938b; Wilde, Torre-Londoño, and Obermeier 2018). The work by this Jesuit was widely recognized by canonic historiographical institutions, such as the Instituto Histórico Geográfico Brasileiro, with which experts in the Jesuit heritage of Brazil also collaborated (Custódio 2018).

9. This orientation is also represented by certain historiographies of the missions, such as that of Jesuit Carbonell de Masy, in a book that, significantly, appeared in the fifth centenary of the Spanish Conquest of America (Carbonell de Masy 1992).

10. Globalization and the intervention of "experts" from European coun-tries in the heritage and conservation policies in Chiquitos and Moxos had immediate effects in the reconfiguration of local memories and the introduc-tion of dramatic generational cuts in the experience and practice of music in the local context. This cut has concrete effects in ritual gestures as shown in the ostensible contrast of performance techniques of elderly sermon preachers (*sermoneros*) and young musicians.

11. Similar depictions of the civilizing role of music in early globalization can be found in the most diverse contexts of Latin America and the world. The Conception of Chiquitos monument has a remarkable resemblance with one located in the Oita district in Japan, where the Jesuits are supposed to have introduced Western music in the sixteenth century. The district is famous for being the place of a music festival devoted to Martha Argerich and one of the most famous tourist destinations of the island.

12. Some authors have described the direct involvement of *myba* communi-ties in the official heritage policy from the beginning of the twentieth century (Ribeiro 2017). See especially those based at Universidade Federal de Rio Grande do Sul (de Souza et al. 2007; de Souza and Taddeu 2005; de Souza et al. 2005; de Moraes et al. 2009).

13. Recent ethnographic research has emphasized the capacity of Indig-enous peoples to incorporate materials, objects, and ideas as an open attitude to the outside constitutive of their non-monolithic conception of identity.

These Indigenous conceptions imply rethinking time and spaces as reversive and continuous categories (Fausto and Heckenberger 2007; Monod-Becquelin and Molinié 1993; Albert and Ramos 2002; Santos-Granero 2009).

14. A few kilometers from the site of Trinidad in Paraguay, the communities of Pindó and Guaviramí got involved in a national program oriented to promote tourism (von Thüngen 2021).

Semiotic Policies in Conflict at São Miguel Arcanjo Mission (Brazil)

ADRIANA SCHMIDT DIAS

After the collapse of the Jesuit project in South America, the Guarani missions had different fates. Their buildings were dismantled, their stones were used as construction material for new colonial settlements, and their memories were eventually erased from the founding narratives of the nascent national states that redrew the borders of the Southern Cone (Baptista and dos Santos, 2009). In 1983, the aesthetic vision of the baroque ruins of the missions' church of São Miguel Arcanjo in Brazil prevailed in the process of its nomination by the International Council of Monuments and Sites (ICOMOS) to the UNESCO World Heritage List because it was the only example with a complete tower and facade among the remaining buildings from the Jesuit missions period in South America (Figure 5). The following year, Argentina presented the candidacy of the four missions with the best-preserved architectural structures in its territory (San Ignacio Mini, Santa Ana, Nuetra Señora de Loreto, and Santa Maria Mayor), and ICOMOS unified the proposals, making the Jesuit missions of Guarani the first transnational asset inscribed on the UNESCO's List. A decade later, two more missions' ruins from Paraguay (Jesús de Tavarengué and Santísima Trinidad del Paraná) were included in the original proposal.

Today around 20,000 persons from the Mbyá-Guarani Indigenous People currently live in the missions' region, more than half in Paraguay, with the remainder divided between Brazil and Argentina. The relationship between the Mbyá and the missions' ruins varies according to the heritage policies of each country. In Paraguay and Argentina, official history and ethnology question the relationship between the Mbyá and the missionary Guarani, which calls into question their traditional land claims (Briones 2012). In Brazil, between 2004 and 2014, the Mbyá-Guarani who live near São Miguel Arcanjo were involved in a project led by the Brazilian governmental heritage agency to document their ethnic appropriation

of the ruins as an Indigenous intangible asset. When the National Historical and Artistic Heritage Institute (IPHAN) registered the ruins of São
Miguel Arcanjo as "Tava, Place of Reference for the Mbyá-Guarani," it officially brings the "new arrivals of the margins" to the governmentality
regimes of heritage practices (Bhabha 1998). During this process, however,
São Miguel's ruins become a place of performance for distinct and conflicting notions of "being in time": the Western historicity and its notion
of heritage as opposed to the Mbyá-Guarani historicity and its notion of
belonging.

Usually, it is accepted without discussion that states and multinational
agencies have the right (and indeed the obligation) to protect, promote,
and define patrimonial assets. This right is accompanied by a profound
naturalization of institutional operations on heritage issues. But what happens when this right is challenged and faced by alternative conceptions
of history, memory, and life? The struggle of the Mbyá-Guarani to defend
their historical sense of the missions is a political act to avoid submission
to institutional discourses that promote diversity but disable differences
and depoliticize other symbolic fields (Wilde 2003). To the Mbyá, the

FIGURE 5. Ruins of São Miguel Arcanjo. (Photo by Adriana Dias, 2013)

ruins of the missions are not a monument of their defeat in the past but a place that gives visibility to their struggles at the present for the right to a transnational Indigenous territory. This case, analyzed here, highlights the following question: What can be expected from the heritage policies, in addition to thinking the Indigenous past as a consumable commodity, as something that is sold as an experience of the exotic and ghostly related to the Western fetishistic obsession with ruins?

The Missions and the Heritage Policy in Brazil

The Western concept of heritage comes from the notion of paternal inheritance (the Roman legal notion of *patrimonium*) as a legacy of civilizing sense that keeps tradition alive by recognizing the artistic and historical value of monuments. According to Pomian, heritage's objects are semiophores—in other words, monuments and museum collections work as an external memory, preserved and created by a given society at a given time. Heritage, therefore, expresses a certain order of time where the representation of the past (the historiographical operation) celebrates the choices of the present about what to remember and what to forget (Pomian 2019).

The modern historicity regime, initiated with the French Revolution, constructed the notion of Western nations as saviors of collective memory, whose function is to safeguard and protect the masterpieces and relics of the past. After World War II, patrimonial policies were oriented to preserve the future for a common benefit (as universal heritage), resulting in a multiplication of heritage protection international commitments, sponsored by UNESCO. In these patrimonial policies, there is a debt of the present with the past (to be preserved), but also with the future (to be guaranteed) (Hartog 2013 [2003]).

At that moment, the restoration of an ideal of civilization was engendered from a globalizing agenda, a kind of cultural and scientific utopia, associated with conservation. UNESCO's post-war projects defended the equivalence of different national histories, narrating the idea of a world history that was, therefore, instrumental for the constitution of civilization itself. In practice, however, UNESCO's heritage policies, which would culminate in the 1972 Convention on World Heritage Sites, were configured as a late scientific imperialism based on academic authority and the idea of the superiority of European heritage expertise and practices. From the 1950s onward, UNESCO began to play the role of an agency specializing in disseminating good preservation practices to less developed nations. Preserving the past was integrated with the potential for economic exploitation of monumental splendor, guaranteeing a future for the ruins through cultural tourism. This is a change from a utopian and humanist ideology, engendered in the post-war context, to a technocratic and developmentalist ideology, typical of the Cold War, that disciplined member states to list and conserve sites in their territories through the creation of a specialized bureaucracy (Meskell 2018).

In Brazil, the first heritage policies originate from a compromise between a renewing cultural movement, modernism, and an authoritarian policy represented by Getúlio Vargas's dictatorship (1937–45). In the 1920s, Brazilian modernism brought together liberal and conservative intellectuals into a critical agenda to the political and cultural models in force. The modernist intelligentsia understood as its social mission to build an authentic Brazilian tradition in opposition to the dominant European paradigms. The theme of heritage appears among modernists as a means of creating the symbols of modernity by recognizing the authentic (and, therefore, universal) character of expressions of popular and Native Brazilian culture. Historical and artistic heritage in Brazil has been an object of public protection since the Constitution of 1934 through the National Service (Institute, since the 1970s) of Historical and Artistic Heritage (SPHAN/IPHAN), created in 1937. As SPHAN employees, modernist intellectuals (mainly artists, writers, and architects) become ideologues of the modern state and co-participants in the construction of a mythical basis for the origin of national culture and history (Fonseca 2017a).

In 1937, the architect Lucio Costa visited São Miguel Arcanjo to evaluate its preservation conditions for patrimonial registration by SPHAN. The resulting report recommended that the remnants be kept in a "state of ruin" to only evoke the memory of the missionary experience and, at the same time, "present an absence" of what was lacking around them, the Indigenous that "let themselves be shaped by the powerful will of the Jesuit" (Costa 1937, referenced in Chuva 2017a, 186). São Miguel's church was listed in 1938 as a Brazilian artistic heritage, and a museum was built next to it in 1940 to house a collection of dozens of baroque statues, most of which were confiscated by force from local places of worship (Bauer 2006) (Figure 6).

FIGURE 6. Museum of the missions, São Miguel Arcanjo. (Photo by Adriana Dias, 2013)

The heritage registration of São Miguel also brought a didactic read-ing to the missions, consolidating the "Jesuit paradigm" in traditional Bra-zilian historiography and considering that the Indigenous had little (or even no) understanding of the artistic and historical experiences lived there. Likewise, this perspective understands that after Christianization, the "civilized" Guarani would have merged into colonial society after the collapse of the missions, giving rise to a mestizo population, and would not have descendants living as Indigenous peoples (Baptista and Boita 2019; Marchi 2018a).

From the 1990s, a postmodern regime of historicity enters the scene in the heritage economy, where conserving the past (and the environment) opens the possibility of renewing the future perspectives of new national identities, celebrating differences, and reframing collective memories. The "patrimonialization racing" that started then responds to strategies that celebrate "places of memory" as active heritage spaces, constantly built, rebuilt, and consumed by the interactions with different agents. Through commemorating the patrimonial value of places, heritage policies denationalize the past, making it a category of individual understanding and belonging. The monuments become a locus of multiple and unpredictable representations, and for historical analysis the past becomes a field of multiple possibilities, open to the study of histories that were interrupted, avoided, destroyed, and forgotten by the modern narratives (Hartog 2013 [2003]; Ricoeur 2018 [2000]).

The "authoritarian and excluding heritage practices" in Brazil concentrated in the apparent neutrality of IPHAN's technical choice, which remained unquestionable until the end of the military dictatorship (1964–85) (Miceli 1987). With redemocratization arises the demand for an expansion of the concept of cultural heritage that favored the exercise of citizenship. In the Constitution of 1988, the state becomes responsible for protecting and preserving the manifestations of popular, Indigenous, and Afro-Brazilian cultures, expressed in material and immaterial assets. This policy, however, only became effective in 2000 with the creation of the National Intangible Heritage Program, whose registration methodology was defined by IPHAN in 2006 through the National Inventory of Cultural References (NICR). The registration of intangible assets in Brazil is based on four categories: knowledge and everyday ways of doing, celebrations (rituals and parties), forms of expression, and places of collective cultural practices (places of cultural reference). The methodology elected by IPHAN derives from UNESCO's 1999 and 2003 conventions about the intangible heritage. In this way, the process must have the prior consent of the holders, who also participate in the development of the safeguard plan (Fonseca 2017b).

Between 2002 and 2016, heritage policies were transformed into instruments of reparation and affirmative policies. These changes expanded the Brazilian heritage stock, but the foundations of the dominant modernist paradigm have not been overcome (Chuva 2017b). Analyzing the heritage assets listed by IPHAN until 2016, the record of Indigenous and Afro-Brazilian intangible assets reinforces the mystique of "cultural authenticity" deriving from modernist canons invented in the Vargas Era, situating the Indigenous peoples in pristine environments, as the Tukano, Arauak, and Maku communities of São Gabriel da Cachoeira in Amazonas, or in historical contexts, as the Mbyá Guarani and the Jesuit missions in Rio Grande do Sul (Marins 2016).

The Mbyá-Guarani and the Jesuitic Missions

The current Guarani nations are an assemblage of ethnic groups that speak languages and/or dialects of the Tupi-Guarani linguistic family, among which are Mbyá, Ñandeva (or Xiripá), Kaiwá (or Pãi), Chiriguano (or Awa), and Paraguayan Guarani, in addition to Xetá, Aché (or Guayaki), Izoceño (or Chané), and Tapieté. The Guarani Indigenous peoples have their histories linked to the national histories of Brazil, Argentina, Uruguay, Paraguay, and Bolivia, totaling a population of at least 65,000 people affected by different land situations. Of this total, around 30,000 people are Kaiowá-Guarani who live in Paraguay and Brazil and 20,000 people are Mbyá-Guarani, of whom 11,500 live in Paraguay, 4,400 live in the South and Southeast Brazil, and 3,500 live in the province of Misiones in Argentina (Assis and Garlet 2004; Brighenti 2010; Melià, Saul, and Muraro 1987).

In Brazil, the Kaiowá-Guarani territory is circumscribed to Mato Grosso do Sul state, in a ruthless land dispute with agribusiness. Since the 1980s, Kaiowá have been articulating themselves in political movements for land demarcation and for the preservation of tradition, playing an important political role for the Indigenous rights recognition by the Brazilian state, ensured by the Constitution of 1988 (Baniwa 2012). In turn, when Mbyá-Guarani lost their traditional territories by the expansion of soy monocultures in La Plata Basin from the 1960s, they dispersed in a network of small village nuclei (the "tekohá"), spread over a large spatial area, that extend from the forests between the

Paraná and Uruguay rivers to the Atlantic coast, transcending the national borders between Brazil, Argentina, and Paraguay. It was this atomized pattern of land use that allowed Mbyá to "invisibility" for the non-Indians (which they call *juruá*) and which permit them to keep their traditional way of life, the *ñande reko*. Unlike the Kaiowá, attached to a single territory, it was in the intensification of residential mobility in the territory that the Mbyá were able to safeguard culture and conquer new spaces in continuous expansion (Assis and Garlet 2004; Ladeira 2007). The Mbyá recognized themselves as part of the Guarani Nation, but Brazilian public policies classify them by their country of birth. Therefore, Mbyá's current high mobility, especially between Argentina and South Brazil, conflicts with the legal framework used by the Brazilian government to evaluate the Native demand for land since the Constitution of 1988 (Brighenti 2010).

To test the methodology of the NICR, in 2004 the Department of Intangible Heritage (DPI) of IPHAN started an experimental project to register Indigenous heritage among the Mbyá of the Jesuitic missions region (Marchi 2018b; Marins 2016). The initial idea of this project was to update IPHAN's discourse on the historical missionary experience in the Archaeological Park and in the Museum of São Miguel to better serve the public of 40,000 visitors per year, mainly students, as well as to arrange some way to include the Mbyá who live in the village of Tekohá Koenju in the patrimonial universe of São Miguel Arcanjo. Founded in the 1990s in a forested area in the São Miguel Archaeological Park, the Koenju village had its land situation defined by the Rio Grande do Sul state in 2000, with the demarcation of an Indigenous reserve of 236 hectares, 28 kilometers from the ruins. Today, around 200 Mbyá live in Tekohá Koenju; their livelihood is based on traditional agriculture and handicrafts sales on the porch of São Miguel Museum.

Coordinated by an anthropologist hired by IPHAN with the collaboration of other researchers and Indigenous leaders, a first phase of the NICR among the Mbyá was developed between 2004 and 2008 with the objective of recording traditional knowledge. In 2006 and 2007, IPHAN organized two meetings with Mbyá political leaders in São Miguel to discuss the process of registering and safeguarding Guarani cultural references. The second meeting brought together 400 Mbyá from different villages of Brazil, Argentina, and Paraguay to hold rituals and parties, and for many it was an opportunity to see the São Miguel ruins for the first time.

After these meetings, "the Mbyá political leaders started to criticize the idea that São Miguel was a creation of the Jesuits. For them, São Miguel already existed as tekohá of the ancient Guarani, and they were the ones who invited the priests to teach them how to work the stone of the ruins" (Pires 2007, 161). IPHAN's position in relation to the Guarani reaction was divided at that time. "While part of the technicians supported the application of the inventory, another was radically opposed to the performance (and the investment of resources) of the heritage agency with Indigenous populations" that "spoiled with their misery the baroque landscape left by the Jesuit missionaries" (Moraes 2010, 45).

As a result, in 2007 a preliminary NICR was presented, defending some parameters established by the Mbyá for the patrimonialization of their intangible heritage in relation to the missions' ruins: (a) the respect of the secrecy of the Mbyá culture; (b) the demarcation of forest areas as Mbyá traditional land; and (c) the guarantee of mobility. In turn, the inventory incorporated the Native term "Tava Miri" for the physical remnants of São Miguel Arcanjo. In the final report, anthropologists suggested that beyond an "invented tradition" that linked the Mbyá to the Guarani of the missions, there is a mythical version of the missions' ruins in Mbyá cosmology (Souza et al. 2007). They are Tava Miri, a "spiritualized stone village" that will shine as the gods' dwelling place at the end of this earthly world (Souza and Morinico 2009, 310–13). For the anthropologists, "in the Mbyá language, the term advocates a relationship between stone (*ita*) and person (*ava*): Tava (the "place where people live"). The adjective 'Miri' provides an ethereal and heavenly aura to the place" (Moraes 2010, 50). The ethnological approach emphasized an eschatological vision as a central element of the Indigenous narrative about the ruins, as expressed in the following passage:

> At the end of the world, the stones of the ruins and the wooden statues in São Miguel will "come back to life," say the Mbyá-Guarani. . . . "Primeval" here is used in the sense that Tava Miri São Miguel will become full again, to the point of transforming itself into another abode of the gods. The terrestrial stratum will recover its divine and spiritual properties and São Miguel will be able to be inhabited again

by the Mbyá converted into immortal men. São Miguel is understood as an example of a place where Yvy marae'i (the Land without Evil), one day, may shine again. (Souza and Morinico 2009, 315)

The ethnological approach offered by the first NICR triggered a series of political tensions among the Mbyá, especially by keeping the focus of the analysis on the meaning of the ruins in a cosmological time and disregarding the role that it has in the present as a locus of Indigenous rights claims. In this context of questioning the results of the first INRC by the Mbyá, in 2009 IPHAN decided to expand the Mbyá cultural inventory to other Brazilian states, and new safeguard actions were proposed. One of the initiatives with greatest impact in this second moment of the Mbyá NICR were the workshops held by the NGO "Video in the Villages,"[1] coordinated by Vicente Carelli, in which two young Mbyá leaders from Tekohá Koenju, Ariel Ortega and Patrícia Ferreira, participated. This workshop gave rise to the documentary *Mokoi tekoa, petei jeguatá: Duas aldeias, uma caminhada* (2009), followed by the films *Bicicletas de Ñhanderú* (2011), *Desterro Guarani* (2011), and *Tava, a Casa de Pedra* (2012), all directed by Ortega and Ferreira.

In this film production, the Indigenous directors are also characters, and the script is created during the filming process, faithful to the notion of the prophetic walk (*jeguatá*). The films are vectors of the "beautiful words" (*ayvu porã*), inspired by mythical ancestor Ñhanderu, and the narrative focus is the dialogue between the filmmakers and the elderly, constructed in a didactic way so that the no-Indians, the *juruá*, could understand the truth about the Mbyá. Likewise, cinema was the instrument of cultural register chosen by the Mbyá because it is a vehicle that respects orality and preserves memory for future generations (Wolf 2019). According to Ariel Ortega:

> Nowadays, most communities already have schools and children are no longer growing up like they used to, they don't sit by the fire during the afternoon . . . [to hear the] leaders to talk about our culture, our way of being Guarani. Nowadays technologies are arriving very quickly within the village, such as cell phones, social networks, computers, television. Cinema is very important for us to have our own materials, filmed within the village by ourselves. . . . All of this is shown within the village, and we also watch the work of other villages to find out how

our village is different, what the difficulties are, the territorial problems. Cinema is a Western tool, but I am using it to defend myself and to tell another story, mine, which is within the village. (Ortega, interview for Wittmann and Téo, 2018, 160, 162)

In this second stage of the INRC was also presented the proposal formal training for Mbyá researchers so that they could take control of the documentation of their own cultural practices. The result was the identification and mapping of "Xondaro," a ritual fight-dance that represents the defense of the traditional territory and the production of the documentary *Tava, a Casa de Pedra* (2012), directed by Ariel Ortega and Patrícia Ferreira, which forms the instructional documentation for the Registration Process of Intangible Heritage[2] approved by the IPHAN Advisory Board in 2014 (IPHAN 2014).

In the film, Tava, Ortega, and Ferreira demonstrate the conflicts between distinct notions of Mbyá and *juruá* historicity, performed in the spheres of heritage. In a statement in the film, Ariel Ortega argues that "to continue the ancestral journey, we have to follow the path open to us to give visibility to the Guarani struggles for the right to land and life." In the reports of the elders recorded in the documentary, for the Mbyá the missions are solely *tava* (ruins), symbolizing the eschatological dilemma that orders Guarani cosmology, yesterday, today, and always: the opposition between the *yvy vai*, the earthly world, shared with the *juruá*, which is imperfect, marked by ruin, aging, death, and oblivion; and *yvy marãey* (land without evils) and *yvyju mirí* (perfect land), the celestial world, resplendent and divine, that awaits the Guarani who protects the good living of tradition in earthly life (*ñande rekó*).

The individual and collective destiny of the Mbyá in the imperfect material world is to be a vehicle for the soul-words of Ñhanderu, the creator of life, to escape death and ascend, with body and soul, to the perfect land (Ladeira 2007). In the narratives recorded in the film *Tava*, the elders teach that the demiurges built the earthly world by walking and demarcating sacred places so that their children could know where to build their villages and plant their gardens and thus maintain the *ñande rekó*. The stone houses (*tava*) of the Jesuits were built by the work of the Guarani who have lived in these sacred places since the beginning of the world. The Guarani who believed in the priests became Christians and went to live in stone houses, lost themselves in the material world of the *juruá*, and perished. But for the Guarani who hide in the forests as the Mbyá and keep the tradition alive, the ruined stone houses of the Jesuits are testimony to the decay that awaits those who stray from the *ñande rekó*.

For the Mbyá, the stone houses were only *Miri* (divine) for the Guarani that adopt Christianity in the past, but not for the present-day Mbyá Guarani who understand the ruins as landmarks for reclaiming their ancestral rights. Considering the Indigenous criticisms, the *Miri* suffix suggested by anthropologists in the first phase of the INRC was removed from the heritage designation, and after a decade of negotiations with IPHAN, the Mbyá defined the title of the Registry of São Miguel as a Brazilian Indigenous intangible asset as "Tava, Place of Reference for the Guarani People" (IPHAN 2014).

Conclusion

Since the nineteenth century, the paradox that the ancient ruins are needed to build modern nations has become established in heritage policies. Ruins are fascinating to the Western imagination as a kind of utopia in reverse, which eternally evokes a romantic longing for a time irretrievably lost. The ruins are "ghostly" heritage assets because they represent the hiatus between a previous state of life and its rebirth through restoration when they are transformed into monuments. By reflecting the materiality of historical experience, from a genealogical perspective, the symbolic capital of ruins, therefore, is an arena for dispute, negotiation, and contestation by different groups and social agents (Hamilakis 2007; Huyssen 2014).

The ruins of the Jesuit missions of the province of Paraguay theatricalize the past in contemporary scenarios full of controlled, promoted, and commercialized heritage meanings. The Mbyá semiotic disputes around the ruins of São Miguel Arcanjo, visited here, indicate a reordering of local hierarchies in defense of more horizontal configurations of heritage appreciation. Once the Mbyá understood "the ritual path" of patrimonial bureaucracy, their leaders mobilized to formulate a proposal that better represented their cultural demands in the present for the recognition of territorial rights that transcend national borders (Pires 2007).

The Mbyá struggle for self-determination over the ten years of the negotiation with IPHAN reflects, on a local scale, a broader debate about the absence, until recently, of specific UNESCO policies regarding Indigenous heritage rights. Only in 2018 the debate on world cultural heritage begins to officially consider the demands of intra-national agents, "enclaves within Nations" represented by Indigenous peoples and ethnic groups who fight for autonomy to define, preserve, and use their material and immaterial heritage (Colwell and Joy 2015, 113). The publication in 2018 of UNESCO's "Collaboration Policy with Indigenous Peoples" reaffirms a decade later the commitments made in the 2007 in the "United Nations Declaration on the Rights of Indigenous Peoples" regarding self-determination, autonomy, participation in decision-making, and defense of cultural, identity, and territorial rights. However, this process was quite turbulent at the highest levels of UNESCO, extending since 2000, when a first effort was made for Indigenous Peoples to have a voice in the processes of naming their heritage by the World Heritage Committee (Meskell 2013).

However, the case of São Miguel Arcanjo also demonstrates how the ethereal evocations of the modernist ghost continue to haunt the heritage agendas that surround the missions ruins. The ruins of São Miguel Arcanjo are a sign of the tragic, where history takes place as a catastrophe, loss, war, and destruction. But they are also "arché" of the Brazilian modern nation: "It is genesis that goes back to the roots and, therefore, points to the bases of belonging" (Pesavento 2007, 61). In the logic of patrimonialization of cultural landscapes related to Indigenous history oriented by the ICOMOS and UNESCO, the mission ruins operate as the setting of an abandoned ghost town, where the contemplative relationship with the monument serves to activate the historical memory. For these reasons, the ruins of São Miguel Arcanjo are only sacred (*miri*) for the heritage gaze of architects, historians, archaeologists, anthropologists, and tourists.

For example, after the registry of São Miguel as a Brazilian Indigenous intangible asset, tekohá Koenju was included in the local commercial circuits that attempt the demands for authenticity of the tourism imaginary eager to consume exotic products (Salazar and Zhu 2015). In this scenario, the Mbyá political struggles in the present are shadowed by the still strong civilizing rhetoric of the Jesuits in the imaginary of the missions for the tourists, renewed every year in the religious pilgrimages to the Caaraó

FIGURE 7. Caaraó sanctuary. (Photo by Adriana Dias, 2013)

Sanctuary, near São Miguel, the mythical place where the Jesuit Roque Gonzalez, canonized in 1988, was killed by the Guarani in 1628 (Barcelos 2016) (Figure 7). As well, the agendas of the modernist ghost continue to echo in the São Miguel church every night in the "sound and light show," in which script the ruins themselves are alive and tell the public their history of resistance as a materialization of a romantic utopia, inspired by Christian values.

For Indigenous peoples, archaeological sites and mission ruins are testimonies of the lives of their ancestors that connect "the physical and the spiritual, the past and the present" to inspire the continuous fight to preserve the legacy of tradition for future generations (Colwell and Joy 2015, 121). Therefore, for the Mbyá-Guarani the Jesuit stone houses continue to be a warning of the ruin that awaits the Guarani who move away from tradition. As well documented in recent Mbyá filmography, it is to the invisibility of the forests of Argentina and Paraguay that the Mbyá should return every time they feel lost in the world of the *juruá* in Brazil, because it is there that the secret of tradition can be kept, far from the eyes of state heritage agents.

References

Assis, Valéria, and Ivori Garlet. 2004. "Análise sobre as populações Guarani contemporâneas: Demografia, espacialidade e questões fundiárias." *Revista de Indias* 64 (230): 35–54.

Baniwa, Gersem. 2012. "A conquista da cidadania indígena e o fantasma da tutela no Brasil contemporâneo." In *Constituições nacionais e povos indígenas*, edited by Alcida Ramos, 206–36. Belo Horizonte: Editora da UFMG.

Baptista, Jean, and Tony Boita. 2019. "Patrimônios indígenas nos 80 anos do Museu das Missões: Etno-história e etnomuseologia aplicada à imaginária missional." *Boletim do Museus Paraense Emílio Goeldi (Ciências Humanas)* 14 (1): 189–205.

Baptista, Jean, and Maria Cristina dos Santos. 2009. *As ruínas: A crise entre o temporal e o eterno*. Vol. 3, *Dossiê missões*. São Miguel das Missões: Museu das Missões.

Barcelos, Artur. 2016. "Narrativas materiais: As missões jesuíticas e seu sistema solar patrimonial." In *Espacios misionales en diálogo con la globalidad Iberoamérica*, edited by Maria Laura Salinas and Lia Renata Quarleri, 225–51. Resistencia: Universidad Nacional del Nordeste.

Bauer, Letícia. 2006. "O arquiteto e o zelador: Patrimônio cultural, história e memória em São Miguel das Missões (1937–1950)." Master's thesis. Porto Alegre: Universidade Federal do Rio Grande do Sul.

Bhabha, Homi. 1998. *O local da cultura*. Belo Horizonte: Editora da UFMG.

Brighenti, Clovis. 2010. *Estrangeiros na própria terra: Presença Guarani e estados nacionais*. Florianópolis: Editora da UFSC.

Briones, Claudia. 2012. "Os direitos territoriais dos povos indígenas na Argentina." In *Constituições Nacionais e Povos Indígenas*, edited by Alcida Ramos, 158–204. Belo Horizonte: Editora da UFMG.

Colwell, Chip, and Charlotte Joy. 2015. "Communities and Ethics in the Heritage Debate." In *Global Heritage: A Reader*, edited by Lynn Meskell, 112–30. Oxford: Blackwell.

Chuva, Márcia. 2017a. *Os arquitetos da Memória: Socio gênese das práticas de preservação do patrimônio cultural no Brasil (anos 1930–1940)*. Rio de Janeiro: Editora UFRJ.

———. 2017b. "Possíveis narrativas sobre duas décadas de patrimônio de 1982 a 2002." *Revista do Patrimônio Histórico e Artístico Nacional* 35: 79–103.

Fonseca, Maria Cecilia. 1997a. *O patrimônio em processo: Trajetória da política federal de preservação no Brasil*. Rio de Janeiro: Editora UFRJ.

———. 1997b. "A salvaguarda do patrimônio cultural imaterial do IPHAN: antecedentes, realizações e desafios." *Revista do Patrimônio Histórico e Artístico Nacional* 35: 157–69.

IPHAN. 2014. *Dossiê de registro: IPHAN TAVA—Lugar de referência para os Guarani*. http://portal.iphan.gov.br/uploads/ckfinder/arquivos/Dossie_da _Tava_Lugar_de_Referencia_para_o_Povo_Guarani(1).pdf.

Hamilakis, Yannis. 2007. *The Nation and Its Ruins: Antiquity, Archaeology and National Imagination in Greece*. New York: Oxford University Press.

Hartog, François. 2013 [2003]. *Regimes de historicidade: Presenteísmo e experiências do tempo*. Belo Horizonte: Autêntica.

Huyssen, Andreas. 2014. *Culturas do passado-presente: Modernismos, artes visuais, políticas da memória*. Rio de Janeiro: Editora Contraponto.

Ladeira, Maria Inês. 2007. *O caminhar sob a luz: Território Mbyá à beira do oceano*. São Paulo: UNESP.

Marchi, Darlan de Mamann. 2018a. "O patrimônio antes do patrimônio em São Miguel das Missões: Dos Jesuítas à UNESCO." PhD diss. Pelotas: Universidade Federal de Pelotas.

———. 2018b. "Patrimônio cultural imaterial em lugar patrimonial consagrado: O registro da Tava em São Miguel das Missões." In *Memória & Patrimônio: Temas e debates*, edited by Eduardo Knack, Maria Letícia Ferreira, and Rita Poloni, 199–219. Porto Alegre: Editora Fi.

Marins, Paulo César Garcez. 2016. "Novos patrimônios, um novo Brasil? Um balanço das políticas patrimoniais federais após a década de 1980." *Estudos Históricos* 29 (57): 9–28.

Melià, Bartomeu, Marcos Saul, and Valmir Muraro. 1987. *O Guarani: Uma bibliografia etnológica*. Santo Ângelo: Fundames.

Meskell, Lynn. 2013. "UNESCO and the Fate of the World Heritage Indigenous Peoples Council of Experts (WHIPCOE)." *International Journal of Cultural Property* 20: 155–74.

———. 2018. *A Future in Ruins: Unesco, World Heritage and the Dream of Peace*. Oxford: Oxford University Press.

Miceli, Sergio. 1987. SPHAN: "Refrigério da cultura oficial." *Revista do Patrimônio Histórico e Artístico Nacional* 22: 44–47.

Moraes, Carlos Eduardo de. 2010. "A refiguração da Tava Miri São Miguel na memória coletiva dos Mbyá-Guarani nas missões/RS, Brasil." Master's thesis. Porto Alegre: Universidade Federal do Rio Grande do Sul.

Pesavento, Sandra. 2007. "Missões, um espaço no tempo: Paisagens de memória." In *Fronteiras do Mundo Ibérico: Patrimônio, território e memória das Missões*, edited by Sandra Pesavento and Ana Lucia Meira, 51–63. Porto Alegre: Editira da UFRGS.

Pires, Daniele. 2007. "Alegorias etnográficas do Mbyá Rekó em cenários interétnicos no Rio Grande do Sul (2003–2007): Discurso, prática e holismo Mbyá frente às políticas públicas diferenciadas." Master's thesis. Porto Alegre: Universidade Federal do Rio Grande do Sul.

Pomian, Krzysztof. 2019. "Relics, Collections, and Memory." *Acta Poloniae Historica* 119: 7–26.

Ricoeur, Paul. 2018 [2000]. *A memória, a história, o esquecimento.* Campinas: Editora da Unicamp.

Salazar, Noel, and Yujie Zhu. 2015. "Heritage and Tourism." In *Global Heritage: A Reader*, edited by Lynn Meskell, 240–58. Oxford: Blackwell.

Souza, José Otávio Catafesto de, and José Cirilo Morinico. 2009. "Fantasmas das brenhas ressurgem nas ruínas: Mbyá-Guaranis relatam sua versão sobre as missões e depois delas." In *História do Rio Grande do Sul*, vol. 5, *Povos indígenas*, edited by Tao Golin and Nelson Boeira, 301–30. Passo Fundo: Editora Méritos.

Souza, José Otávio Catafesto de, Carlos Eduardo Moraes, Daniele Pires, José Cirilo Morinoco, and Mônica Arnt. 2007. *Tava miri São Miguel Arcanjo, Sagrada Aldeia de Pedra: Os Mbyá-Guarani nas Missões.* Porto Alegre: IPHAN.

Wilde, Guillermo. 2003. "Imaginarios oficiales y evocaciones locales: Los usos del pasado jesuítico Guarani." *Avá* 4: 53–72.

Wittmann, Luisa, and Marcelo Téo. 2018. "Entrevista com Ariel Ortega, cineasta Mbyá-Guarani." *Fronteiras: Revista Catarinense de História* 31: 159–63.

Wolf, Ivarnice. 2019. "A produção videográfica dos Guarani: Entre o político e a arte." Master's thesis. Vitória: Universidade Federal do Espírito Santo.

Notes

1. "Apresentação," *Vídeo nas aldeias*, http://www.videonasaldeias.org.br /2009/vna.php?p=1.

2. "Tava Lugar de Referência para o Povo Guarani," YouTube, https://www .youtube.com/watch?v=wVH5MUF01U0.

Teaching Missions, Training Citizens
The California Missions as Curriculum

ELIZABETH KRYDER-REID

Introduction

Research on missions, as on other historic sites, typically focuses on their history and materiality and, at times, their afterlife as tourist destinations and their import in contemporary political and social fields of power. It is instructive to also consider missions as curriculum in both formal and informal learning contexts. In the case of the California missions, the current state history-social science framework says, "Building missions from sugar cubes or popsicle sticks does not help students understand the period and is offensive to many." Instead, it positions the missions as "sites of conflict, conquest, and forced labor" (California State Board of Education 2016). The framework adopted in 2016 stands in sharp contrast not only to prior state-sanctioned curricular frameworks, but to the historical interpretation at many of the mission sites themselves. The discourse surrounding both the curriculum and mission sites highlights the highly contested meanings accorded the California missions as public heritage sites and signals the divergent interests of stakeholders in the state's historical narrative. The revised framework also invites exploration of the particular role of missions in US public memory and the ways in which their narratives and counternarratives reveal the tensions of religion and heritage. Finally, the particular circumstances surrounding the intersections of California mission history and public education illuminate the fissures of the settler colonial ideologies and the politicization of teaching US history in this third decade of the twenty-first century.

The twenty-one California missions were established by Franciscans in the late eighteenth and early nineteenth centuries as part of Spain's expansion into Alta California (Haas 2014; Hackel 2005; Jackson and Castillo 1995; Lightfoot 2005; Madley 2019; Sandos 2004). Secularized in 1833, many missions became private property for a short time under

Mexican rule. Under American governance and during a time of systematic state-sponsored violence to subjugate Native people throughout the state (Lindsay 2012; Madley 2016), the mission properties were restored to the Catholic Church in 1865. With the exception of two sites run by the California Department of Parks and Recreation, the missions are still owned and operated by the Catholic Church in various administrative capacities (parishes, Diocesan Center, universities, etc.). Not only were the missions significant sites in the colonial conquest of Native peoples and lands, but they have become central to the narratives of California history. They are complex heritage sites, therefore, that blend multiple functions—places of worship, historic sites, destinations for both sacred and civic pilgrimages, and sites of public education.

As sites for the production of heritage, the California missions have played a well-documented role in the construction of what has been called the "Spanish fantasy past" (Kryder-Reid 2016; Lorimer 2016; McWilliams 1946; Kropp 2006; Thomas 1991). This richly imagined version of colonial history not only celebrates a romanticized Mediterranean aesthetic, but it presents that fantasy past as a white-centered, Christian, triumphalist narrative that marginalizes Indigenous people and erases the oppression and dispossession of the colonial project. It elevates the Franciscan padres, particularly the missions' founder, Junípero Serra, as the heroes of the narrative. Furthermore, this valorized history has been promulgated in cultural productions as varied as pageants and performances, literature and art, tourism and marketing, and through a wide range of material culture including the mission landscapes (DeLyser 2005; Deverell 2004; Kropp 2006; Kryder-Reid 2016; Lorimer 2016). The public memory practices associated with the missions have developed over a century and a half, and they are entangled with political interests, economic incentives, and cultural identity. As such, mission discourses and memory practices are both a reflection of the broader settler colonial narrative and an active part of the construction of heritage.

A critical heritage lens (Gentry and Smith 2019; Harrison 2012; Lehrer, Milton, and Patterson 2011; Winter 2013) interrogates the intersections of heritage and power relations such as those entangled in "nationalism, imperialism, colonialism, cultural elitism, Western triumphalism, social exclusion based on class and ethnicity, and the fetishising of expert knowledge" (ACHS 2012). Similarly, critical pedagogy encourages students to critique structures of power and oppression (Freire 1970; Kincheloe 2008). A productive entry into a critical examination of the construction of heritage at the California missions, therefore, is their place in curriculum, including both the formal educational practices of state-sponsored education and the distributed practices of informal learning settings. This chapter explores the history and ideological implications of the California missions as pedagogical instruments and offers observations on the particular place of missions in American social studies education.

Social Studies Curriculum

In the face of deeply entrenched, widely practiced, and romanticized California mission narratives, the curriculum covering the missions has been a long-standing arena for the contestation of the state's historical narrative. In that sense, the missions are just one thread in the complex tapestry of the politics of public education in the United States. It is worth noting that while the US colonies were among the first to pass compulsory education laws (Perkinson 1995), and while the role of public education has long been debated, it is widely agreed that education's purpose is not simply the transfer of knowledge, but instead that educating youth contributes to the public good (Miller 1992; Bankston and Caldas 2009; Evans 2020). The notion of an educated citizenry may seem an obvious and central value for any society, but just what that citizen is to know and why has had widely divergent objectives (Adams 2019; Bankston and Caldas 2009; Church 1976; Dewey 1899; Miller 1992; Reese 2005; Bickford and Clabough 2022). Writing at the end of the nineteenth century, Conway McMillan argued that "education at the schools—social education—has therefore not only the duty of stimulating the individual to do his best as an individual, but more fundamentally it must from its very nature so mould him that he will be the best as a member of society" (McMillan 1896, 334).

The history of US curriculum is particularly charged regarding the role of social studies—a field, as curriculum historian Ronald Evans has noted, that serves as "a tangible forum through which Americans have struggled over competing visions of the good society and the desirable future" (Evans 2006, 321). Since the introduction of social studies into public schools in 1916, the goals have been articulated in terms of promoting social welfare, whether conceived as citizen education to inculcate national values and build cohesive community or more progressive outcomes of training critical, self-reflective thinkers and "sustaining individuals and groups from the ravages of urbanization and industrialization" (Saxe 1991, 3). Throughout the twentieth century, public education, particularly history and social studies, has often been entangled in the battles of those who want to encourage identification with shared values of community and nation and those who want to support individual, critical engagement with the world and to grapple with complex perspectives and divergent experiences.

Education scholar E. Wayne Ross has examined the role of curriculum in building a democratic society, particularly in the context of neoliberal trends of "antidemocratic impulses of greed, individualism, and intolerance" and advocated for the idea that social studies can and perhaps even should be a part of the "pursuit of dangerous citizenship" (Ross 2017). In his examination of *The Social Studies Wars* Evans argues that there at least five competing camps that have shaped the direction of social studies teaching: (1) traditional historians who emphasize historical factual content mastery; (2) advocates of teaching social science methodologies; (3) educators drawing on techniques of business and industry to prepare students for life roles; (4) those influenced by John Dewey and promoting a reflective and issues-centered curriculum; and (5) the related critical pedagogues who encourage critical examination of power structures and envision social studies as instrumental in transforming American society (Evans 2004). Others have characterized the factions somewhat differently (e.g., Kliebard 1986, Hertzberg 1981), but all agree that the trends are predicated on the shifts in the broader fields of power in American society, as well as enduring structural racism in the field of education itself (Bickford and Clabough 2022). Evans has observed a predominant pattern that social studies curriculum has tended toward more traditional, discipline-based principles during conservative times and toward "experimentation, child-centered and inquiry or issues-oriented curricula during liberal times" (Evans 2006, 317).

Given the increasingly polarized US politics over the first two and a half decades of the twenty-first century, history and social studies curriculum has become particularly contested as proponents of divergent views have waged their culture wars in textbooks and curricular standards in K-12 and higher education. As Kenneth Teitelbaum has phrased it . . .

Curriculum conflicts are not just *about* our politics; they *are* our politics. They are one of the ways in which we wrestle with each other over not just what is "good" in life and what is not, but also *who* is good and who is not. (Teitelbaum 2022, 49; emphasis in the original)

For example, local school board meetings have become more frequently disrupted with protests over critical race theory, inclusion of minoritized histories, and LGBTQ heritage. Florida governor and presidential hopeful Ron DeSantis made education a key battleground in his "war on woke," including legislation restricting what can be taught in K-12 classrooms and "reform" of curriculum and policies promoting diversity and equity in Florida's public universities (Kaufman-Osborn 2023). In one of the more prominent initiatives, President Donald Trump established the "1776 Commission" (in reaction to the *New York Times'* 1619 project) to support what he called "patriotic education." Should the goal of this commission be ambiguous, President Trump's 2020 speech at the National Archives made his agenda clear:

Our mission is to defend the legacy of America's founding, the virtue of America's heroes, and the nobility of the American character. We must clear away the twisted web of lies in our schools and classrooms, and teach our children the magnificent truth about our country. We want our sons and daughters to know that they are the citizens of the most exceptional nation in the history of the world. (Trump, September 17, 2020).

In contrast to the president's vision of history classes valorizing American exceptionalism, some academics, educators, cultural critics, politicians, and others continue to advance critical pedagogy, decolonizing curriculum, and other strategies to address the history of social and racial injustice in America's past (e.g., Leslie et al. 2021; Ross 2017).[1] These perspectives may be seen in contrast to those interested in preserving narratives of white supremacy, nationalistic rhetoric, exclusion of marginalized communities, and avoidance of contentious topics and painful histories. For example, the Texas legislature has debated numerous bills that seek to conscribe how history is taught, particularly around issues related to race and racism (Romero 2021). South Dakota's latest social studies standards draft reduced the references to the state's Indigenous history and culture, aligning with Governor Kristi Noem's recent statements in support of "honest, patriotic education that cultivates in our children a profound love for our country" (Matzen 2021). It is hardly surprising, therefore, that in this time of increasingly strident critiques of long-standing, white-centered histories reinforcing narratives of American exceptionalism and settler colonial ideologies, the California missions are a heritage hot spot, and their role in curriculum is contested.

California Missions as Curriculum

As in most states in the US, California's fourth-grade social studies curriculum provides students an opportunity to delve into the state's history. The role of the missions in that narrative for many years followed a typical pattern: it began with a brief overview of Native California life before the arrival of Europeans (aka "prehistory"), followed by the story of the missions' establishment, which signaled the beginning of history with all the markers "civilization" (Keenan 2019, 2021; Kryder-Reid 2015; Schneider et al. 2019). For example, *A Child's History of California* (Flower 1949), a mid-twentieth-century fourth-grade textbook still in use in California in 1971, contained twenty-six chapters, one of which (chapter 2) was devoted to "The first people to live in California" and one (chapter 9) on "The California missions" (Figure 8). In Chapter 2 the text focuses primarily on material culture and presents the early history of Native California as a static society, stating, "In the Indian mounds there is little change. The Indians did not learn to make better tools than the first Indians had made. In all the years that went by, the Indians did not change very much or improve their ways of making things to use" (Flower 1949, 22). The chapter devoted to the California missions merits quoting at length.

> The mission fathers were happy. Father Serra was the happiest of all. To build missions in California and teach the Indians were what he had dreamed of doing for many years. The mission fathers made friends with the Indians. They taught them to help in the missions. . . . Before the Spanish came, the Indians did not plant seeds. They did not raise any food. They did not water the ground to make things grow. . . . Everyone at the missions was busy. There was much work to be done. . . . In some places, the Indians were friendly and peaceful. They liked the fathers. They were glad to come to the mission to live and work.

ᕦ ·· ᕤ

Table of Contents

FIGURE 8. Table of contents, Enola Flower, *A Child's History of California*, 1949.

. . . . . [Following secularization] The fathers were very sad at leaving. The Indians were very unhappy to say good-by to the good fathers. The Indians were like children. They could not take good care of themselves. Some of them ran away to Indian villages where they could be wild and did not have to work. Others tried to take care of the fields

and orchards as the fathers had taught them. But they needed someone to tell them what to do and how to do it. (Flower 1949, 55, 57–59,
64–65)

The textbook, written for nine- and ten-year-olds, not only promulgated
the imagery of benevolent nurturing pastors training the childlike, grateful Native peoples, but it was premised on many of the common markers
of Western cultural superiority—domesticated plants and animals, disciplined labor practices, and technological advancement. The text is notable not only for its Western-centric cultural superiority, but also for its
lacunae. The text erases the violence and dispossession central to the colonial project. It excludes California Indigenous peoples outside the missions and ignores the ongoing presence of Native communities, to name
but a few of its problematic messages.

In addition to its didactic prose, Flower's text also includes an exercise
that, while never a part of the state-mandated curriculum or state standards, was a widely distributed practice of making mission models. In the
list of suggested activities, Flower includes having students create "an
imaginary tour of the missions . . . developed by illustrated reports or soap
sculpture or clay modeling." As has been discussed elsewhere, that practice endured for at least seventy years as children-built mission models that
replicated the familiar tropes of the benevolent, productive, cultivated,
beautiful landscape (Gutfreund 2010; Keenan 2019, 2021; Kryder-Reid
2015). These mission models became discursive objects, as they were displayed in libraries, museums, amusement parks, fairs, and at the mission
sites and museums (Collins 2021; Kryder-Reid 2015). These miniaturized
missions not only reproduced a triumphalist settler colonial narrative, but
with their colorful gardens, tiny fountains, contemplative Franciscans, and
gold bells, they amplified California booster imagery of a "new Eden." They
materialized a nostalgic, romanticized, aestheticized vision of California's
past (Figure 9).

The lessons taught at and through the missions have reflected the
changing politics of the times. In the early twentieth century, the missions
were seen as a peaceful oasis in the face of increasing urbanization and
the pace of modern life. During the post–WWII era, the missions were
presented to elementary students as an object lesson of American progress
and white Christian values (Gutfreund 2010). During the 1960s, politically

FIGURE 9. Model of Mission San Gabriel made by a fourth grader on display at the mission in 2013. (Photo by Elizabeth Kryder-Reid)

conservative figures such as Max Rafferty, California superintendent of public schools from 1962 to 1970 and the first elected rather than appointed person to serve in the position, used their power to resist what they saw as anti-establishment influences. Rafferty's 1961 speech "The Passing of the Patriot," given at La Cañada School in the northeast suburbs of Los Angeles, advocated teaching "traditional values" to counter what he saw as the rising immorality of the "sideburned" and "unwashed" youth (Rafferty 1961; Herrera 2019). Rafferty's rhetoric not only increased his reputation as a conservative firebrand but presaged the sentiments of Reagan-era educational reform and Trump's speech at the National Archives: "Education during the last three decades has deliberately debunked the hero. If it is ugly to teach children to revere the great Americans of the past, to cherish the traditions of our country, to hate communism and its creatures, then I say let's be ugly" (Rafferty 1961, quoted in Gutfreund 2010).

In counterpoint to this triumphalist framing of the missions in the California curriculum, activists and scholars, particularly Indigenous scholars, have advocated for more critical histories and for curriculum reform. Rupert Costo (Cahuilla) and Jeannette Henry Costo (Cherokee) were among the early activists promoting revising state educational standards. They published the influential *The Missions of California: A Legacy of Genocide* (Costo and Costo 1987), founded the American Indian Historical Society, and started the Indian Historian Press (Herrera 2019). Native scholars such as Jack Norton (1979) and Edward Castillo (1991) and their allies (Haas 2011, 2014) also produced cogent histories that centered Indigenous perspectives. Others directly addressed the problematic messages of the curriculum (e.g., Gutfreund 2010; Keenan 2019, 2021; Miranda 2013; Schneider et al. 2019; Trafzer and Lorimer 2014). In publications, hearings, editorials, blogs, art installations, and public speaking, these scholars and activists worked to shift the dominant narrative of the formal curriculum and to challenge racist informal practices such as dressing up in Indigenous clothing and the mission model project. In one of the more biting critiques, Deborah Miranda posed a thought experiment where schoolchildren are tasked with an assignment much like the mission model project, but they are first asked to create a slavery plantation as the reconstructed environment and then a German concentration camp (Miranda 2013). These curriculum debates are not merely about matters of factual accuracy or acknowledgment of multiple perspectives, but of naming and addressing the enduring harm of white supremacist narratives in contemporary society. They call out how the teaching of the missions in California state-sponsored curriculum has perpetuated the slow violence of settler colonial ideologies. Rupert Costo articulated the ongoing harm of the curriculum for Indigenous people, saying, "There is not one Indian in the whole of this country who does not cringe in anguish and frustration because of these textbooks. There is not one Indian child who has not come home in shame and tears" (Costo, quoted in Herrera 2019).

In the past decade there has been significant progress in California curriculum reform, particularly in the representation of Indigenous history. One of the most influential factors has been the formation in 2014 of the California Indian History Curriculum Coalition (CIHCC). Begun as an informal coalition of educators, tribal scholars, and Native activists, the group has developed an annual Indian Curriculum Summit to create Indian-vetted curriculum and resources as well as advocate for meaningful change (Schneider et al. 2019). The goal is to center Native experience and include California Indian voices in the content that California children learn in school. Educational institutions have also taken a lead in this curriculum reform effort. Since 1994, Sacramento State's annual Multicultural Education Conference (MCE) has promoted California Indian participation and included the Miwok Nation on whose land the MCE meets.

A significant benchmark of curriculum reform has been the adoption of new state standards in 2016 that, as noted in the introduction to this chapter, specifically call out the problematic California mission projects. The new standards, along with the broader interest in incorporating more critical perspectives and more Indigenous voices, have spurred several new curriculum projects. A prominent example is the Stanford History Education Group (SHEG), which works to improve education by creating free curriculum and, according to their website, has had more than ten million downloads of their "Reading Like a Historian" curriculum and "Beyond the Bubble" assessments (SHEG). Their California mission curriculum, available in English and Spanish, invites students to use primary sources to better understand Spanish treatment of Native Americans in Alta California under the mission system. Students first examine two nineteenth-century paintings and read through accounts that vary in their depiction of conditions at the missions. Specifically, they read an excerpt from a book written by an American novelist, a newspaper letter written by a Scottish-born citizen of Mexico, the account of a French naval officer, and an excerpt from an interview with a Native American born at the San Luis Rey Mission. After viewing the images and reading the accounts, students are encouraged to consider the context of the sources and to ask why the artists and authors might have presented more or less favorable representations of mission life. Following this investigation of the sources, the concluding question posed in the curriculum is, "Which of the documents would you use if writing a history of the Mission System? Which would you discard? Why?" (SHEG)

Other recent curriculum development efforts suggest that work remains to be done. For example, the Huntington Library developed "Exploring the California Missions," which poses a relatively straightforward question—"How did the Native Californians and the Franciscans impact one another?," inviting students to investigate that question in the context of "Everyday life" and of "Spirituality." Like the Stanford curriculum, the Huntington lesson plan uses primary documents, such as a list of provisions and an early nineteenth-century painting, but it uses them to focus on the material culture of the colonial encounter. The framework encourages comparisons of different tools and foodways but avoids any interrogation into the fundamental power relationships, strategic goals, or health consequences of colonization, let alone the violence and dispossession of the mission system. The desired learning outcome is for students to understand, "While it can be easy to come to simple conclusions about their relationship, the Native Californians and the Franciscans affected each other in varied and complex ways" (Huntington Library—Exploring the California Missions).

Top-down state-mandated standards tell only a part, however, in the story of how the California missions operate as curriculum. A site called "Teachers Pay Teachers" offers a window into a more distributed curriculum development resource. The site markets itself as "the world's most popular online marketplace for original educational resources" and the "go-to platform created by teachers, for teachers to access the community, content, and tools they need to teach at their best" (Teachers Pay Teachers). In this online marketplace, founded in 2006, teachers (purported to be a community of more than seven million educators) can access a catalogue of over five million pieces of educator-created content. A search for "California mission" in September 2021 yielded 565 results including PowerPoints, posters, lesson plans, reading passages and questions, flip book templates, Google classroom activities, and a "Distance learning California missions digital breakout escape room." One of the offerings, "The Living History of Father Serra, Founder of the California Missions," is a document including instructions and a script so that teachers can act "like your favorite padre, Father Serra himself." The description promises that, "with a quick costume change and 10 minutes of preparation, you will transform your classroom or MPR into a 45-minute interactive experience that will captivate your listeners and catapult you into rock star status." The cost is $4.99 and has a 5 out of 5-star rating in the reviews. The premise of educator-produced content available to other educators, along with the idea that teachers who have developed innovative, effective curricular materials should be able to profit from it, are commendable. But the site illustrates the challenge of creating meaningful change and incorporating Native voices and perspectives into California social studies classrooms. Even though the traditional mission project is no longer sanctioned in the state standards and curriculum reform advocates have pleaded, "Repeat after us, say no to the mission project" (Tran 2017), making models is a long-standing practice, and most of the resources on the Teachers Pay Teachers site still refer to the mission project. Furthermore, it is challenging for educators, however well-intentioned, to realize the new goals of conveying the range of experiences at the missions, incorporating Indigenous voices, and presenting a more complex view of the missions, let alone connecting past events with their contemporary consequences.

California Mission Sites as Curriculum

Just as school curriculum has mobilized the missions as a purveyor of ideas about California's past, so too the mission sites serve as places of pedagogy. In a volume exploring missions as heritage, it is useful to think critically about the particular role of religious sites in creating didactic experiences and operating as spaces of public memory (Buggeln, Paine, and Plate 2017; Buggeln and Franco 2018). As historical missions and (mostly) Catholic-owned heritage sites, the missions operate in a complex intersection of contemporary faith-based communities and sectarian heritage as well as a variety of local, state, and national discourses and of Indigenous communities and others who identify a shared affinity with the sites. To understand the ways in which mission heritage operates as curriculum, it is illuminating to examine what stories are told at the sites, whose voices are heard, and who has the authority to make those interpretive decisions. Because of their functions as both historic sites and worship homes of faith-based communities, the missions also raise issues about the separation of church and state. A particular point of contention has been the use of taxpayer dollars to support restorations, especially following crises such as the 1925 earthquake at Santa Barbara, the 2003 earthquake that nearly destroyed Mission San Miguel, and the 2020 fire at Mission San Gabriel (Kryder-Reid 2018). The tension between secular and religious heritage has also been manifested in the representation of the past along many of the same fissures seen in the California school curriculum debates. For example, the long-standing battles over mission founder Fr. Junípero Serra's canonization and the recent vandalism of his statues exemplify the contested role of the missions in California public memory (Hackel 2018; Kagan 2018; Komanecky 2018; Pineda 2018) (Figure 10). Venerated saint to some, perpetrator of cultural genocide to others, Serra's polarizing significance is only one of many manifestations, albeit a highly visible one, of the tensions between the heroic church and priest-centered narratives and the goals of those operating both within and outside Catholic institutions who seek a more inclusive, decolonized history (Black 2020; Denzin 2021).

As with curriculum reformers, some mission curators, interpreters, and other historic site administrators have begun to address their presentation of the past to tell more inclusive stories and to address the trauma of colonization. Much has been written about the public interpretation in mission museums, landscapes, and programs and the ways they replicate the dominant narratives often characterized as the "Spanish Fantasy Past" of California's colonial history (Dartt-Newton 2011; Kryder-Reid 2014, 2016; Panich 2016; Thomas 1991). In a time when culture wars are being fought through textbooks and state curriculum, some mission administrators, educators, and museum staff are reckoning with the sites' complex and painful history and are working with Native scholars and activists who are seeking to change those narratives. For example, Mission La Purísima, one of the two missions that are state parks, has redesigned its visitor center to foreground Native voices and experiences. Mission San Gabriel has a long-standing partnership with the Gabrielino-Tongva, and they have conducted traditional ceremonies at the mission. Native scholar Deana Dartt has proposed that the missions join the International Coalition of Sites of Conscience (Dartt-Newton 2011), and while no missions have joined to date, the Santa Barbara Trust for Historic Preservation has joined. They operate El Presidio de Santa Bárbara State Historic Park (under an agreement with California State Parks) and the Santa Inés Mission Mills. In addition, curators at California cultural heritage institutions such as the Huntington and the Autry have developed exhibitions looking critically at California's colonial past through a decolonized lens and privileging Indigenous and other marginalized voices.

A prominent example is the Critical Mission Studies project, a collaboration of UC faculty and California Indian Research partners that "supports Indigenous perspectives on the California colonial missions and their aftermath. Through reconsideration of the missions as both physical places and objects of interpretation, we pursue new research collaborations that

FIGURE 10. Father Manuel Diaz examining the Serra statue in front of Mission San Gabriel following an attempt to decapitate the sculpture and the application of red paint in November 2017. (Photo by Archdiocese of Los Angeles)

surface both Native and Mexican / Mexican American voices in the history of California and the US. Our research fosters more complex, multidimensional public engagements with difficult and traumatic histories" (Critical Mission Studies n.d.). Other Native-led efforts are similarly informing interpretation at the missions and bringing a critical lens to mission history and recasting the fundamental narrative (Byram et al. 2018; Lightfoot and Lopez 2013). For example, rather than write about the missions as sites of oppression, scholars are framing them as Indigenous spaces, investigating how the Indians created Native spaces within the mission property boundaries and documenting survivance strategies for those displaced from their homelands (Acebo 2020; Schneider 2015; Schneider and Panich 2019; Silliman 2001). As University of California Berkeley professor Peter Nelson (Coast Miwok) has put it, California Indian studies have shifted from "research 'on' to research 'with, for, and by' Indigenous people" (Nelson 2021). Furthermore, this Indigenous-led scholarship is predicated on Native communities working as partners rather than as subjects or informants, and the goal of the collaborations is to support the "empowerment, health, and well-being of our communities" (Nelson 2021).

Conclusion

There are currently efforts to decolonize both education and heritage fields (Leslie et al. 2021) as well as numerous examples of people working to Indigenize California history in schools and historic sites. The California missions are well-positioned to be agents of change, and they have the potential to be exemplars in the broader context of American social studies curriculum. Roland Evans's (2004) articulation of the five goals of social studies teaching discussed earlier are relevant for the future of California missions as curriculum. Do interpreters and teachers want students to master historical factual content, to reflect on central issues facing our democracy and society, to encourage critical examination of power structures, and to be an active part of transforming American society? As tourist destinations for hundreds of thousands of visitors seeking to understand and connect with California's colonial history, the missions offer informal learning experiences that have the potential to shape public understanding of the past and of its ongoing role in California contemporary social and political power dynamics. There are hopeful signs, but the history of social studies curriculum teaches us that the pendulum is fully capable of swinging back and that the politics of the past are an instrument for wielding power in the present. As Keenan has argued, the enduring practices of the mission project persists despite generations of critique because it continues to serve relevant ideological interests. In an example of what he terms "ritual avoidance," the mission project is "a repeated social practice that relies on the designed obscuring of known information that would threaten a narrative central to the identity of a dominant group" (Keenan 2021, 110). A critical history of the missions is essential not only to reckon with the history of colonial-era oppression and harm, but to face what religious scholar and founder of PRRI (Public Religion Research Institute) Robert P. Jones has called "the unholy relationship between American Christianity and white supremacy" (Jones 2020).

Roy Rosenzweig and David Thelen (1998) published a study seeking to assess how people thought about history—what it was, where they got their information, and what sources they trusted. In 2019 the American Historical Association (AHA) partnered with Fairleigh Dickinson University to revisit those questions assessing "public perceptions of, and engagement with, the discipline of history and the past" (AHA 2021). The results of the two studies, conducted nearly twenty years apart, were surprisingly similar in many ways. People surveyed in both studies thought of history primarily as facts—names, dates, and events. They also found museums and historic sites to be among the most trustworthy sources, although they were only ranked in the middle of sources frequently consulted. The authors of the AHA 2021 report noted that while a significant majority of respondents reported trusting historical institutions, "there are measurable differences in those views as a function of such factors as age and political affiliation. Moreover, those favoring an explanatory view of history showed signs of greater interest in, and perhaps empathy for, peoples and events far removed from the respondents." In short, attitudes about the role of interpretation and analysis correlate with both personal identity and identification with others. The data crystalize what many have observed across the US—namely, the increasing politicization of teaching history in schools and in historic sites and public spaces. So, yes, historic sites are political. Curriculum is political. And social studies is more important than ever for training citizens in the core values of our nation. The question is whether that curriculum has the courage to acknowledge the painful injustices of our past and whether it can create the space to include all voices and experiences.

References

Acebo, Nathan Patrick. 2020. "Re-Assembling Radical Indigenous Autonomy in the Alta California Hinterlands: Survivance at Puhú." PhD diss. Stanford, CA: Stanford University.

ACHS—Association of Critical Heritage Studies. 2012. Manifesto. https://www.criticalheritagestudies.org/history.

Adams, Erin. 2019. "Economics and the Civic Mission of Social Studies Education: Two Critiques of Neoclassicism Citizenship, Social and Economics Education. *Citizenship, Social and Economics Education* 18 (1): 16–32.

American Historical Association. 2021. "History, the Past, and Public Culture: Results from a National Survey." https://www.historians.org/history-culture-survey.

Bankston, Carl, and Stephen Caldas. 2009. *Public Education America's Civil Religion: A Social History*. New York: Teacher's College Press.

Bickford, John, and Jeremiah Clabough. 2022. "A Guided History into Racist Curriculum, Pedagogy, and Policy: Then and Now." *Social Studies* 113 (3): 109–24.

Black, Charlene Villaseñor. 2020. "Rethinking Mission Studies." *Latin American and Latinx Visual Culture* 2 (3): 3–7.

Buggeln, Gretchen, and Barbara Franco, eds. 2018. *Interpreting Religion at Museums and Historic Sites*. Lanham, MD: Rowman & Littlefield.

Buggeln, Gretchen, Crispin Paine, and Brent Plate, eds. 2017. *Religion in Museums: Global and Multidisciplinary Perspectives*. New York: Bloomsbury.

Byram, Scott, Kent Lightfoot, Rob Cuthrell, Peter Nelson, Jun Sunseri, Roberta Jewett, Breck Parkman, and Nicholas Tribcevich. 2018. "Geophysical Investigation of Mission San Francisco Solano, Sonoma, California." *Historical Archaeology* 52 (2): 242–63.

California State Board of Education. 2016. "History Social Science Framework for California Public Schools." https://www.cde.ca.gov/ci/hs/cf/documents/hssframeworkwhole.pdf.

Castillo, Edward. 1991. *Native American Perspectives on the Hispanic Colonization of Alta California*. New York: Garland.

Church, Robert. 1976. *Education in the United States: An Interpretive History*. New York: Free Press.

Collins, Ashley Paige. 2021. "Idyllic Imperialism: The California Mission Replica at the Louisiana Purchase Exposition, 1904." PhD diss. Athens: University of Georgia.

Costo, Rupert, and Jeanette Costo. 1987. *The Missions of California: A Legacy of Genocide*. San Francisco: Indian Historian Press.

Critical Mission Studies. n.d. https://criticalmissionstudies.ucsd.edu/.

Dartt-Newton, Deana. 2011. "California's Sites of Conscience: An Analysis of the State's Historic Mission Museums." *Museum Anthropology* 34 (2): 97–108.

DeLyser, Dydia. 2005. *Ramona Memories: Tourism and the Shaping of Southern California*. Minneapolis: University of Minnesota Press.

Denzin, Norman. 2021. "Forty Acres and a Mule: Reparation Blues." *Cultural Studies ↔ Critical Methodologies* 21 (6): 521–26.

Deverell, William. 2004. *Whitewashed Adobe: The Rise of Los Angeles and the Remaking of Its Mexican Past*. Berkeley: University of California Press.

Dewey, John. 1899. *The School and Society*. Chicago: University of Chicago Press.

Evans, Ronald. 2004. *The Social Studies Wars: What Should We Teach the Children?* New York: Teachers College Press.

———. 2006. "The Social Studies Wars, Now and Then." *Social Education* 70 (5): 317–21.

———. 2020. *Fear and Schooling: Understanding the Troubled History of Progressive Education*. London: Routledge.

Flower, Enola. 1949. *A Child's History of California*. Sacramento: California State Department of Education.

Freire, Paulo. 1970. *Pedagogy of the Oppressed*. New York: Herder and Herder.

Gentry, Kynan, and Laurajane Smith. 2019. "Critical Heritage Studies and the Legacies of the Late-Twentieth-Century Heritage Canon. *International Journal of Heritage Studies* 25 (11): 1148–68.

Gutfreund, Zevi. 2010. "Standing Up to Sugar Cubes: The Contest over Ethnic Identity in California's Fourth-Grade Mission Curriculum." *Southern California Quarterly* 92 (2): 161–97.

Haas, Lisbeth. 2011. *Pablo Tac, Indigenous Scholar: Writings on Luiseño Language and Colonial History, c. 1840*. Berkeley: University of California Press.

———. 2014. *Saints and Citizens: Indigenous Histories of Colonial Missions and Mexican California*. Berkeley: University of California Press.

Hackel, Steven. 2005. *Children of the Coyote, Missionaries of Saint Francis: Indian-Spanish Relations in Colonial California, 1769–1850*. Chapel Hill: University of North Carolina Press.

———. 2018. "Introduction: Junípero Serra; New Contexts and Emerging Interpretations." In *The Worlds of Junípero Serra: Historical Contexts and Cultural Representations*, edited by Steven W. Hackel, 1–12. Berkeley: University of California Press.

Harrison, Rodney. 2012. *Heritage: Critical Approaches*. New York: Routledge.

Herrera, Allison. 2019. "Indigenous Educators Fight for an Accurate History of California: The Golden State Is Ignoring a History of Violence against Native Americans." *High Country News*, April 29.

Hertzberg, Hazel W. 1981. *Social Studies Reform, 1880–1980*. Boulder, CO: SSEC.

Huntington Library. n.d. "Exploring the California Missions—Everyday Life." http://missionhistory.org/pdf/Everday_Life_QG.pdf. Accessed October 5, 2021.

Jackson, Robert, and Edward Castillo. 1995. *Indians, Franciscans, and Spanish Colonization: The Impact of the Mission System on California Indians*. Albuquerque: University of New Mexico Press.

Jones, Robert. 2020. *White Too Long: The Legacy of White Supremacy in American Christianity*. New York: Simon & Schuster.

Kagan, Richard. 2018. "The Invention of Junípero Serra and the "Spanish Craze." In *The Worlds of Junípero Serra: Historical Contexts and Cultural*

   Representations, edited by Steven Hackel, 227–56. Berkeley: University of
   California Press.

Kaufman-Osborn, Timothy. 2023. "Not Just a War on 'Woke.'" *Inside Higher Ed.*
   May 22, 2023. https://www.insidehighered.com/opinion/views/2023/05/22
   /not-just-war-woke.

Keenan, Harper Benjamin. 2019. "Selective Memory: California Mission
   History and the Problem of Historical Violence in Elementary School
   Textbooks." *Teachers College Record* 121 (8): 1–28.

———. 2021. "The Mission Project: Teaching History and Avoiding the Past
   in California Elementary Schools." *Harvard Educational Review* 91 (1):
   109–32.

Kincheloe, Joe. 2008. *Critical Pedagogy Primer.* New York: Peter Lang.

Kliebard, Herbert. 1986. *The Struggle for the American Curriculum, 1893–1958.*
   Boston: Routledge and Kegan Paul.Komanecky, Michael. 2018. "The Public
   Consumption of Junípero Serra." In *The Worlds of Junípero Serra: Historical
   Contexts and Cultural Representations*, edited by Steven Hackel, 257–84.
   Berkeley: University of California Press.

Kropp, Phoebe. 2006. *California Vieja: Culture and Memory in a Modern
   American Place.* Berkeley: University of California Press.

Kryder-Reid, Elizabeth. 2014. "Marking Time in San Gabriel Mission Garden."
   *Studies in the History of Gardens & Designed Landscapes: An International
   Quarterly* 34 (1): 15–27.

———. 2015. "Crafting the Past: Mission Models and the Curation of California Heritage." *Heritage & Society* 8 (1): 60–83.

———. 2016. *California Mission Landscapes: Race, Memory, and the Politics of
   Heritage.* Minneapolis: University of Minnesota Press.

———. 2018. "California Mission Trail." In *Interpreting Religion at Museums and
   Historical Sites*, edited by Gretchen Buggeln and Barbara Franco, 23–57.
   Lanham, MD: Rowman & Littlefield.

Lehrer, Erica, Cynthia Milton, and Monica Eileen Patterson, eds. 2011.
   Curating Difficult Knowledge: Violent Pasts in Public Places. New York:
   Palgrave Macmillan.

Leslie, Angela, Varja Watson, Rose Borunda, Kate Bosworth, and Tatianna
   Grant. 2021. "Towards Abolition: Undoing the Colonized Curriculum."
   Journal of Curriculum Studies Research 3 (1): 1–20.

Lightfoot, Kent. 2005. *Indians, Missionaries, and Merchants: The Legacy of
   Colonial Encounters on the California Frontiers.* Berkeley: University of
   California Press.

Lightfoot, Kent, and Valentin Lopez. 2013. "The Study of Indigenous Management Practices in California: An Introduction." *California Archaeology* 5 (2):
   209–19.

Lindsay, Brendan. 2012. *Murder State: California's Native American Genocide, 1846–1873*. Lincoln: University of Nebraska Press.

Lorimer, Michelle. 2016. *Resurrecting the Past: The California Mission Myth*. Pechanga, CA: Great Oak Press.

Madley, Benjamin. 2016. *An American Genocide: The United States and the California Indian Catastrophe, 1846–1873*. New Haven: Yale University Press.

———. 2019. "California's First Mass Incarceration System: Franciscan Missions, California Indians, and Penal Servitude, 1769–1836." *Pacific Historical Review* 88 (1): 14–47.

Matzen, Morgan. 2021. "'Political Football' or 'Mountain out of a Molehill'? South Dakota Officials Clash over Indigenous Education Standards." *USA Today*, August 12, 2021.

McMillan, Conway. 1896. "The Sociological Basis of School Education." *Education* 16 (6).

McWilliams, Carey. 1946. *Southern California Country: An Island on the Land*. New York: Duell, Sloan and Pearce.

Miles, James. 2021. "Curriculum Reform in a Culture of Redress: How Social and Political Pressures Are Shaping Social Studies Curriculum in Canada. *Journal of Curriculum Studies* 53 (1): 47–64.

Miller, Ron. 1992. *What Are Schools For: Holistic Education in American Culture*. Brandon, VT: Holistic Education Press.

Miranda, Deborah. 2013. "Post-Colonial Thought Experiment." In *Bad Indians: A Tribal Memoir*, 186–91. Berkeley, CA: Heydey.

Nelson, Peter. 2021. "Where Have All the Anthros Gone? The Shift in California Indian Studies from Research 'on' to Research 'with, for and by' Indigenous Peoples. *American Anthropologist* 123 (3): 469–73.

Norton, Jack. 1979. *Genocide in Northwestern California: When Our Worlds Cried*. San Francisco: Indian Historian Press.

Panich, Lee. 2016. "After Saint Serra: Unearthing Indigenous Histories at the California Missions." *Journal of Social Archaeology* 16 (2): 238–58.

Perkinson, Henry. 1995. *The Imperfect Panacea: American Faith in Education*. New York: McGraw Hill.

Pineda, Baron. 2018. "'First Hispanic Pope, First Hispanic Saint': Whiteness, Founding Fathers and the Canonization of Friar Junípero Serra. *Latino Studies* 16: 286–309.

Rafferty, Max. 1961. *The Passing of the Patriot*. Reprint. New Rochelle, NY: America's Future.

Reese, William. 2005. *America's Public Schools: From the Common School to "No Child Left Behind."* Baltimore: Johns Hopkins University Press.

Romero, Simon. 2021. "Texas Pushes to Obscure the State's History of Slavery and Racism." *New York Times*, May 20.

Rosenzweig, Roy, and David Thelen. 1998. *The Presence of the Past: Popular Uses of History in American Life*. New York: Columbia University Press.

Ross, Wayne. 2017. *Rethinking Social Studies: Critical Pedagogy in Pursuit of Dangerous Citizenship*. Charlotte: Information Age.

Sandos, James. 2004.*Converting California: Indians and Franciscans in the Missions*. New Haven: Yale University Press.

Saxe, David Warren. 1991. *Social Studies in Schools: A History of the Early Years*. Albany: State University of New York Press.

Schneider, Khal, Dale Allender, Margarita Berta-Ávila, Rose Borunda, Gregg Castro, Amy Murray, and Jenna Porter. 2019. "More Than Missions: Native Californians and Allies Changing the Story of California History." *Journal of American Indian Education* 58 (3): 58–77.

Schneider, Tsim. 2015. "Placing Refuge and the Archaeology of Indigenous Hinterlands in Colonial California. *American Antiquity* 80 (4): 695–713.

Schneider, Tsim, and Lee Panich. 2019. "Landscapes of Refuge and Resiliency: Native Californian Persistence at Tomales Bay, California, 1770s–1870s." *Ethnohistory* 66 (1): 21–47.

Silliman, Stephen. 2001. "Theoretical Perspectives on Labor and Colonialism: Reconsidering the California Missions." *Journal of Anthropological Archaeology* 20 (4): 379–407.

Stanford History Education Group (SHEG). n.d. Website. About page. https://sheg.stanford.edu/about. Accessed October 5, 2021.

Teachers Pay Teachers. n.d. https://www.teacherspayteachers.com/. Accessed September 15, 2021.

Thomas, David Hurst. 1991. "Harvesting Ramona's Garden: Life in California's Mythical Mission Past." In *Columbian Consequences*, vol. 3, *The Spanish Borderlands in Pan-American Perspective*, edited by David Hurst Thomas, 119–57. Washington, DC: Smithsonian Institution.

Teitelbaum, Kenneth. 2022. "Curriculum, Conflict, and Critical Race Theory." *Phi Delta Kappan* 103 (5): 47–53.

Trafzer, Clifford, and Michelle Lorimer. 2014. "Silencing California Indian Genocide in Social Studies Texts." *American Behavioral Scientist* 58 (1): 64–82.

Tran, Tuyen. 2017. "Repeat after Us: Say No to the Mission Project." *California History Social Science Project*, May 23, 2017.

Trump, Donald. 2020. Remarks by President Trump at the White House Conference on American History. September 17. Posted on the National Archives Museum, Washington DC, website. https://trumpwhitehouse.archives.gov/briefings-statements/remarks-president-trump-white-house-conference-american-history/.

Winter, Tim. 2013. "Clarifying the Critical in Critical Heritage Studies." *International Journal of Heritage Studies* 19 (6): 532–45.

Note

1. These issues of curriculum reform are relevant in other settler colonial contexts. See, for example, Miles (2021) on how Canadian political and social initiatives to redress "historical wrongs" have informed curricular revisions.

Native Heritage and the California Missions

A Collaborative Approach at Mission Santa Clara

LEE M. PANICH AND CHARLENE NIJMEH

Introduction

Missionaries working with various colonial governments established hundreds of missions in the lands that today comprise the United States. Perhaps the best known are the Franciscan missions associated with the Spanish Borderlands of La Florida, Texas, the Pueblo Southwest, and California (Thomas 2014; Weber 1990). Across this vast region, the vagaries of natural deterioration, intentional preservation, and subsequent development have led to stark discrepancies in the physical attributes of mission sites—both in terms of their standing architecture and what has survived below ground in the archaeological record. These patterns, in turn, have shaped the different ways in which generations of Native people, historians, archaeologists, and the public have engaged with these places as explicit sites of heritage. One commonality, however, is that the heritage meaning ascribed to the Franciscan missions—from the perspective of the dominant society, at least—typically represents foundational European claims to the North American continent. The missions, in other words, have come to represent Euro-American heritage, despite the fact that they were constructed for and by Native people.

In California, the most visible heritage discourse surrounding the twenty-one Franciscan missions established under Spanish and Mexican rule similarly focuses on their European roots. Where they have been preserved, the individual mission structures are often the oldest colonial establishments in any given municipality, and taken collectively, the mission chain and the associated Camino Real provide a common heritage lens through which to view the region's Euro-American past. Indeed, mission-themed businesses, architectural styles, and place names proliferate across the California landscape (Kryder-Reid 2016; Rawls 1992; Thomas 1991). In contrast, this framing excludes the tens of thousands of

Native people who lived and worked at the missions—a pattern that is especially common in the use of mission motifs in popular culture. To the extent that mission sites, their associated museums, and state-sanctioned pedagogical materials do discuss Native Californians, they are too often presented as static foils to the civilizing project of the region's Franciscan missions (Dartt-Newton 2011; Kryder-Reid 2016 and this volume; Lorimer 2016; Schneider et al. 2019).

Yet Native communities have long resisted both the Eurocentric interpretation of the California missions and the historical amnesia around the suffering and disruption that missionization caused among the region's tribal communities (e.g., Castillo 1989; Costo and Costo 1987; Field, Leventhal, and Cambra 2013; Galvan 2013). Over the past decade, these tensions have taken on new forms with the canonization of the eighteenth-century missionary Junípero Serra in 2015, a failed (for now) attempt to nominate California's El Camino Real to the UNESCO World Heritage List, and the renewed protests against racial injustice in the United States that began in the summer of 2020. The Native critique highlights the structural and physical violence perpetrated against Indigenous people by the Franciscans and other Euro-American colonists in the late eighteenth and early nineteenth centuries, as well as the continued erasure of Indigenous people from heritage discourse surrounding the missions today in the twenty-first century (Chilcote 2015; Galvan and Medina 2018; Lopez 2015; Miranda 2013; Ramirez and Lopez 2020; Schneider et al. 2019; Schneider, Schneider, and Panich 2020; Haas, this volume). These interventions are a clear indictment of the "fantasy heritage" of the missions as bucolic European outposts, but also raise the question of what constitutes a site of Indigenous heritage in twenty-first-century California.

As Tsim Schneider, a citizen of the Federated Indians of Graton Rancheria, has argued elsewhere, the contemporary heritage landscape leaves Native people out of heritage narratives at sites dating from the colonial period to the present day. For example, sites of colonial violence—missions, forts, and the like—are celebrated as part of the foundation of California's Euro-American history, while Indigenous heritage is typically relegated to parks and other "natural" areas that rhetorically place Native people in the past (Schneider 2019). Of course, many natural preserves are indeed important for contemporary California Indian people because they are home to myriad culturally important species of plants and animals and often conceal the remains of ancestral sites that have been spared destruction by agricultural activities and suburban sprawl. But they nevertheless leave out the centuries between the Spanish invasion in the late eighteenth century and today. Without discounting the importance of the deep past, how do heritage sites commemorate the violence of colonialism and honor the survivors? Is it possible to see the California mission as sites of Indigenous heritage, as troubled as that heritage is?

We examine this question through the example of ongoing collaborative approaches to mission heritage at Mission Santa Clara on the campus of Santa Clara University (SCU). At Santa Clara, the role of the mission in local historical narratives has been similar to that of the twenty other Franciscan missions of Alta California. For instance, Santa Clara is known officially as "The Mission City," while Ohlone people—whose ancestors built the mission complex and comprised Mission Santa Clara's initial Native population—have been largely absent from broader celebrations of the mission and its history. This chapter presents the various ways that the local Ohlone community has been involved in shaping mission heritage in both unofficial and official capacities. With regard to the latter, the chapter will focus on SCU's recent Ohlone History Working Group, for which Ohlone leaders and university personnel collaboratively assessed the existing heritage infrastructure associated with Mission Santa Clara and made recommendations for improving it in ways that center long-term Ohlone presence. While more work remains to be done, this process reflects a growing consensus in California that the story of the missions should focus on and be told by those whose ancestors experienced Spanish colonialism firsthand (Schneider, Schneider, and Panich 2020).

Making Heritage at Mission Santa Clara

Franciscan missionaries founded Mission Santa Clara de Asís at the southern end of San Francisco Bay in 1777, in an area known to local Ohlone people as Thámien. It operated into the 1840s, though the mission church had to be moved several times as a result of natural disasters such as flooding and earthquakes (Skowronek and Wizorek 1997). Over the course of its existence, some 9,000 Native individuals were baptized at the mission, the vast majority of them Native people from local Ohlone tribes, and, after 1810, from more distant Yokuts and Miwok groups. This diverse community lived in the large mission *rancheria*—the Spanish term for Native Californian settlements—that included both adobe apartment blocks and more traditional conical dwellings made from tule, a local wetland reed (Figure 11). Indigenous people were alienated from the mission lands over the course of the 1830s and 1840s as the territory was claimed by Mexican-era elites and ultimately by settlers from the United States (Panich 2020; Shoup and Milliken 1999). The Jesuits founded Santa Clara College—known today as Santa Clara University—at the site of Mission Santa Clara in 1851.

While the former mission church has always been at the geographic center of the Santa Clara campus, it only took on significant heritage value in the late nineteenth and early twentieth centuries as local residents appealed to the antiquity of Mission Santa Clara as a historical tie to Euro-American heritage. As at other California mission sites, some of the first evidence of this shift came with the construction of formal gardens that created a romanticized image of the colonial period (McKevitt 1979, 126, and Kryder-Reid 2010, 2016). By the early twentieth century, the public perception of the mission expanded beyond aesthetic value to one of historical importance. In 1907, crews digging a utility line unearthed portions of the third mission quadrangle and its associated cemetery. Though the cemetery in particular had been marked on maps for decades, this "discovery" gave rise to a celebration of Mission Santa Clara's role in the colonization of western North America (Panich 2022). The excavations themselves were widely covered in the regional press, including articles in the *Evening News* (1907) from neighboring San Jose and the *San Francisco Chronicle* (1907a)—the latter of which extolled "bones of hundreds of Indians discovered in Town of Santa Clara." As far as we know, no descendants of the Native people were notified that their ancestors' remains had been disturbed.

Instead, the proto-archaeological excavation of the mission site and associated cemetery coincided with a wave of heritage-making at Mission Santa Clara that would last over two decades. Just a few weeks after the rediscovery of the third mission complex, the university and local leaders held a landmark day to commemorate what they viewed as "the advent of civilization and Christianity" in the region (*San Francisco Chronicle* 1907b). It was also around this time that the campus literary

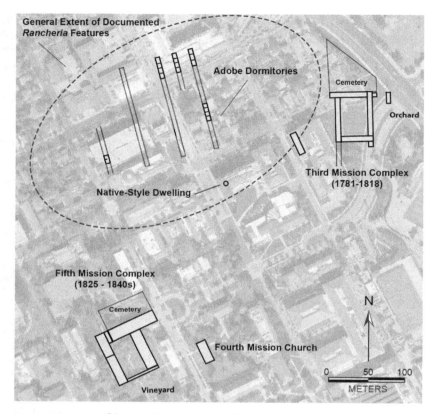

FIGURE 11. Map of layout of Mission Santa Clara (as revealed through archaeology) over modern Santa Clara University campus.

magazine, the *Redwood*, began regularly featuring essays praising the Franciscans, who in the words of one author offered "a beacon of light in the Aboriginal darkness" (Duffey 1907, 109). Shortly thereafter, in 1912, the first buildings constructed in the Mission Revival architectural style appeared on campus, flanking the mission church (McKevitt 1979). Further construction work at the third mission site unearthed more human remains and evidence of the mission quadrangle throughout the 1910s and 1920s, disturbances that caught the attention of the local media time and again, cementing Mission Santa Clara as a place where a romantic Euro-American past could be authentically engaged (Hylkema 1995, 41–43; Panich 2022).

These early examples of heritage-making at Mission Santa Clara persisted into the late 1920s with the construction of a new replica mission church. The remnants of the fifth mission church—originally erected a century earlier—had been remodeled significantly, and the structure was ultimately destroyed by fire in 1926. This loss allowed the university to rebuild the mission church as a larger-than-life replica that would anchor the rapidly developing campus. The new mission church and a replacement bell donated by King Alfonso of Spain were jointly dedicated on Columbus Day in 1929 (McKevitt 1979, 216–21). This celebration, tied to the founding mythology of the United States, was the culmination of Eurocentric heritage-making at Mission Santa Clara in the early twentieth century. As was typical for the time, these events are not known to have included any Ohlone people whose ancestors had lived and worked at Mission Santa Clara. In fact, the exclusion of Ohlone voices from instances of mission heritage in the early twentieth century is part and parcel of broader discourses in which the field of anthropology and the United States government both declared the Ohlone to be extinct in the mid-1920s (Field et al. 1992; Leventhal et al. 1994; Panich 2020). The Ohlone, wrote the famed California anthropologist Alfred Kroeber (1925, 464), were "extinct so far as all practical purposes are concerned."

The heritage of Mission Santa Clara was again in the spotlight in the 1980s and 1990s. This period saw still further archaeological work at the site of Santa Clara's third mission complex, events that fed into the nationwide celebrations of the 500-year anniversary of Columbus's first voyage to the Americas. The archaeological mitigation was associated with the re-routing of a local highway that cut through the SCU campus and again disturbed the cemetery associated with the third mission, as well as the foundations of the church and other mission structures (Hylkema 1995). The work fostered new public discussions about the mission, its legacy, and relation to the Columbian Quincentenary. For example, the university and the City of Santa Clara set aside a portion of the third mission site as an archaeological park in 1991; shortly thereafter, the university worked with the U.S. National Park Service to erect informational plaques as part of the Juan Bautista de Anza National Historic Trail. By the end of the decade, the campus heritage landscape also included a statue of Franciscan missionary Junípero Serra (Baines et al. 2020; Panich 2022). Yet, as described later, these more recent attempts at heritage-making did not fully include Ohlone people as partners. While Ohlone representatives were consulted about the disturbances to the third mission cemetery, the public discourse surrounding the mission and its history remained firmly Eurocentric in its outlook, expressions of what the Muwekma Ohlone Tribe and affiliated scholars have called "the politics of erasure" that serve to limit Indigenous sovereignty in the San Francisco Bay area and across California (Field, Leventhal, and Cambra 2013).

Ohlone Presence at Mission Santa Clara

Despite their exclusion from the official heritage discourse at Mission Santa Clara, the Ohlone community has found ways to maintain their connection to the site. As stated by Charlene Nijmeh, Chairwoman of the Muwekma Ohlone Tribe, the missions are "kind of the core of our history" in that the mission system impacted everyone through forced relocation, indoctrination, and, in many cases, death. Given the fact that some 7,500 Native individuals are buried at Mission Santa Clara, along with others who were laid to rest in a large precontact Ohlone village nearby, one major area of concern has long been the treatment of human remains and associated funerary objects inadvertently disturbed during construction on the SCU campus. Federal and state laws governing cultural resources—originally enacted in the late 1960s and early 1970s—require varying levels of consultation with tribal groups, particularly when human remains are encountered. While these regulations are far from ideal (e.g., Gnecco and Dias 2015), they have provided an opportunity for Ohlone communities to have a say about the treatment of their ancestors.

As noted previously, the first instance of Ohlone participation in CRM archaeology at Mission Santa Clara was associated with a highway realignment project that disturbed portions of the third mission cemetery in the 1980s (Hylkema 1995). Since then, various Ohlone representatives—including Andrew Galvan and members of the Muwekma Ohlone Tribe—have worked on numerous CRM projects at Mission Santa Clara, both as construction monitors and as "Most Likely Descendants" (MLDs), the officially designated spokesperson for tribal consultation when human remains are inadvertently discovered. One notable project took place in 2009, when ground-disturbing activities again revealed portions of the cemetery associated with the third mission complex. The Muwekma Ohlone Tribe's own CRM firm, the Ohlone Families Consulting Services, was hired to complete the mitigation. At the conclusion of the project, the partial remains of sixteen individuals were reburied at the site, and the area itself was renamed in the Chochenyo Ohlone language as the *Clareño muwékma ya túnnešte nómmo* [where the Clareño Indians are buried] site (Leventhal et al. 2011). While the tribe has renamed other ancestral sites affected by construction, the renaming of the mission cemetery is an especially powerful way to reclaim the space from Eurocentric heritage interpretations (Panich et al. 2024).

Archaeology is not the only realm where the Ohlone community has provided a counter-narrative to the dominant heritage discourses at Mission Santa Clara and other nearby missions. For example, Andrew Galvan has been curator of Mission Dolores in San Francisco for nearly two decades and has used his role there to reinsert Ohlone history into the physical interpretive space as well as guided tours (Galvan 2013; Galvan and Medina 2018). While formal relationships outside of CRM consultation have been less well developed at Santa Clara, members of the Muwekma Ohlone Tribe have long worked with SCU's de Saisset Museum, including on the construction of a traditional tule house in the mid-1980s. Representatives from various Ohlone groups have also collaborated with the de Saisset in the years since, including a major renovation and redesign of its California History exhibit, which was completed in 2019. Similarly, SCU faculty have invited Ohlone leaders from several groups to speak in classes and other campus events (Lueck and Panich 2020; Lueck, Kroot, and Panich 2021), a practice that goes back decades. However, it was not until very recently that a centralized approach has crystalized to center Ohlone voices at Mission Santa Clara.

Collaborative Approaches at Mission Santa Clara

The long-standing but largely unofficial relationships between members of the Ohlone community and SCU are today beginning to operate within new, more formalized channels. It is important to note here that the Muwekma Ohlone Tribe (and related descendant lineages) have ancestors that lived across large portions of the San Francisco Bay region and who were associated with Missions San Francisco, San José, and Santa Clara. Therefore, their involvement at SCU is just one of many relationships they have with universities, government agencies, and other organizations. These connections take many forms, and while interpersonal relationships are crucial, so too are institutional structures that can endure over time. Also important is a willingness on the part of non-Natives to listen and allow Indigenous voices to take precedence. In the words of Charlene Nijmeh, "Being invited to the table to share our story—I think that's what makes a good working relationship."

While individuals and particular units have in the past invited members of the Ohlone community to collaborate on projects at SCU, the formalization of the relationships between the university and tribes is ongoing. This process has been driven by a number of factors, including continued outreach on the part of Ohlone representatives, SCU student activism, increasing interest in these issues by SCU faculty and staff, and by top-down programs implemented by the university administration. SCU students, for example, have long advocated for a more inclusive campus climate, adding issues surrounding Indigenous representation to their concerns over the course of the late 2010s. Meanwhile, faculty and staff also began seeking more official ways to address the erasure of Ohlone people from campus public memory. These efforts were reflected in the adoption of an official university land acknowledgment and first annual Indigenous Peoples' Day celebration, both in 2018. These developments coincided with the renovation of the California History exhibit at the campus's de Saisset Museum (Baines et al. 2020, 5).

In 2019, Fr. Michael Engh—who was at that time president of SCU—appointed a working group to examine how the university interprets Mission Santa Clara and Native heritage more broadly, with the intent of better acknowledging long-term Ohlone presence. In a 2019 email communication to the SCU campus announcing the formation of the working group, Engh thanked the Ohlone community for their continued efforts, stating, "For some time, it has been clear to me that the University has needed to identify better ways to acknowledge the Ohlone history of Mission Santa Clara de Asís at Santa Clara University. It is important to honor these Ohlone ancestors and their descendants in a way that is concrete, meaningful, and forward-looking."

The resulting Ohlone History Working Group (OHWG) consisted of representatives from Ohlone communities as well as SCU administration, faculty, staff, and the student body. Both coauthors of this chapter were part of the OHWG: Charlene Nijmeh represented the Muwekma Ohlone Tribe of the San Francisco Bay Area, and Lee Panich is on the SCU faculty. The group met several times in 2019 and early 2020 to review the existing monuments and public interpretive markers related to Mission Santa Clara and to discuss how best to modify the existing heritage landscape to center Ohlone voices and experiences. The final report was released in the summer of 2020 (Baines et al. 2020).

Assessing Monuments to Mission Heritage

One important outcome of the OHWG has been to gather information on the history and current disposition of markers and monuments at SCU dedicated to the heritage of Mission Santa Clara and, less frequently, the Ohlone and other Native people. This work is in keeping with other trends in public memory, such as the National Monument Audit recently conducted for the United States (Monument Lab 2021). For SCU, the full inventory is available in Baines et al. (2020), but we highlight some of the main findings here to demonstrate the variety of ways that mission heritage is conveyed and to assess where current conditions fail to acknowledge Native presence (for similar analyses of other California mission sites, see Dartt-Newton 2011; Kryder-Reid 2016; Lorimer 2016). We present overviews of composite landscapes at the current mission church on the site of the fifth colonial-era mission, the third mission complex (the fourth location is totally unmarked; the first and second sites are not on the SCU campus), and the Native *ranchería*, as well as specific monuments and markers that both exist within and crosscut those three main areas.

Mission Church and Surroundings

The centerpiece of the twenty-first-century SCU campus is the mission church. As noted, this structure was completed in 1928 and is an enlarged replica of Mission Santa Clara's fifth church, which itself was constructed in the 1820s (Panich 2015; Skowronek and Wizorek 1997).

Like many other missions in California, the Santa Clara mission church still operates as a place of worship and therefore contains few didactic materials. Five interpretive panels with brief textual explanations are located near the entrance to the church, only one of which focuses on the history of Ohlone people and their engagement with the Franciscan mission system. A pamphlet with a self-guided tour is available to visitors interested in further information, but likewise focuses primarily on the church itself. Outside the mission church, the remnants of the former mission quadrangle enclose an area known as the "Mission Gardens," which are planted with roses, wisteria, and other ornamentals. Within this general area of campus, there are a number of monuments and markers that speak to the site's Spanish colonial heritage. These include a California State Historic Landmark plaque (dedicated in January of 1980) and a small informational board that describes the garden area. In front of the church stands a replica mission bell. Directly to the north of the mission church lies a separate rose garden enclosed by a low adobe wall. This area encompasses a portion of the mission cemetery that was in use from the early 1820s until 1851, during which time approximately 2,500 individuals (mostly Native people) were laid to rest there. The site itself is unmarked, and the rose garden is not currently open to the public (Figure 12).

Despite the ersatz nature of the current structure, the mission church and the surrounding gardens appeal directly to the heritage sensibilities

FIGURE 12. Rose garden at site of cemetery associated with the fifth mission church. Reconstructed mission church in background.

of Californians steeped in the region's mission mythology. The gardens, for example, are a familiar motif at nearly all California mission sites (Kryder-Reid 2010). That the cemetery associated with the fifth mission complex is today an unmarked rose garden is not entirely surprising, given that most mission sites generally downplay the sheer numbers of Native people interred on their premises (Dartt-Newton 2011, 102). Even the replica mission bell fits within common heritage themes from throughout the region. It is one of thousands that were placed in the early twentieth century along Highway 101, the approximate route of El Camino Real, in an early effort to increase automobile-based tourism in California (Kropp 2006; Ramirez and Lopez 2020). In sum, then, the current mission church and the surrounding area fit neatly within existing—yet historically inaccurate—tropes of architecturally significant churches, beautiful gardens, and a fleeting presence of Native people.

Third Mission "Archaeological Park"

The site of Santa Clara's third mission complex offers only slightly more interpretation. This location of Mission Santa Clara was in use for the longest duration and dates to the period between 1781, when construction began, and 1818, when the site was abandoned after a series of earthquakes. The church was officially blessed in 1784.

Much of the original mission quadrangle is preserved below ground in an "archaeological park" dedicated in 1991 after a major highway project impacted the site. A large cross marks the location of the former mission, below which a handful of plaques commemorate its founding and the dedication of the park. Offering a sense of the scale of the original mission structures, concrete paver stones are set into a grassy lawn, and adjacent streets and sidewalks demarcate the outline of the former mission compound as revealed by archaeological investigations (Figure 13). Despite the intent of the archaeological park to prevent future development directly on top of the former mission quadrangle, recent construction for the SCU school of law did affect a portion of the third mission complex and associated archaeological deposits (Peelo et al. 2015). A large cemetery is directly north of the site of the third mission church and is partially built over by a street and residential dwellings. It was originally in use from around 1781 until the early

FIGURE 13. Third site of Mission Santa Clara. Note paver stones in grass demarcating original foundation locations and Juan Bautista de Anza National Historic Trail informational board. School of Law building in background.

1820s. The cemetery holds the remains of approximately 5,000 individuals, nearly all of whom were Native people.

Given that the third site of Mission Santa Clara was the longest-serving location of this particular mission during the colonial period, it is historically significant in various ways. For Ohlone people and other Native Californians, this site arguably has the greatest association with—and made the greatest impact on—their ancestors. Yet the interpretive and commemorative materials at the site notably omit any mention of the fact that Ohlone and other Native people lived, worked, and were buried there, with one plaque in particular referring to the mission's large Indigenous population simply as "the many dwellers who lived around the mission" (Panich 2022). And whereas the cemetery associated with the fifth mission church is partially enclosed by a rose garden, the third mission's larger cemetery is totally unmarked. This situation persists despite the fact that the cemetery has been disturbed several times since the early twentieth century and was recently renamed as Clareño Muwékma Ya Túnneště Nómmo [where the Clareño Indians are buried] by the Muwekma Ohlone Tribe (Leventhal et al. 2011; Panich 2015).

Mission Ranchería

The Native neighborhood at Mission Santa Clara—known historically as the mission *ranchería*—appears to have remained in the same general location during the periods of use of the third, fourth, and fifth mission churches, from the early 1780s until the 1840s. During that time, this area was home to a total of nearly 10,000 Native individuals, with the annual population approaching 1,400 in most years during the height of the mission period. Recent archaeological mitigation work in the area has revealed scores of features related to Native life at the mission, including the remnants of several adobe dormitories, at least one traditional-style Indigenous dwelling, a possible sweat lodge, and pits of various utilitarian and ceremonial functions (e.g., Allen et al. 2010; Peelo et al. 2018; Potter, Mirro, and Wheelis 2021).

Despite this massive investment in archaeology, the public acknowledgment of the site is minimal. The primary marker is a textured outline of the foundations of a portion of a dormitory that was used to house Native families cut into the pavement of a parking garage (the dormitory foundations were destroyed during the construction of the garage). There is also a small interpretive panel on a pillar near the textured concrete outline. Ironically, both elements are obscured to casual observers because of their placement directly within the parking area reserved for the university's Jesuit community.

Juan Bautista de Anza Trail Informational Panels

Cross-cutting these two main mission locations are a series of interpretive panels associated with the Juan Bautista de Anza National Historic Trail. These panels describe subjects such as the layout of the Mission Santa Clara agricultural and industrial complex, the five mission sites, and the changing façade of the mission church. Only one is dedicated to discussing the history and culture of the Ohlone people. A similar panel was erected near the third mission church as part of the mitigation process when Native burials were disturbed at the third mission site in 2009; however, input from the Muwekma Ohlone Tribe is conspicuously missing from the panel, despite their involvement in the archaeological component of the project (Leventhal et al. 2011).

Junípero Serra Statue

At the time of the OHWG inventory, a life-sized statue of eighteenth-century Franciscan missionary Junípero Serra stood within the gardens surrounding the Santa Clara mission church. Serra is often referred to as "California's Founding Father" (e.g., Hackel 2013), a designation that grew with the importance of mission heritage over the course of the twentieth century. As mentioned, Serra is a controversial figure in California, given his role in the establishment of the Alta California mission system. While some Native people—including Andrew Galvan, curator at Mission Dolores—supported the canonization cause, the elevation of Serra to a saint of the Roman Catholic Church was criticized by many tribal groups (Panich 2016; and see Haas, this volume). The bronze statue at SCU is one of nearly one hundred identical statues donated by the William H. Hannon Foundation to mission sites and Catholic schools and colleges throughout California. William H. Hannon, a real estate developer and supporter of the Serra canonization cause, used the statues as a way to raise awareness of Serra's life work (Kryder-Reid 2016, 225–28).

Plaque to Peter H. Burnett

Though it is not related to the mission period per se, Ohlone representatives—and in particular, Andrew Galvan—had specifically asked that the OHWG review a plaque dedicated to the memory of Peter H. Burnett and his family that hung inside the mission church. Burnett was California's first American governor, but his legacy is marred by his racist beliefs and actions. Most relevant for our collective work at Mission Santa Clara is the fact that Burnett promised a "war of extermination" against Native people during his brief term as governor of California (Nokes 2018).

The Burnett plaque was placed in the spring of 1930, shortly after the opening of the reconstructed mission church following the fire of 1926 (*Santa Clara* 1930). In addition to being a prominent convert to Catholicism, Peter Burnett was on the first Board of Trustees of Santa Clara College, the institution that is today Santa Clara University, and the Burnett family remained closely connected to the university well into the twentieth century. Today, SCU continues to maintain a Peter Burnett Award for public service.

Recommendations and Actions

As detailed in the OHWG report (Baines et al. 2020), released in the summer of 2020, the group found that the existing heritage landscape at SCU and Mission Santa Clara does not adequately acknowledge Ohlone history, their experience under the mission system, or the continued Ohlone presence in the greater San Francisco Bay region. Our findings, moreover, mirror national trends in the US in which public monuments predominantly commemorate war and conquest as well as white male individuals (Monument Lab 2021). Yet, monuments are not static. In thinking about how to implement changes to the heritage landscape at SCU, the OHWG separated the markers and monuments into three distinct clusters. These were grouped by priority, but also roughly by geography.

The highest priority was the group of markers within and immediately surrounding the mission church. This area is not only the center of the SCU campus, but also attracts visitors who come to see the mission church, as well as schoolchildren visiting on field trips as part of the California fourth-grade curriculum. While the exact details remain to be decided, the general recommendations include an enhanced interpretive exhibit that details Ohlone involvement in the mission system and at least one statue or monument dedicated to Ohlone culture or specific Ohlone individual(s). The report also stresses the need to acknowledge the Ohlone and other Native people buried at the two mission cemeteries, as well as at a precontact village site on the SCU campus. Though the group recommended commemorating the cemeteries with a physical memorial and informational plaques, there was also a consensus that these materials should highlight the richness and diversity of Ohlone life before, during, and after the mission period. Based on this recommendation, an interactive digital memorial was designed with the Muwekma Ohlone Tribe and installed in the de Saisset Museum in the autumn of 2023. It includes the names of all 7,612 Native individuals listed in the mission's death records, as well as biographies of select historical individuals and video interviews with contemporary tribal members.

The second-highest priority area included the third mission quadrangle and the Juan Bautista de Anza National Historic Trail markers. The third mission site is near the main entrance to the SCU campus and therefore could attract significant numbers of visitors. To that end, the OHWG recommended updating the National Historic Trail information boards and other plaques at the site to better reflect Ohlone perspectives on their ancestors' experiences at Mission Santa Clara. The group also suggested enhancing the visibility of the paver stones that mark the mission quadrangle and etching culturally appropriate words or phrases in the local Chochenyo Ohlone language into the hardscaping. The third and final grouping of markers included the mission *ranchería* as well as several geographically discrete locations on campus, where mission heritage is referenced through artwork or displays.

Though most of the recommendations will require further collaboration and will likely take years to complete, two actions were taken shortly after the release of the report on the recommendation of the OHWG. The Junípero Serra statue was removed almost immediately in the summer of 2020. This took place at a moment when mission sites and statues of colonists were being targeted during the social justice protests that were sweeping the US following the intense public scrutiny of a wave of police killings of Black Americans. The short-term decision was framed as a preventative measure to protect the statue from vandalism, but the OHWG strongly recommended further conversations between the SCU and Ohlone communities to think about how best to interpret the Serra statue should it be reinstalled. The Peter H. Burnett plaque was also removed in 2020. Like the Serra statue, the OHWG saw educational value in a forthright presentation of the painful history of Burnett's advocacy of genocide but felt that such discussions would be better contextualized within the campus museum rather than inside the mission church. With California under shelter-in-place orders because of the Covid-19 pandemic, no formal gathering was held to mark either occasion.

The original charge of the OHWG was to review the historical markers and monuments related to mission and Indigenous heritage at SCU. However, the group also recognized the need to acknowledge the continued Ohlone presence today in the twenty-first century. As such, an additional set of forward-looking recommendations was included in the report. For example, the university announced the creation of the Ohlone and Muwekma Ohlone Scholarship fund to support students whose ancestors were associated with Mission Santa Clara and other California missions. The first recipient of the scholarship, from the Muwekma Ohlone Tribe, matriculated to SCU in the autumn of 2023.

Discussion and Conclusion

The work of the OHWG provided an opportunity to assess how heritage is made at Mission Santa Clara from a collaborative, interdisciplinary perspective. The existence of the working group has helped formalize relationships that will, we hope, lead to durable structures of partnership and accountability at SCU. Still, the findings suggest much work to be done to more fully acknowledge the complex, and often painful, connections between the mission and today's thriving Ohlone community.

In thinking about how best to acknowledge and represent these connections, it will be imperative to incorporate perspectives from a broad segment of Bay Area Ohlones and to think carefully about how to contextualize the mission period in the broader scope of Ohlone history. While the focus of the OHWG was specifically on Mission Santa Clara, there exist many other heritage sites that are of great importance for the Ohlone community as a whole and for specific Ohlone families or individuals. As noted, the Muwekma Ohlone Tribe regularly renames ancestral sites—most of which date to times prior to the Spanish invasion—in the Chochenyo Ohlone language. Similarly, Ohlone people of various affiliations gather annually at Coyote Hills, a local park that holds what remains of multiple Ohlone villages that were occupied more than 2,000 years ago. This event acknowledges the site's deep Indigenous history but also celebrates continued Ohlone presence in the San Francisco Bay area today. From this vantage point, Mission Santa Clara is just part of that longer, and perhaps more interesting, history. Indeed, the mission period is valued more by some members of the Ohlone community than others in part because of the painful legacy of missionization and how it has been portrayed over the past two centuries.

Similarly, Mission Santa Clara needs to be understood within the broader context of mission heritage as presented throughout the region. There exist twenty other mission sites in California, each with varying relationships to local Native communities and with different approaches to presenting their history to the public. This is not necessarily a unique situation in the US, where historic sites are managed by a jumble of private entities, educational institutions, and local, state, and federal governments, but it is an additional challenge to creating a more balanced view of missionization and other difficult chapters in North American history.

Writing about how historic sites do or do not offer a full accounting of the horrors of chattel slavery and the humanity of enslaved Africans, Smith (2021, 289) remarks, "Many of these places directly confront and reflect on their relationship to that history; many of these places do not. But in order for our country to collectively move forward, it is not enough to have a patchwork of places that are honest about this history while being surrounded by other spaces that undermine it" (Smith 2021, 289).

The same could be said for the California missions. There, the presentation of historical narratives across the region's twenty-one mission sites is both constrained and enabled by their current disposition, which includes ownership, level of architectural preservation, and legacies of historical and/or archaeological research. Most of the California missions today remain part of the Catholic Church. These sites vary widely regarding interpretive material, rhetorical strategies, and inclusion of Indigenous voices. As other chapters in this volume discuss, the overall pattern has been to celebrate the European heritage of the missions while largely ignoring the contributions of Native Californians as well as the tragic human toll of the mission system (see Dartt-Newton 2011; Kryder-Reid 2016; Lorimer 2016). An important exception to this has been at Mission Dolores, in San Francisco, where—as noted—Andrew Galvan has worked to center Ohlone history and culture in the public presentation of the mission and its heritage (Galvan 2013; Galvan and Medina 2018).

The record of the public sector is similarly checkered. Three California missions—La Purísima, San Francisco Solano, and Santa Cruz—are wholly or partly administered as historic parks by the State of California's Department of Parks and Recreation. These sites also have a relatively long history of archaeological research, and the museums and associated interpretive materials largely present a balanced discussion of the most difficult aspects of mission history. For example, at Sonoma State Historic Park, which includes Mission San Francisco Solano, the names of all the Native Californians buried at the mission are etched in a black stone memorial, evoking the Vietnam War Memorial at the US National Mall in Washington. In a poignant editorial choice, the names of children who died at the mission are indicated with an asterisk to underscore the terrible human suffering that was synonymous with the missions. Yet, in a situation that exemplifies the inertia of earlier forms of celebratory mission heritage, interpretive panels within the mission structure itself do not mention Native people in any capacity.

Santa Clara stands out as the only California mission site to be located on a university campus. While still under the umbrella of the Catholic Church, the educational goals of the institution and the presence of a diverse set of stakeholders beyond parishioners provide opportunities for deeper reflection on the role of the mission as a heritage site. For example, the original Santa Clara mission was founded by the Franciscans but today exists on the campus of a Jesuit university in a city that has historically had a large Catholic population—to say nothing of the thousands of students who pass by the reconstructed mission church and gardens in their daily lives, imprinting memories of the space that are completely at odds with the harsh realities of life there two centuries earlier. These varied viewpoints undermine universalizing heritage narratives—as seen in the seemingly doomed attempt to add California's Camino Real to the UNESCO world heritage list over the past decade (Ramirez and Lopez 2020)—and instead encourage us to allow the Ohlone and other Native Californian communities to share their own history with a broader audience.

At Mission Santa Clara, the Ohlone community has steadfastly insisted that the mission does have heritage value to them. It is certainly not the only site of importance for Ohlone people, nor do all Ohlone individuals see Santa Clara or other missions in the same light. Throughout the OHWG process, a central commitment has been to keep working with the local Ohlone community to ensure that their story is told accurately. As Charlene Nijmeh states, "It's a painful story. But it's a story that needs to be told for what it is, the truth." Ohlone perspectives on Mission Santa Clara resonate with those of other Native Californians. While none condone the whitewashing of mission history, it is important to recognize that the erasure of Native experiences from mission heritage does more than simply give Euro-Americans an opportunity to forget the mistreatment of Native people. It also strips the humanity from those Native people who experienced missionization first-hand—their trials, but also the texture of their daily lives. The truth of the California missions must be told, and at Santa Clara our hope is to present it in a way that shows how Native people maintained relationships with each other and with important places before, during, and after the Spanish colonial period.

References

Allen, Rebecca, Scott Baxter, Linda Hylkema, Clinton Blount, and Stella D'Oro. 2010. "Uncovering and Interpreting History and Archaeology at Mission Santa Clara." Report to Santa Clara University, Santa Clara.

Baines, Lauren, Andrew Galvan, Alan Leventhal, Catherine Moore, Charlene Nijmeh, Lee Panich, Margaret M. Russell, Rebecca M. Schapp, and Robert Senkewicz. 2020. "Ohlone History Working Group Report." Santa Clara University. https://www.scu.edu/media/offices/diversity/pdfs/V10.2_OHWG_CombinedReportFINAL.pdf.

Castillo, Edward. 1989. "The Native Response to the Colonization of Alta California." In *Columbian Consequences*, vol. 1, *Archaeological and Historical Perspectives on the Spanish Borderlands West*, edited by David H. Thomas, 377–94. Washington, DC: Smithsonian Institution.

Chilcote, Olivia. 2015. "Pow Wows at the Mission: Identity and Federal Recognition for the San Luis Rey Band of Luiseño Mission Indians." *Boletín: Journal of the California Missions Studies Association* 31 (1): 79–87.

Costo, Rupert, and Jeannette Henry Costo, eds. 1987. *The Missions of California: A Legacy of Genocide*. San Francisco: Indian Historian Press.

Dartt-Newton, Deana. 2011. "California's Sites of Conscience: An Analysis of the State's Historic Mission Museums." *Museum Anthropology* 34 (2): 97–108.

Duffey, George. 1907. "The Coming of the Cross." *Redwood* 7: 108–9.

Evening News. 1907. "Workmen Unearth Human Remains." October 2.

Field, Les, Alan Leventhal, and Rosemary Cambra. 2013. "Mapping Erasure: The Power of Nominative Cartography in the Past and Present of the Muwekma Ohlones of the San Francisco Bay Area." In *Recognition, Sovereignty Struggles, and Indigenous Rights in the United States: A Sourcebook*, edited by Amy E. Den Ouden and Jean M. O'Brien, 287–309. Chapel Hill: University of North Carolina Press.

Field, Les, Alan Leventhal, Dolores Sanchez, and Rosemary Cambra. 1992. "A Contemporary Ohlone Tribal Revitalization Movement: A Perspective from the Muwekma Costanoan/Ohlone Indians of the San Francisco Bay Area." *California History* 71 (3): 412–31.

Galvan, Andrew. 2013. "Old Mission Dolores, Under New Management: An Open Letter." *News from Native California* 26 (4): 11–13.

Galvan, Andrew, and Vincent Medina. 2018. "Indian Memorials at California Missions." In *Franciscans and American Indians in Pan-Borderlands Perspective: Adaptation, Negotiation, and Resistance*, edited by Jeffrey M. Burns and Timothy J. Johnson, 323–31. Oceanside, CA: American Academy of Franciscan History.

Gnecco, Cristóbal, and Adriana Schmidt Dias. 2015. "On Contract Archaeology." *International Journal of Historical Archaeology* 19 (4): 687–98.

Hackel, Steven. 2013. *Junípero Serra: California's Founding Father.* New York: Hill and Wang.

Hylkema, Mark. 1995. *Archaeological Investigations at the Third Location of Mission Santa Clara de Asís: The Murguía Mission, 1781–1818 (CA-SCL-30/H).* Oakland: California Department of Transportation.

Kroeber, Alfred. 1925. *Handbook of the Indians of California.* Bureau of American Ethnology Bulletin, no. 78. Washington, DC: Smithsonian Institution.

Kropp, Phoebe. 2006. *California Vieja: Culture and Memory in a Modern American Place.* Berkeley: University of California Press.

Kryder-Reid, Elizabeth. 2010. "Perennially New: Santa Barbara and the Origins of the California Mission Garden." *Journal of the Society of Architectural Historians* 69 (3): 378–405.

———. 2016. *California Mission Landscapes: Race, Memory, and the Politics of Heritage.* Minneapolis: University of Minnesota Press.

Leventhal, Alan, Les Field, Hank Alvarez, and Rosemary Cambra. 1994. "The Ohlone: Back from Extinction." In *The Ohlone Past and Present: Native Americans of the San Francisco Bay Region,* edited by Lowell J. Bean, 297–336. Menlo Park, CA: Ballena Press.

Leventhal, Alan, Diane DiGiuseppe, Melynda Atwood, David Grant, Rosemary Cambra, Charlene Nijmeh, Monica V. Arellano, Sheila Guzman-Schmidt, Gloria E. Gomez, and Norma Sanchez. 2011. "Final Report on the Burial and Archaeological Data Recovery Program Conducted on a Portion of the Mission Santa Clara Indian Neophyte Cemetery (1781–1818): Clareño Muwékma Ya Túnnešte Nómmo [Where the Clareño Indians Are Buried] Site (CA-SCL-30/H), Located in the City of Santa Clara, Santa Clara County, California." Report to Pacific Gas and Electric Company, Santa Clara, CA.

Lopez, Valentin. 2015. "Foreword." In *A Cross of Thorns: The Enslavement of California's Indians by the Spanish Missions,* by Elias Castillo. Fresno, CA: Craven Street Books.

Lorimer, Michelle. 2016. *Resurrecting the Past: The California Mission Myth.* Pechanga, CA: Great Oaks Press.

Lueck, Amy, and Lee Panich. 2020. "Representing Indigenous Histories Using XR Technologies in the Classroom." *Journal of Interactive Technology & Pedagogy* 17.

Lueck, Amy, Matthew Kroot, and Lee Panich. 2021. "Public Memory as Community-Engaged Writing: Composing Difficult Histories on Campus." *Community Literacy Journal* 15 (2): 9–30.

McKevitt, Gerald. 1979. *The University of Santa Clara: A History, 1851–1977.* Palo Alto, CA: Stanford University Press.

Miranda, Deborah. 2013. *Bad Indians: A Tribal Memoir*. Berkeley, CA: Heyday.

Monument Lab. 2021. *National Monument Audit*. Monument Lab and the Andrew W. Mellon Foundation. https://monumentlab.com/monumentlab -nationalmonumentaudit.pdf.

Nokes, R. Gregory. 2018. *The Troubled Life of Peter Burnett: Oregon Pioneer and First Governor of California*. Corvallis: Oregon State University Press.

Panich, Lee. 2015. "Mission Santa Clara in a Changing Urban Environment." *Boletín: Journal of the California Mission Studies Association* 31 (1): 36–45.

———. 2016. "After Saint Serra: Unearthing Indigenous Histories at the California Missions." *Journal of Social Archaeology* 16 (2): 238–58.

———. 2020. *Narratives of Persistence: Indigenous Negotiations of Colonialism in Alta and Baja California*. Tucson: University of Arizona Press.

———. 2022. "Archaeology, Indigenous Erasure, and the Creation of White Public Space at the California Missions." *Journal of Social Archaeology* 22 (2): 149–71.

Panich, Lee M., Monica V. Arellano, Michael Wilcox, Gustavo Flores, and Samuel Connell. 2024. "Fighting Erasure and Dispossession in the San Francisco Bay Area: Putting Archaeology to Work for the Muwekma Ohlone Tribe." *Frontiers in Environmental Archaeology* 3 (2024): frontiersin .org/journals/environmental-archaeology/articles/10.3389/fearc.2024 .1394106/full.

Peelo, Sarah, John Ellison, Stella D'Oro, Clinton Blount, and Lorie Garcia. 2015. "Phase I Resource Identification and Phase II Evaluation of Significance and Assessment of Impacts for the Unified Facility for the School of Law Project." Report to David J. Powers & Associates, San Jose, CA.

Peelo, Sarah, Linda Hylkema, John Ellison, Clinton Blount, Mark Hylkema, Margie Maher, Tom Garlinghouse, Dustin McKenzie, Stella D'Oro, and Melinda Berge. 2018. "Persistence in the Indian *Ranchería* at Mission Santa Clara de Asís." *Journal of California and Great Basin Anthropology* 38 (2): 207–34.

Potter, James M., Mike Mirro, and Brenna Wheelis. 2021. *575 Benton Street Project, Santa Clara California*. Vol. 1, *Data Recovery at Site CA-SCL-30H*. Report to Prometheus Real Estate Group. San Mateo, CA.

Ramirez, Renya K., and Valentin Lopez. 2020. "Valentin Lopez, Healing, and Decolonization: Contesting Mission Bells, El Camino Real, and California Governor Newsom." *Latin American and Latinx Visual Culture* 2 (3): 91–98.

Rawls, James. 1992. "The California Mission as Symbol and Myth." *California History* 71 (3): 342–61.

San Francisco Chronicle. 1907a. "Find a Mission Burial Ground." October 3.

———. 1907b. "Will Celebrate City's Birthday." October 28, 3.

Santa Clara. 1930. "Slab Placed to Memory of Governor." May 8.

Schneider, Khal, Dale Allender, Margarita Berta-Ávila, Rose Borunda, Gregg Castro, Amy Murray, and Jenna Porter. 2019. "More Than Missions: Native Californians and Allies Changing the Story of California History." *Journal of American Indian Education* 58 (3): 58–77.

Schneider, Tsim. 2019. "Heritage In-Between: Seeing Native Histories in Colonial California." *Public Historian* 41 (1): 51–63.

Schneider, Tsim D., Khal Schneider, and Lee Panich. 2020. "Scaling Invisible Walls: Reasserting Indigenous Persistence in Mission-Era California." *Public Historian* 42 (2): 97–120.

Shoup, Laurence H., and Randall T. Milliken. 1999. *Inigo of Rancho Posolmi: The Life and Times of a Mission Indian*. Novato, CA: Ballena Press.

Skowronek, Russell, and Julie Wizorek. 1997. "Archaeology at Santa Clara de Asís: The Slow Rediscovery of a Moveable Mission." *Pacific Coast Archaeological Society Quarterly* 33 (3): 54–92.

Smith, Clint. 2021. *How the Word Is Passed: A Reckoning with the History of Slavery across America*. New York: Little, Brown.

Thomas, David Hurst. 1991. "Harvesting Ramona's Garden: Life in California's Mythical Mission Past." In *Columbian Consequences*, vol. 3, *The Spanish Borderlands in Pan-American Perspective*, edited by David H. Thomas, 119–57. Washington, DC: Smithsonian Institution.

———. 2014. "The Life and Times of Fr. Junípero Serra: A Pan-Borderlands Perspective." *Americas* 71 (2): 185–225.

Weber, David. 1990. "Blood of Martyrs, Blood of Indians: Toward a More Balanced View of Spanish Missions in Seventeenth-Century North America." In *Columbian Consequences*, vol. 2, *Archaeological and Historical Perspectives on the Spanish Borderlands East*, edited by David Hurst Thomas, 429–48. Washington, DC: Smithsonian Institution.

Heritage at Stake

The Contemporary Guarani and the Missions

CRISTÓBAL GNECCO

There are two main ways to engage the missions the Jesuits established in pre-Republican times amidst the Guarani in what are now southern Brazil, northeastern Argentina, and southeastern Paraguay. One is historical in the canonical sense—that is, the missionary story happened in the past, and what remains of the missions is just ruins, material witnesses to their former existence. Their contemporaneity, that of the ruins and the missions, does not trouble that historical sense or bring any relevance to its deployment. Their contemporaneity does not exist. Better, they are not contemporary, but events/things of the past (not *from* the past, but *of* the past, implying an understanding of the past as past, self-contained, unreachable to any current concern). The second way is ethnographic. The missions (and their ruins!) mean something to the people that interact with them, a *something* that is endowed with heritage meanings that are far from being consensual, although the hegemonic meaning crafted centuries ago still pictures them as an endless source of civilizational inspiration. The missions and their legacy are thus fully contemporary. This latter way is the one I have chosen to follow in this essay, which is centered in the relationship of the Guarani with the missions, in two senses: (a) the one granted to them by scholars and institutional agents—that is, a relationship seen and considered from afar; and (b) the one they feel and think they have—that is, a relationship from within. As seen from these relationships (sometimes conflicting, sometimes complementary), the very meanings of the missions as heritage are at stake.

The missions involved two main actors and their cultural traditions: the Jesuits and the Guarani; the culture of the latter was a target of the culture of the former. We have two protagonists, then, whose presence as words oscillates in a fascinating way. In the profuse discursive production about the missions (academic, official, touristic, heritage-related, advertising) the Jesuit name prevails, agreeing to a primacy not only historical but also moral; after all, it was the Jesuits who reduced the Guarani, and not the other way around—although missionary apologetics thought that this was the case, that the priests were reduced by the Indians in an act of divine sacrifice. Even more, the name "Guarani" only appeared recently in the description of the Southern Cone missions, perhaps starting after 1992 (with the commemoration of the fifth centenary of the European arrival in the Americas), when the Indigenous agency was highlighted.

The heritage meanings accorded to the missions have changed through the years. They were initially marked by the fact that the missionary project went from being a successful civilizing experiment (autonomous, relatively peaceful, protective, and bucolic) to, in the eighteenth century, being a threat to imperial and national policies. Thus, their memory survived unevenly in the national discourses of Brazil, Paraguay, and Argentina, as well as in ethnic memories. The UNESCO declaration of the ruins as world heritage prompted a resignification of their meaning and a collision of varied interests because, before, they were just regional and national patrimonies. What has been patrimonialized in/of the missions?—the general idea of civilization, to be sure, not the legacy of the societies subdued by that idea. That idea was genocidal, violent, and imposed on the indigenes because it was solidly based on the belief that it was better, superior, more advanced; it was based, that is, on the then undiscussed assumption that there were natural hierarchies articulated by racial and religious criteria. That is why in the relationship between the Jesuits and the Guarani, what has counted for the most part is the place of the former, not that of the latter. What has mattered most is the modernity that the Jesuits still represent. In that story (save in some academic fields) the Guarani are mute, the weakest link in the missions' narrative chain. Has that changed with the recent heritage processes to which the ruins of the missions have been subjected? Not so much, except in Brazil (for the reasons I will describe). The fact that both benefited from their encounter (the Jesuits gaining souls and the Guarani gaining security and stability) can never deny that the missions meant an imposed reduction and an ethnocide.

The civilizational imprint of the missions still lingers, no matter that their ruins now stand in three different countries with quite different national histories. It is a legacy from a colonial era that, for the most part, has been condemned in those histories—rhetorically, for the ideal

of civilization still moves on at a great speed, now dressed as development, of which heritage process is but a part; its impacts (destruction,
dispossession, infringement of cultural and natural rights) are as terrible
nowadays as they were before. Because of this, at least since the late
nineteenth century, the missions have become subjected to heritage
attention and, eventually, to heritage declarations, even global. Their coloniality, however, has rarely been explicitly dealt with—save by some historians. In this sense, disciplinary and heritage interventions are additional
layers in the hardening of the mission experience as civilization. History
is not being rewritten by archaeological and heritage discourses; the history
we already know (as recounted by those who won), the history celebrated
and commemorated in countless mnemonic spaces (from classrooms to
TV and movie documentaries, from the media to the apparent seclusion of
homes, from heritage sites to a plethora of booklets, posters, and books), is
being recast time and again. That history, recounting a story of the past as
past, insistently bypasses that what happened then is inextricably linked to
what happens now: the Guarani selling handicrafts in the ruins (Figure 14)
and struggling to survive in minuscule reservations, deprived of their
former territories and their cultural scaffolding, are a consequence of the
mission experience, of the place of Indigenous peoples in the nation-state
and in post-national societies, of the concerted work of academic
disciplines—archaeology among them.

The Guarani and the Missionary Story

The relationship between the Guarani that currently live in the region,
where the Jesuit established their missions in the seventeenth century, and
the historical Guarani, reduced in colonial times by that religious enterprise, is highly contested. For some people there is no relationship at all
between those two populations—which is tantamount to saying that the
current Guarani have no historical relation to the missions; for others, the
former are heirs of the latter. This essay intends to describe the different
positions on the subject as they have been articulated by scholars and heritage officials as well as by Indigenous peoples. Disciplinary arguments
(historical, anthropological, linguistic) usually exclude the political context in which they unfold, while political arguments ignore the academic
context. Further, the difference among the three countries—the choice

FIGURE 14. A Mbyá Guarani family selling handicrafts outside the museum in the ruins of the São Miguel mission, Brazil. (Photo by Adriana Dias, 2013)

of one position to the detriment of the other—is a product of the place of their others in their national stories, to the imprint of Catholicism, and to the uneven unfolding of academic traditions.

An assessment of heritage interventions on the mission experience (through the ruins, that is) cannot be comprehensively seen if the focus is not placed over the Guarani—the main subjects (for subjection) of such an experience. The presence of the Guarani in the missionary story, that story that lingers until today through patrimonialization, is obscure, opaque, and unequal and demands to ask: why patrimonialize the ruins of the missions in the first place, such objects-signs of a project that, in any case and from wherever you look at it (with a little or a lot of empathy, with a little or a lot of contempt), was part of the conquest of America, one of the biggest genocidal enterprises in history? Why patrimonialize precisely those ruins, eloquent witnesses of the submission of the Guarani to civilization, witnesses of their reduction? Because they are part of a *good genocide*, let's say, if something so absolutely abominable can actually be conceived? But is it not what humanism has always done to justify colonialism and its violence if it leads to civilization, to get these poor Indians out of their primitive, primordial condition? So, yes, an object-sign that is a part of a genocidal enterprise can be patrimonialized. Moreover, it *must* be patrimonialized. Although heritage erases the original meaning, say, of what it patrimonializes and imposes new meanings, is it not in this case the UNESCO heritage narrative as humanistic as the act of civilization of the Jesuits, that would bring together one humanism with another—one of the sixteenth century with another of the twenty-first century, that would come to point out, then, that humanism is a same totemic (and violent) animal that has only changed its skin? Would not this come to re-signify the act of civilization and to renew its validity, now as development (through heritage)? Since the ruins were elevated to world heritage at the same time as the creation of the Common Market of the Southern Cone, the search for a common history and, above all, for common commodities has been notorious. The missions have not escaped that search: their utopian value became an exchange value to which development clings forcefully.

Having asked these basic questions about the heritage meaning of the missions, their protagonists are exposed, those of then and now: the Guarani, the Jesuits, the *encomenderos*, the settlers, the colonial and republican officials, the historians and the anthropologists, the heritage agents. They intersect, those protagonists, and erase the boundaries between past and present. The missions and their ruins are central icons in the imaginary of three nation-states in which they now stand because they helped to build what Rita Segato (2007) called *national formations of otherness*, historical regimes of creation of the others of the nation and, now, of the post-nation. To ask about the missions from the vantage point of those formations is to ask about the place of their others, the place of the Guarani, and to find that theirs is a rather opaque place filled in uneven ways in Argentina, Brazil, and Paraguay during the last two centuries.

The first thing that calls my attention when I ask about the place of the Guarani in the missions is the lack of consensus, not so much historical but contemporary. The canonical and dominant narrative about the missions was conservative, unidirectional, and static: it was an apology of the civilizing deeds of the missionaries without recognizing the indigenes' agency and, if that, even history. But the historiography on the Guarani of the missions has changed, and it now investigates their active role (e.g., Wilde 2009; Neumann 2015; Chamorro 2017), moving away from the idea of their essential passivity, which accorded, until recently, the central role of the story to the Jesuits. There, in that question about the agency of the Guarani in the missions, a certain new consensus begins to form. The same thing does not happen when the question moves from the ghostly character of the missionary Guarani to the utter concretion of the contemporary Guarani; in other words, when one asks about the relationship between today's Guarani, especially the Mbyá, and the Guarani of the missions. There dissent reigns, as if the real bodies (individual and, above all, social) challenge the possibility of establishing unequivocal answers. Dissension reigns because the place of the current Guarani in the missionary story is no longer just an academic issue, as in the case of historiography (still dominated by disciplinary preoccupations), but rather a political one. This dissent can be seen by comparing the narratives about the missions and their others in the three countries.

In Brazil, the story of the missions had the Jesuits as protagonists until the 1980s, when a dramatic change occurred: protagonism passed on to the Guarani due, mostly, to academic militancy, especially around the demarcation of Indigenous lands. As a result, the relationship of the Mbyá with the Guarani of the missions is not a matter of discussion any longer but of documentation (in ethnographies, workshops, documentaries). In the juridical dispute on land issues, temporal and territorial continuity matters much, and being heirs of the Guarani of the missions provides fine rhetorical fuel to the Mbyá and their academic supporters. This does not happen in Argentina and Paraguay, where the approach to the issue is academic, not political—and where, not coincidentally, regulations for the demarcation of Indigenous lands are either nonexistent or not widely applied. In those two countries there is little doubt: the current Guarani are not thoroughly related to the Guarani of the missions, and, therefore, their relationship with the ruins (and the memories they trigger) is rather ethereal. To put it another way: while in Brazil the issue is already clearly discursive, in the other two countries it remains substantive; while in Brazil it abandoned the positivistic limits of disciplinary research and the modern criteria of reality, in Argentina and Paraguay such an abandonment (such an escape) is still far from happening.

Anthropologists in Argentina and Paraguay claim not to know expressions of the Mbyá about the missions or their ruins, implying that they are not interested in them or are totally unrelated. But, if so, should not that disinterest or distance be the reason for an investigation still unattended? It would not seem possible to affirm that the Mbyá are unrelated to the Guarani of the missions, that they are not their heirs, except from the claims of truth of the modern disciplines and their monological channel of communication. In this, as in so many other things, disciplinary truths are ideologically veiled: the missionary work is celebrated (even if the emphasis falls on the Jesuits, inferiorizing the Guarani, poor infantile souls) while, at the same time, a place is denied to the contemporary Guarani, who are said to have "arrived" in the missions area not long ago (even after the Eastern Europeans who populated the region since the late nineteenth century and who have created a very curious "missionary culture") and whose life elapses between poverty and welfare.

The differences among the three countries in this issue are also a result of different and, to a certain extent, closed academic traditions. They do not know each other well, despite a certain fluidity and exchange. If the missions were a question of frontiers, not only geographic but also cultural, their academic research is another form of frontier, not because such research is positioned in the frontier—in the postcolonial sense of Anzaldúa (1987)—but because it establishes rigid and quite insurmountable borders: the historians here, the anthropologists there; the Brazilians here, the Paraguayans there, as before the Indians of the missions here, the forest Indians there. Borders between themes, then, but also between academic traditions. This partitioning is typically modern (and colonial, of course, if I see the issue as expressing the coproduction of modernity and coloniality).

There is more on the role of the disciplines in structuring the coloniality of the narrative of the missions (see Gnecco and Dias 2021). Archaeology and heritage pretend "to give voice to ethnic minorities and subaltern, oppressed, disadvantaged, or marginal segments who could not record their own history" (Lima 1993, 228). The coloniality spoken in those word is astonishing: it is modernity who gives voice to the oppressed, who could not record their own history. This is a long story by which modernity indulged in telling the history of those who subdued because they were incapable of doing so and ultimately because they didn't have history—not only because they didn't have letters, but also because they didn't exist in the very time from where history is recounted. Archaeologists and historians continue to thicken the colonial archive described by Walter Mignolo—"From such a philosophy of language and writing, it should come as no surprise that Spanish men of letters appointed themselves to write down the history that Amerindians could not properly write because of their lack of letters" (Mignolo 1995, 129)—and feed the unending tension between those who live in their memories and those who name themselves to write the history of other memories that did not live but contemplate from afar, even if in awe, but academically and aseptically.

If archaeology utterly eludes Indigenous life—simply because it is not there to grasp it—what are mission archaeologists after? Let's see what Arno Kern (1998a, 12, 19) has to say in that regard: "The aim is to elaborate a new memory that will be accessible to the community in the form of an expanded and reinterpreted cultural heritage. . . . These archaeological remains allow the production of an important social memory." What "important social memory" is he talking about? That of the Guarani, subdued by the mission experience? If it were so, the most we could say is that Indigenous historicity would be trampled by the temporality of modernity. But this is not the case, even though public (even Indigenous) archaeology would welcome it. The archaeologists are not concerned with Indigenous social memory, not even when they talk of collaboration or participation of non-academics in their research. That concern falls, if anything, on the side of anthropologists and historians, another expression of the compartmentalization of reality by disciplinary frames. No. The social memory Kern is talking about is that produced by archaeology: a curious "social memory" built upon the shared idea that the past is buried and somehow encrypted/codified in things. (The procedures for uncovering/decoding have changed through the years, from unregulated common sense to highly ritualized scientific protocols; the definition and meaning of what is covered/codified and hence awaiting to be uncovered/decoded for the sake of archaeological knowledge, have not. The latter is thoroughly naturalized.) If this "social memory" is not that of the Guarani but of archaeology, which is its place? Which is its relation with the community (an anthropological token for Indigenous diversity)? Well, their rapport is directional, teleological, and mono-logical: archaeology, as a part of the modern-colonial way of enacting reality, teaches its "social memory" to the unfortunate Others, those poor fellows without history, as we are constantly reminded: "We still have the task of discovering the most important data of this cultural transformation that led the Guarani to cross the level of Prehistory to History" (Kern 1998b, 69). Great! The Guarani are now in the hands of historical writing, that of the archaeologists, where they can safely abandon their premodern darkness.

It would be amusing, if it were not tragic, to read Kern (1998b, 67) again, stating that "archaeological documents inform us about the daily life of the Natives without the ideological distortions of the conquering white." Archaeology appeals to a reified, non-ideological reality (a single and unified reality out-there, a reality as is, an empirical reality), while historical accounts are fooled by interpretations. The conquering white speaks (ideologically) through history, while a neutral, external, objective truth speaks through archaeology. Archaeology un-deforms historical deformations! Hard to believe. Mission archaeology in the hands of practitioners such as Kern cannot be but a part of the ongoing modern-colonial (onto) logic.

The heritage story partakes of the epistemological and ontological ruptures established by the modern-colonial order, the most prominent of which in this regard is that between the Indigenous past and the disciplinary present: from the temporality of modernity (the temporality of heritage, that is), the time of the others is studied, assessed, gauged . . . and objectified. (There is an additional rupture, also disciplinary, with colonial underpinnings all over: history deals with documents—which therefore are part of culture—heritage with "material culture," a parcel of the natural world, that of the Others and their things. Of course, this is not an immanent division, but the way modernity partitioned its reality to distribute it among the disciplines.) Such a rupture can be seen from a disciplinary perspective: the Guarani of the missions (as part of the ruins and through their objects, if not as objects themselves) are dealt with by heritage, while current Guarani are the concern of anthropology, as if there were not a circular relation between past and present, as if what happened then was unconnected with what happens now. There are no communicating vessels between anthropology and archaeology (each of them preserving their parcel of knowledge, their parcel of otherness) regarding the current Guarani and the mission experience—which the Guarani inherited, mythologized, and still sense as violent and catastrophic—which is tantamount to saying that there are no connections between the present and the past, as if they were just events in the arrow of time that simply pass, but do not connect. The present thus discards the past as something that happened and disappeared, but that does not linger; as something that can be delivered to the firm grip of heritage. Historical connections between mission and current Guarani are thus severed. The unacknowledged deep logic in all this, the logic that makes the heritage agents feel comfortable, is that mission Guarani vanished into thin air; being so, they don't have to deal with the awkward presence of the Guarani they nowadays spot selling handicrafts outside the ruins—not to say when the Guarani press for their cultural and historical claims (which are the domain of the anthropologists, anyway, in the modern distribution among disciplines). Although historians have documented that this was not the case—that mission Guarani did survive, disperse, mingle, went to work into the cities (Neumann 1996; Wilde 2001; Poenitz 2012), heritage bypasses historical findings. This is not surprising, though, because the archaeological discourse to which it recurs speaks to a centuries-old archive that talks about catastrophes, disappearances, ruptures, degradation. The mission Guarani, say archaeologists and heritage agents, may have well been the ideal civilized Indians, but the destitute current Guarani can only be their degraded, yet disconnected, heirs. Disciplines thrive amidst a praised civilization and an overlooked misery—as if they had not participated in their joint constitution. Mission Guarani were a part of a civilizational time (as they were subjected to it), while current Guarani belong to another time—premodern, primitive, savage, in short, Indigenous.

The way the Guarani are dealt with by heritage has yet another angle. Heritage interventions, formerly restricted to elevating to patrimony certain things (usually monuments, such as the ruins of the missions), gained momentum when heritage education was initiated, especially since so-called public and historical archaeologies became new exports from the metropolitan world in the 1980s, received with utmost relief in the periphery. The argument about heritage education posits that past evidence exposed by archaeology can be converted into heritage and then taught to local populations. Heritage education programs are booming as a means of countering the critiques archaeology receives from the outside world, especially regarding its esoterism and its isolation from various stakeholders, mostly local. Heritage education programs have allowed archaeology to become socially responsible—an expression formerly reserved to corporations, a symptom that archaeology has entered a corporate phase. The arrogance, coloniality, and utter modernity of heritage education are obvious: they pretend that local populations are ignorant about their pasts, which can only exist if exposed by the discipline (in the modern sense of unearthing, unveiling, stripping—that is, digging); and they make heritage educators the redeemers of the past, history, and even the cultures of local populations. The compensatory politics engaged through heritage education is not politics for the common good but plain and simple corporate politics. Corporate social responsibility, it is worth recalling, is a one-way action by which capitalism "gives back" to the people (normally local populations affected by development projects) whatever it deems worth giving—usually unimportant crumbs far removed from mitigating the social and environmental harm caused by such projects. Social responsibility, as altruistic action, acts along local resistance; while the former is widely publicized as good, the latter is routinely criminalized and silenced. The co-existence of social responsibility and local resistance and the uneven treatment they receive (in the media, in the legal systems, in the administrative apparatus) highlight that the former supports and reproduces capitalism, which is disdainful of local struggles that challenge its operation (Gnecco and Dias 2015, 689). Despite this (or, perhaps, because of it), de Moraes (2014) and Focking (2018) praise heritage education linked to mission archaeology. Communities, in their opinion, are eager to participate in what archaeology and heritage have to offer: "In the field of archaeology, it is possible to see that professionals are increasingly observing that communities have a sense of belonging to their own past and want to participate effectively in decision-making processes in order to bring their own ideas of heritage appreciation" (de Moraes 2014, 18). This is not surprising, either. Ever since Vine Deloria (1992, 598) put collaboration between archaeologists and Indigenous peoples at the forefront of a new form of (noncolonial) relationship, it became a token for socially and politically committed archaeologists; it even became a morality on its own. Collaboration with and participation of formerly disenfranchised parties is one of the aims of most brands of activist archaeologies—to which heritage education in mission archaeology would certainly subscribe. Both have been premised in the democratic agenda of a widened archaeology (and heritage), socially and politically accountable to a host of new actors by fostering inclusion and sharing. Yet, bringing other peoples to share the bounty of archaeology and heritage (the cosmology of modernity) is a one-way inclusion that disregards crucial issues such as time, descent, space, and living as they are considered and experienced by not-so-modern worldviews. The sharing collaboration offers is fully developed within the conception of modern democracy and has become a new disciplining routine where, more often than not, what is shared is just the temporality of modernity. Again, the "social memory" being shared is that built and spread by heritage, not by Indigenous agendas.

The Current Guarani and the Missions

I watch a group of Guarani youngsters watching *The Mission*, a 1986 film directed by Roland Joffé that portrayed the so-called "Guarani wars" of the 1750s—which were not wars at all, but vicious massacres inflicted on the Guarani that resisted the order to vacate the mission in which they had been living in what is now Brazilian territory. I watch them because they have been filmed watching the film in the documentary *Tava, a Casa de Pedra* (Ferreira et al. 2012), made by Guarani filmmakers about the significance of the missions and their ruins for current Guarani populations. A film within a film, then, and an outsider watching two films unfolding, intertwining, telling how history is written by those who win, how it is contested by those who lose; telling how the very collectives marginalized and silenced by the authority of "heritage" engage with it, yet from a different ontology that questions its very meaning (that of "heritage") and, notably, its utter naturalization.

Seen from the discursive corner, not from the disciplinary one, the sharp separation between the Guarani of the missions and the contemporary Guarani has catastrophist overtones and is a part of the reproduction of the civilized/savage dichotomy; a part of the enlightened meaning of heritage (the missionary Indians *in* the ruins, the contemporary Indians *outside* them, selling handicrafts: an insulting, shameful contrast, worthy of the heritage act, as disinterested from the fate of the new Indians as it is concerned about the fate of the old Indians); a part of academic traditions (the Indians of the missions with the historians and the current Indians with the anthropologists, without communicating vessels, each of them preserving their parcel of knowledge and, therefore, their parcel of otherness); a part, alas, of the denial of coevalness (Fabian 1983). If this issue is seen instead from the discursive corner (which is also political), other things begin to emerge, even in terms of ontological divergences and multiplicities. The spaces for multiplicity must be gained in a field of struggle that has already been defined as a political ontology, centered "on the conflicts that ensue as different worlds or ontologies strive to sustain their own existence as they interact and mingle with each other" (Blaser 2009, 877). The consideration of multiplicity is ontological; the consideration of versions of reality that oppose or collide is epistemological. While the former offers openness, freedom, creativity, the latter guarantees disciplinary closure. It is up to mission archaeologists to keep feeding the modern-colonial project or to engage multiplicity (to engage not-so-modern cosmologies) in alternative, generous, and caring ways.

In the memory of the Mbyá the missionary story, but not its modern patrimonial conversion, is a firm historical source, quite relevant for their struggle for territory and self-determination. It has been noted that there is a mythical place called *Tava Miri* of great cultural importance because it is "recognized as a work left by the ancestors of the current Mbyá-Guarani . . . *Tava Miri* as a source of knowledge of the Mbyá because it marks their union with the gods" (de Moraes 2010, 15). *Tava Miri* keeps "a kind of 'petrified message' left to his descendants about the fact that life is made by successive challenges, that it is worthwhile to fight against death and decomposition knowing that victory is almost impossible, but motivated by the idea that there is an immortality and a fullness of existence here and beyond this world" (de Souza and Morinico 2009, 314). Yet, some of the elders interviewed in the film *Tava, a Casa de Pedra* (Ferreira et al. 2012) are quite certain that the ruins are not Tava Miri—the sacred dwelling, to be found elsewhere, in the beyond, even perhaps in a place akin to the Christian heavens—but just Tava, a temporary dwelling left by the gods in their walk toward the "land without evil": "In the places where they stopped to rest [the Nhanderú, the gods], they built the Tava, which were their temporary abodes, before reaching the sacred abodes. For this reason, the Mbya Guarani follow the Tava, who were left behind by the Nhanderú Mirim, as they indicate the way to reach the sacred dwellings. However, since the arrival of the Juruá (non-Indigenous), the

Mbyá Guarani peoples have never been able to reach the sacred dwellings again, due to the Juruá interference with the *mbya reko* (Guarani Mbyá way of being). . . . It was along the path of the Nhanderu Mirim that they built the Tava, large stone houses. Among these Tava are the missionary reductions, built together with the Jesuit priests: but for the Guarani ancestors, it was about the journey in search of Nhanderu."[1] At any event, whether Tava Miri o Tava, the ruins are important cultural referents for the current Guarani. Their relevance is purely utopian, both as a no-place and as a horizon of possibility. The Mbyá, however, do not engage with the authority of the heritage discourse from a different perspective, as if it were just an epistemological issue; they engage the ontological peculiarity of their historical narrative aside from how "heritage" is conceived and mobilized. Their bearing on heritage, which has not been forcefully articulated yet, is thus ontological. The Guarani population in the missions was dispersed or resettled; if to that fact we add the implementation of strong assimilationist policies in the region (radicalized by the governments of the three independent polities created in the early nineteenth century), it is possible to understand why in Guarani memories the missions embody a sense of community autonomy eventually destroyed and lost. What is the relation of current Guarani with this heritage? Whose heritage it is, anyway? In elevating the missions to heritage (well, their ruins)—regional, national, and nowadays global—has an erasure been exercised over their coloniality? No, it hasn't. Their coloniality is an integral part of them as heritage.

The missions were utopian in a broad sense—that is, they were located nowhere. They were not in a Western country or in the colony, since they were worlds apart in all respects, an unanchored idea—and were, therefore, perfect mirrors of what was possible. But this utopia, as seen from Western eyes, was surgically separated from the ontology of modernity, from the relations of power it established, as if it had not been a fundamental beachhead in its advance over other ontological frontiers. Maybe because of this brutal separation, the utopia of the missions eventually disappeared into thin air. The missions suffered a similar fate. The Jesuits were expelled from Portugal and Spain and their colonies, and their work of conversion came to a halt, as well as what little remained of their buildings, soon turned into ruins. Utopia was devoured by the jungle, like the ruins. It returned, let's say, to its place in nature, to the world of the primitive. But recently, after more than two centuries of twilight, utopia once again showed its face, and, wonderful paradox, it did it in the hands of the contemporary Guarani, those subjects on the margins (in every sense: on the margins of history, the countryside, cities). Nothing can hide, however, that the missions were the ruin of the Guarani. Their ruins, then, are places of consolidation of the Indigenous ruin, of its exaltation (touristic, national, supranational) as a project of civilization. The meaning of a ruin is imposed (because it glorifies, exalts, markets) over the meaning of another. What lingers is the imprint of the ruin as ruin: a vestige of what there was, but an unmistakable emblem of what it remains.

References

Anzaldúa, Gloria. 1987. *Borderlands/La frontera: The New Mestiza*. San Francisco: Spinsters/Aunt Lute.

Blaser, Mario. 2009. "Political Ontology: Cultural Studies without 'Cultures'?" *Cultural Studies* 23 (5–6): 873–96.

Chamorro, Graciela. 2017. *Cuerpo social: Historia y etnografía de la organización social en los pueblos Guaraní*. Asunción: Tiempo de Historia.

Deloria, Vine. 1992. "Indians, Archaeologists, and the Future." *American Antiquity* 57: 595–98.

de Moraes, Carlos Neves. 2010. "A refiguração da tava miri São Miguel na memória coletiva dos mbyá-guarani nas missões/RS, Brasil." PhD diss. Porto Alegre: Universidade Federal do Rio Grande do Sul.

de Moraes, Tobias Vilhena. 2014. "Preservação arqueológica e ação educativa nas missões." PhD diss. Porto Alegre: Universidade Católica do Rio Grande do Sul.

de Souza, José Catafesto, and José Cirilo Morinico. 2009. "Fantasmas das brenhas ressurgem nas ruínas: Mbyá-Guaranis relatam sua versão sobre as missões e depois delas." In *Historia geral do Rio Grande do Sul*, vol. 5, *Povos indígenas*, edited by Arno Kern, Cristina dos Santos and Tau Golin, 301–30. Passo Fundo: Méritos.

Fabian, Johannes. 1983. *Time and the Other*. New York: Columbia University Press.

Ferreira, Patricia, Ariel Ortega, Vicent Carelli, and Ernesto de Carvalho. 2012. *Tava, a Casa de Pedra*. Recife: Vídeo nas Aldeias.

Focking, Gabriel de Freitas. 2018. "Ações educativas na Arqueologia Missioneira (1985–1995)." Master's thesis. Porto Alegre: Universidade Federal do Rio Grande do Sul.

Gnecco, Cristóbal, and Adriana Schmidt Dias. 2015. "On Contract Archaeology." *International Journal of Historical Archaeology* 19 (4): 687–98.

Gnecco, Cristóbal, and Adriana Schmidt Dias. 2021. "A Double Coloniality: The Colonial Underpinnings of Mission Archaeology in South America." In *Routledge Handbook of the Archaeology of Indigenous-Colonial Interaction in the Americas*, edited by Lee Panich and Sara Gonzales, 30–43. London: Routledge.

Kern, Arno. 1998a. "Pesquisas arqueológicas e históricas nas missões jesuítico-guaranis (1985–1995)." In *Arqueologia histórica missioneira*, edited by Arno Kern, 11–64. Porto Alegre: PUCI.

———. 1998b. "Escavações arqueológicas na missão jesuítico-guarani de São Lourenço (RS, Brasil)." In *Arqueologia histórica missioneira*, edited by Arno Kern, 65–96. Porto Alegre: PUCI.

Lima, Tania Andrade. 1993. "Arqueologia histórica no Brasil: balanço bibliográfico (1960–1991)." *Anais do Museu Paulista Nova Série* 1: 225–62.

Mignolo, Walter. 1995. *The Darker Side of the Renaissance*. Ann Arbor: University of Michigan Press.

Neumann, Eduardo. 1996. *O trabalho guarani missioneiro no Rio da Prata colonial, 1640–1750*. Porto Alegre: Martins.

———. 2015. *Letra de indios*. São Bernardo do Campo: Nhanduti.

Poenitz, Alfredo. 2012. *Mestizo del litoral: Sus modos de vida en Loreto y San Miguel*. Posadas: Edición del autor.

Segato, Rita Laura. 2007. *La nación y sus otros: Raza, etnicidad y diversidad religiosa en tiempos de políticas de la identidad*. Buenos Aires: Prometeo.

Wilde, Guillermo. 2001. "Los guaraníes después de la expulsión de los jesuitas: Dinámicas políticas y transacciones simbólicas." *Revista Complutense de Historia de América* 27: 69–106.

———. 2009. *Religión y poder en las misiones de guaraníes*. Buenos Aires: Editorial SB.

Note

1. "As casas de pedra dos Nhanderu Mirim. . . ." https://historiaecultura guarani.org/as-casas-de-pedra-dos-nhanderu-mirim/. Accessed November 3, 2023.

Part II: Local Appropriations of the Historical Meanings of the Missions

Uses and Meanings of the Jesuit Missions of Paraguay

MAXIMILIANO VON THÜNGEN

Introduction

In South America in the seventeenth and eighteenth centuries, the Company of Jesus founded the famous Jesuit missions of the Guarani, also known as Reductions. These settlement towns extended over a broad territory that today includes the northeast of Argentina, the south of Brazil, and the southeast of Paraguay. In these small towns, partially isolated from the rest of colonial society, the Indigenous were to be converted to the Christian religion. Beginning in 1609, priests and lay brothers embarked with the Guarani on an ambitious pastoral undertaking they carried on until 1767, when King Carlos III of Spain decreed the expulsion of the Order from all his domains. During those 150 years, missionaries and Indigenous produced imposing architectural structures and a great many wood carvings, paintings, and other ornamental objects meant to serve in the evangelizing of the Indigenous (Wilde 2008; Sustersic 1999; Plá 2006). The missionaries' expulsion of course damaged the organization and the functioning of the reductions. Most of the objects made in their workshops vanished, and the impressive architectural complexes began a long phase of deterioration.

Around 1975, in a context of growing worldwide interest in preserving cultural goods, a process began in Paraguay of a new appreciation for the heritage of the ancient Guarani missions. Between 1978 and 1981, museums of sacred art were inaugurated in the small towns of Santa María de Fe, Santa Rosa de Lima, Santiago Apóstol, and San Ignacio Guazú. These towns, founded by Jesuits in the colonial period, are located in the territory that today belongs to the department of Misiones, in the south of the country. The same initiative, between 1978 and 1982, restored the reduction of Santísima Trinidad del Paraná. A project instigated by the Jesuits of Nuremberg, Germany, it repaired, between 1989 and 1996, the damage sustained by the church and Jesuit college (*colegio*) of San Cosme y San Damián. In the settlement town of Jesús, the Spanish Agency for International Development Cooperation (AECID) financed the restoration of the reduction in the early 1990s.

This reparation process continues into the present and has had deep cultural, social, and economic consequences for the locals of peasant origin who remain in everyday contact with this heritage (von Thüngen 2021). Recovery of the reduction has created new economic activity connected to tourism and has transformed the uses the local populace makes of the missions in their day-to-day life. Until the 1990s, the communities had enjoyed unlimited access to those spaces. From them people extracted materials with which to build houses and corrals. In these spaces their animals grazed and their children played. Today, the sites are protected and fenced in and attract more and more tourists, both Paraguayan and foreign. Thus, over the last forty years, the local uses and meanings of the material remains of the missions have changed. Despite these changes, the reductions are as present as they ever were in the day-to-day life of those who are conserving them, not only because people attend Mass in them, or work in them—in the case of tour guides—or because they serve, say, as an attraction for entertaining some relative visiting for a weekend. In addition to those uses, the missions are an important element in the shaping of social identities and are perceived by people as an element of their own history.

The reclamation of the missions implies that new discourses and practices related to the questions of how to conserve and administrate cultural heritage are entering into the towns that are conserving them. In those towns, heritage is conceived as something of value to the world at large that must be kept intact for future generations. The history of the shaping of this authorized heritage discourse, as Laurajane Smith has called it, is long and has been dealt with in other works (Hall 1999; Smith 2006). Here, let it suffice to recall that it is linked to the formation of states and of national identities over the nineteenth century. In that context, to construct national narratives shared by all social groups had to contribute toward suppressing social conflicts and allowing all citizens to feel that they were part of a single collective. To that end the states built solemn monuments, created pantheons of national heroes, and protected the ruins of a past always presented as glorious. All these elements were meant to reinforce national identities.

The Convention Concerning the Protection of the World Cultural and Natural Heritage adopted by UNESCO in 1972 was one of the most important milestones leading toward the formation of an authorized heritage discourse. This text, ratified by almost all states around the world, construes cultural heritage as almost invariably constituted by an architectural heritage. A precedent for this convention, the Venice Charter (1964), had established, in its article 9, that a monument can be restored only in exceptional instances, and then only respecting its "original essence" (Ciam 1964). For a long time, the excessive privileging of ruins and monuments led to the conservation of heritage resting exclusively in the hands of architects. The populace in contact with the sites, often rural and with scant formal education, lacks the technical knowledge these documents consider necessary to take part in their care. Nowadays more and more academic fields and social actors question that traditional view of heritage. It was the prevailing one, however, in the 1970s, when the restoration work began on the missions in Paraguay. Nor has influence, even now, completely faded away.

In what follows, I will attempt to show how the uses and the meanings of the Jesuit-Guarani cultural heritage of Paraguay have changed since the 1970s. I will analyze what those goods have represented to the residents of their locales and to institutions that took part in their restoration: the Paraguay Secretariat of Tourism (SENATUR), the Catholic Church of Germany and Paraguay, and UNESCO. The data I use come from my stays doing ethnographic work in the south of Paraguay and from historical research in the Jesuit archive in Nuremberg and in the private libraries of those who have instigated restoration projects since the '70s.

Caring for Heritage

In the late 1930s the governments of Argentina and Brazil took their first steps toward preserving the architectural remains of the Jesuit missions (Page 2012). In Paraguay something similar took place later when, in 1973, its government applied to the Organization of American States (OAS) for aid to save the threatened structures (von Thüngen 2021). The OAS sent the architect Graziano Gasparini to assess the state of the sites and determine whether it was feasible to restore them. After various months working in Paraguay, Gasparini wrapped up his report. In his view, recovery operations should start up in Jesús, San Cosme, and Trinidad, the last of these being especially dilapidated. The passage of time and lack of maintenance had reduced this impressive architectural complex to rubble. By the mid-twentieth century, lush vegetation covered its buildings, and the roots of the *guapoí* trees were working their way into the stones of the walls, quickly destroying them.

Gasparini's conception of salvage was close to that of the international documents described previously. It was important not to rebuild the edifice, but rather to protect it from deterioration, without altering what he considered "the original and authentic character of the monument" (Gasparini 1974). Beyond keeping these monuments from destruction, Gasparini proposed creating an infrastructure that would allow for tourism. Tourism, in his plan, was the other side of conservation. In this same period, the governments of Paraguay, Brazil, and Argentina were weighing the possibility of linking up all the Jesuit missions of South America into one international tourist route.

Such a conception of cultural heritage, however, did not take hold immediately in Paraguay. The first measures to reclaim the Jesuit-Guarani legacy were taken by the Paracuaria Foundation, created in West Germany in the mid-'70s with the aim of preserving what was left of the missions of Paraguay. The promoters of this initiative were Paul Frings—a philanthropist closely connected to the Catholic Church in Germany—and the German Jesuits of Nuremberg. Their notion of heritage differed from Gasparini's on one fundamental point: for the creators of Paracuaria, the mission remains were an expression of exemplary religious and cultural values. Restoring the missions would allow not just the enrichment of the church's pastoral work in the south of Paraguay, but would also create new sources of employment for the local inhabitants, most of them small farmers (Frings and Übelmesser 1982). Enhancing the value of their heritage would necessarily foster the cultural, religious, and economic development of the old Jesuit settlements. The bishopric of Encarnación, in whose jurisdiction the reductions are located, the Jesuit Province of Paraguay, and the General Directorate for Tourism (now called National Secretariat of Tourism) also took part in the Paracuaria initiative.

Both this German project and the report of the architect Gasparini reflected a growing international concern for encouraging and overseeing the protection of cultural goods. Both agreed that the legacy of the missions must not disappear; yet they did have differing views of how they should continue to exist. Gasparini valued this legacy for the artistic, architectural, and historical testimony it bore of the colonial past. The members of Paracuaria appreciated this aspect of the heritage as well, yet they thought it should contribute to the economic, cultural, and religious development of the local population. This was the main reason for restoring the wood carvings and for creating museums of sacred art that displayed the pieces from the colonial past that had adorned the sanctuaries. In these museums the local parish priests were to give various courses, catechism workshops, and training in trades. Carvings in wood, which in the past had been objects of worship, should, in the present, support a modern catechism (Frings and Übelmesser 1982).

Both notions of heritage were alien to the local populace: (1) that of Paracuaria, because it was based on an interpretation of the colonial past that they didn't necessarily share. In that interpretation, the reductions related to a golden era in the history of evangelization in Latin America. As such, they had to serve as models for a present that was lost in the labyrinth of modernity; and (2) that of Gasparini, who separated the heritage from the sociocultural circumstances it was situated in. His secular outlook took no account of the campesinos' devoutness or the emotional bonds that joined them to the Jesuit legacy. Nonetheless, though both conceptions were external to the communities, that of Paracuaria showed an awareness—through the local parishes—of the situation in which the largely Catholic populace found itself. For this reason, it started out from a correct diagnosis of the social and economic problems that needed most urgently to be solved.

The notion that the Jesuit heritage ought to contribute to developing the Native populations belonged very much to the theological climate that set in after the Second Vatican Council (1965) and the conference of Latin American bishops convened in Medellín in 1968. In a world by this time labeled "underdeveloped," poverty was already one of the most pressing problems. In the 1960s it was clear that the free-market economy was widening the distance between wealthy and poor countries. In Paraguay, an agricultural modernization led by minority sectors of society and by for-

eign capitals had sped up land concentration. The social consequences of
that process were profound, since a high percentage of the population lived
off family farm production, which was incompatible with the new extensive agriculture.

With the aim of protecting the campesinos' family farming, Jesuits and
inhabitants of Santa Rosa de Lima (in the department of Misiones) formed
the Christians Agrarian Leagues, organizations created to allow small pro-
ducers to sell their products and to work the land on a community basis
(Caravias 2019). Among the peasantry itself, the initiative had widespread
support, but it was violently quelled by the military government of Alfredo
Stroessner in the early 1970s. In this context, the concept of social commitment meant something quite precise to the Jesuits of Paraguay: preach-
ing the Gospel had to be complemented by direct actions on behalf of the
poor. It was in this theological climate that the reclamation work of the
Jesuit-Guarani heritage began.

Restoration of the wood carvings began in 1976 and concluded when
the museums opened. The restoration of Trinidad, something much more
complex, finally came to pass between 1977 and 1982. The General Direc-

FIGURE 15. Current view of the Mission of San Cosme. (© Maximiliano von Thüngen)

torate for Tourism in Paraguay was counting on the reduction's becoming an international tourist attraction. UNESCO saw it as an indispensable architectural monument to conserve for the future. Paracuaria, the bishopric of Encarnación, and the Jesuits hoped that the locals would identify with this heritage and turn it into a religious center for the community. In 1984 Mass was celebrated in Trinidad for the first time in 217 years. In 1993, as a crowning of all these efforts, Jesús and Trinidad were declared World Heritage sites by UNESCO (Figure 15).

Uses and Meanings of the Missions before Their Reclamation

After the Jesuits were expelled in 1767, the buildings in the reductions continued to be part of the day-to-day life of the inhabitants of Trinidad, Jesús, and San Cosme. Imposing monuments in ruins, ambitious but unfinished houses of worship or structures in disrepair, the sites were converted into part of the local landscape, spaces in which the everyday activities of the towns took place; at no point were they totally abandoned (Telesca 2009). Many people in Trinidad recall the existence of a soccer field on the premises of the reduction and a makeshift church functioning in an old construction near the bell tower (Perasso 1992). The cows that grazed amid the old edifices, sheltering from the midday sun, were also part of the day-to-day landscape. Something similar happened in Jesús, where for many years the soil of the main square was tilled to grow food crops. To Native memory, the reductions are inseparable from these activities.

These popular uses were visible above all in San Cosme, where the church and the Jesuit college (colegio) were never abandoned. All the older denizens of San Cosme remember the celebrations, the dances, and the weddings organized in the reduction's courtyard (von Thüngen 2021). Gathering there on dates important to the community were both the residents from the town's urban center and those from its rural fringe. On these occasions, people would tour the ancient rooms and contemplate the peeling or paint-stripped floral-patterned ceilings that survived from the eighteenth century. Children would enter the gardens and use the ancient square as a soccer pitch or to play hide and seek. There was celebrated the most important event of the year, the patron saint's feast day, honoring the physician brothers Cosme and Damian, Christian martyrs. Yet use of the mission was not limited to popular festivals. Up until the 1960s rooms of the ancient *colegio* housed the offices of the justice of the peace and the National Telecommunications Administration, the police precinct, the prison, the school, and the town hall.

In addition to festive and administrative uses, there were other functions more harmful to the structures. From shortly after the expulsion of the Jesuits until well into the twentieth century, stones, irons, tiles, and wood from the reductions were used to build houses, animal pens, and walls (Amaral and Durán 1994). For decades, freely entering the grounds and taking those materials from the buildings was common and accepted practice. In Trinidad, stones from the mission were for such different purposes as carving handicrafts or constructing wells. The architect Gasparini, in his 1974 report, bemoaned the missions' having been turned into quarries of already carved stones. Then, too, the custom of hunting for gold—which, according to many inhabitants of these parts, the Jesuits buried on being expelled—caused damage to courtyards and buildings. These uses started being forbidden in the 1980s as the heritage reclamation work progressed.

If, for decades, the grounds of the mission had been open spaces, today wire fencing protects them and separates them from the street. At the entrance to the sites, a small office of the National Secretariat for Tourism sells tickets and organizes the guided tours. There they lead the ever-growing number of tourists, Paraguayan and foreign, who come to these towns to visit their remarkable churches. Jesús, Trinidad, and San Cosme are run similarly, even if the last of these is not a "world heritage" monument. The three missions form part of the so-called Ruta Jesuítica [Jesuit Path] de Paraguay, a circuit promoted by SENATUR and by commercial organizers linked to the tourist sector. The goal of creating a pastoral use for the sites, so prominent in Paracuaria's original plan, with time has lost its centrality.

To truly "revalue" the missions requires re-educating the towns and residents entrusted with their conservation. "Bringing awareness to the locals," the public servants call it. The practices and heritage-related discourses the state promotes today are transmitted through institutions such as schools, municipal governments, the SENATUR, tourist agencies, and nongovernmental organizations. This task calls for prohibiting many

FIGURE 16. Celebration of the mass in the Church of San Cosme. (© Maximiliano von Thüngen)

practices that before were condoned, such as extracting materials from the reductions or allowing animals inside them. In this way, it is not just the aspect of the buildings that is transformed as their reclamation moves forward, but also the activities and meanings associated with them (Figure 16).

The revived appreciation for the missions brings into local space practices of conservation and management of the sites that at first were alien to the locals, coming as they did from a set of values not their own (von Thüngen 2021). "We don't know to appreciate what we have," I've often heard the Natives complain. Used to seeing the missions as spaces associated with everyday activities, people don't immediately understand what their value as "heritage" consists of. As the sites' reclamation advances, more and more tourists visit the towns. Conservators and architects routinely work at the missions. SENATUR officials and local politicians meet to propose the creation of new tourist attractions in the area. School groups come from all over Paraguay to visit them. With the parade of novelties unfolding before their eyes, the local residents begin to see valuable monuments in these old buildings. "Before, people didn't know we had a historical ruin here. To us it was just a church," the care-taker of one of the reductions told me.

Little by little the populace is being familiarized with the values filter-ing in through the restoration projects. The new representations of the missions, which take them to be highly valuable sites for their history and for their architectural features, don't displace the earlier values, but rather, blend with them. In San Cosme, where the reduction played a central role in the day-to-day life of the town, various conceptions of the site can be observed today. One of these conceptions is markedly local, shaped over a long period of time, ever since the expulsion of the Jesuits. Its salient trait is that it conceives of the site as a church and as a space bound up with everyday social activities. The other conception, formed outside the town, relates to the UNESCO notion of "World Heritage." Only over the past decades, through the restoration projects, has it entered into local space. For the residents of San Cosme the church was for a long time sim-ply their church, and only gradually has it transformed itself in their eyes into a cultural heritage. A similar process to this one can be seen in the other towns.

Differing views of the missions start, then, to intermesh with a collec-tive image bank of each locale. A woman resident of San Cosme, as she enumerated the many uses to which the past had put the reduction, ex-plained to me that for a long time the site had been "abandoned" because no one assigned much value to it. In this context, the term "abandoned" refers to the era in which the reduction was not visited by tourists, or watched over by guards, or kept clean and fenced off. For this woman, the opposite of an abandoned site is one managed as a historical monument. This process is particularly visible in San Cosme, but it can also be found in the other towns. "Forty years ago," a resident of Trinidad told me, "no one knew that the ruins were worth a lot." The reductions emerge from their alleged abandonment when their transformation into cultural goods commences.

A person's occupation or level of formal education influences how quickly he or she is familiarized with the new discourses and practices (von Thüngen 2021). The public workers of SENATUR are the first to as-similate them. It is they who have the task of accompanying tourists on guided tours of the sites and of explaining to them the history of the Guarani settlements. In many cases people's basic motivation for taking an interest in the missions is the chance to earn income from tourist activity. On the other hand, those less familiar with the authorized heritage discourse are people who don't partake of the income that tourism generates—for instance, the fishermen of San Cosme or the farm laborers who live on the rural fringe of the urban centers.

As refurbishment of the missions progresses, the local residents more and more fault one another—and themselves—for not managing to appreciate these sites. Some distance themselves from their community and describe it as unaware for having so long allowed animals to graze on mission grounds. Many of those who should indeed know to appreciate the sites—tourist guides, public workers, former employees in the restoration projects—will take it upon themselves to educate the rest of the community. The new representations associated with heritage are, in this form, expanded vertically, from the state toward the citizens, and horizontally, among the residents themselves. In this process of information spreading and legitimation, the local residents convey their admiration for the Jesuits of the past, represented as bearers of knowledge the local Indigenous did not have, to the tourists of the present, who have the cultural background to appreciate the value of this heritage.

The supposed ignorance that public officials often attribute to people is also the product of the way in which the conservation work has been carried out over the last decades. Instigated by foreign institutions and by the central government from Asunción, these tasks have only marginally involved local residents. Rarely have they been given the reasons that have justified restoring the ruins. Nor have they taken part in directing the work. The number of employees of SENATUR, though it has been rising, is still small. The sense of not being included in the administration of heritage, or of benefiting from the income it generates, leads to local residents feeling that the salvaging of these sites is something oriented toward others outside their communities, like a movie of which they are mere viewers.

Cultural Heritage and Economic Development

As I have briefly mentioned, economic processes affected how local residents perceive the recovery of their heritage. The first steps in reassessing the missions coincided in Paraguay with a crisis in its rural economies.

The development of mechanized agriculture in the 1990s eliminated sources of employment and hastened the concentration of land, encouraging a system of large-scale production (Galeano 2010). In Paraguay, where a high percentage of the population lives in rural areas dedicated to small- and medium-scale rural production, this process has had serious consequences. Ever since the mid-1970s, due to the crisis in family farming caused by agricultural modernization and the ever-greater extension of land given over to soy cultivation, the peasants have been migrating en masse to urban centers (Riquelme and Vera 2015).

The advance of agribusiness has been dizzyingly rapid ever since soy became Paraguay's main export product. The area set aside for growing it has expanded rapidly over the last two decades. The use of genetically modified seeds, beginning in 2000, allows great tracts of land to be cultivated with no need to hire rural workers. Soy revenue in Paraguay exceeds three billion dollars, representing 17 percent of the GDP, and constitutes around 62 percent of exports. In the department of Itapúa, where the Jesuit missions are located, the advent of soy has been rapid, too. Overall, the agro-industrial production model has, in just a few decades, transformed the rural landscape in the region the missions are in. Beginning in the '90s many peasants began to sell their smallholdings, often at low prices, forced to do so by the lack of credit for farm production. In the course of just a few years, agricultural units of between five and twenty hectares have merged with other, larger ones.

In local memory, the past is the locus of a well-being that has vanished. That well-being was not founded merely upon the abundance and quality of food consumed, but rather on social bonds, described as having been of a more tight-knit solidarity than those of today. Frequent among the customs that strengthened intracommunity relations were the *jopói* and the *minga*, Indigenous practices of pre-Hispanic origin focused on redistribution of goods. "A woman neighbor would butcher a cow and divvy it up among all the neighbors. Everyone would go off with a portion," one woman explained to me. Later it would be someone else's turn. Most people had their little parcel of land with animals and crops. These mechanisms of reciprocity and redistribution, still present in the rural world of Paraguay, bred social cohesion and fostered a form of production that steered clear of capital accumulation.

In San Cosme, too, the peasant economies underwent a process like the one I have just described. There, the proximity of the Paraná River enabled agricultural production to be complemented by fishing. On islands reached by sailing in small boats, people would breed cattle, hunt, and farm. The closeness of the Argentine shore of the river allowed the peasants to sell or barter their products for goods they didn't produce locally. A further income for families came from the salaried work of the men on ranches in the area. The building of the Yacyretá hydroelectric dam, between Argentina and Paraguay, radically altered this scenario. The rise of the river when its reservoir overflowed in 1994 flooded 111,000 hectares of rich wetlands and productive land. Until that moment the river had been narrow and pleasant to fish in. Today it is over ten kilometers wide and has become dangerous to sail on. In local memory the dam marks the end of an era characterized by abundant food, social harmony, and the absence of material worries. "They all lived off of Yacyretá Island," I often heard people say. The dam, the advance of agribusiness, and the lack of state support for small local farm production destroyed traditional activities that were not compensated by the creation of alternative sources of employment.

The transformation of the missions into tourist sites has taken place in an economic setting marked by the lack of productive activities and by structural unemployment. This context makes many residents view tourism as their one chance to overcome the problem of unemployment. Nevertheless, to stimulate this activity—many think—people must learn how to "value" the heritage. Knowing the past of the reductions to be able to communicate it to visitors would seem to be one of the conditions for partaking in the revenue tourism is generating. That past, however, really doesn't belong to the local residents; it is a more impersonal one: that of the nation of Paraguay, if not of all humanity. The locals aren't familiar with that history; they must learn it and memorize it. "The people who come here want to know the history of the Jesuits, but that's hard for me, because I don't have books," a woman who owns an inn told me.

Their not knowing the history of the missions means their being shut out of the new opportunities arising around them. In this sense, the power of heritage discourse to convince the local population of its legitimacy implies more than having the backing of institutions such as UNESCO or the Paraguayan state itself. Much more important, apparently, is the hope people place in tourism. The current economic situation explains to a large extent why many locals try to adopt values and practices that come from a discourse that until just recently was largely unfamiliar to them.

Although international tourism to Paraguay has been growing steadily since 1990, local expectations remain unmet. Many complain that they haven't recouped the money they invested in an inn, a restaurant, or a business. Visitors to San Cosme and Jesús usually tour the two towns in the afternoon, then move on to spend the night in some other town in the area. Trinidad is a little better off in this regard, since its hotel infrastructure is more sophisticated than that of the other towns. Yet there too the disappointment is palpable. The lack of regular, adequate revenue from tourism obliges local residents to make ends meet by other means: one woman tries to live off the handicrafts she makes, but she gets her main income from selling clothing imported from China; an artisan in San Cosme depends on the wages he earns working for the town; a woman who owns a newly opened inn lives off what she can sell in her grocery store; the owner of a restaurant sustains himself on what he produces on a small farm.

Interpreting the Past

The "cultural heritage" status the missions now enjoy requires defining their significance in the history no longer of the towns that preserve them, but rather in that of broader collectives: the Paraguayan nation in its ntirety, say, if not all humanity. During the nineteenth and twentieth centuries the political and intellectual elites of Paraguay would debate whether the Jesuit missions form part of the national identity of Paraguay (Telesca 2014). Today in the old reductions we find professional conservationists filling out technical reports. The reductions, separate from the geographical and social space in which they stand, are being fitted into a global scenario whose protagonists are states, nongovernmental organizations, development banks, and international organizations. The reductions, now construed as "World Heritage," are no longer manifestations serving national debate but, rather, universal values.

These days, various representations of the missions circulate within the Jesuit towns. Some people view them as a motor of local development, others as monuments to forced labor in which the Indigenous were exploited in the colonial past. Some see the Jesuits as men of sacrifice, devoted to protecting the Guarani, others as Europeans hungry for riches and power. Some insist that they introduced the Christian faith by peaceful means, others that they did so through violence. Some of these representations entered the towns almost as soon as the reclamation of the missions began, others evolved over a long period, ever since the Company of Jesus was expelled. Among all of them the most visible—spread through official organizations and pamphlets and tourist publicity—are those that depict the missions as an expression of the peaceful encounter between two cultures. In that encounter, the Jesuits contributed what the Indigenous allegedly lacked: writing, architectural and artistic knowhow, and scientific knowledge. Seldom does this narrative incorporate local memories.

Despite the existence of dominant narratives, people integrate the remains of the reductions into their own vision of their history, using them to give meaning to their past, yet above all to their present. They do not mechanically repeat the institutional discourses, but rather others grounded in their own experience, inseparable from that of the town they live in. One notices this even among the tour guides, SENATUR's representatives to the communities and to tourists. They too relate alternative memories that have meaning only in light of local historical experience such as that lived by the communities they are a part of (von Thüngen 2021).

One widely circulating representation found in the texts of tourist pamphlets and publicity depicts the reductions as part of a civilizing process. The Jesuits brought undreamt-of knowledge to the jungle of the Guarani, above all in the fields of science, art, and architecture, but also agricultural and cattle production. Thanks to this new knowledge—I hear the locals saying—the Indigenous were able to move beyond the barbarism in which they lived. Their life before the arrival of the missionaries was steeped in poverty and backwardness. The priests were wise and magnanimous. The Guarani were inept and not very clever, yet they were willing and able to imitate their masters. Except for some occasional disobedience, corrected almost always by verbal reprimands, they adapted without much difficulty to life in the missions. Their economic and social organization could boast barely a single positive aspect. By this interpretation, the past is idealized and freed of conflicts.

Rarely do these "official" memories mention the dismantling of pre-Hispanic forms of organization through evangelization or the pressure exerted on the Indigenes to settle in the mission villages. They describe as benevolent the treatment the fathers showed the Guarani yet fail to mention the Black slaves who worked for the Jesuits on the large estates in Peru. Likewise, they pass over the symbolic violence exerted upon the local religious beliefs and the dependence bred in the Indigenous by the fact that in the reductions, Guarani was adopted as the official language and they were not taught Spanish (Pavone 2007, 123). Few, for that matter, are the references to the semi-collective distribution regimen and the exploitation of the land in the missions during the colonial period.

A sort of counter-memory is expressed by the Guarani Indigenous people who currently live in southern Paraguay, in the region of the old Jesuit towns. In Guaviramí, a small Guarani village located just a few kilometers from Trinidad, people define themselves as different from the non-Indigenous Paraguayans, but also as different from the Guarani who lived in the missions during the colonial period. Their ancestors are not the Guarani "reduced" by the Jesuits, but the rebel Indigenous communities who chose to defend their independence and remain in the forest. It is not the life in the missions that they see as the foundation of their own identity, but rather the order opposed to the "civilizing" project of the Jesuits. At the same time, in order to be able to benefit from the growing tourism and reverse the situation of economy impoverishment in which the historical development of Paraguay has been sinking them, Indigenous people must adapt themselves to the representations and stereotypes that tourists have of them. For example, during the last decade they adopted the custom of wearing white clothes and playing music and songs to entertain an audience that sees a continuity between the Jesuit missions and the actual Guarani populations. Counter-memory, then, but also adaptation.

The tour guides don't reproduce the "official" discourses uncritically. The information they get from SENATUR consists of basic history, which allows them to be autodidacts and choose for themselves what bibliography to read. One guide recounts that the missionaries convinced the Indigenous to move into their settlements by luring them with gifts of iron tools. Others dispute the often-made claim that the religion of the Guarani resembled Christianity. A third quotes the anthropologist Branislava

Susnik by way of questioning some aspect of the most traditional histori-cal interpretations. Thus, each guide's formation is unique. Personal in-terests and formal studies play a major role in this variance. At this point there is a visible difference between the tourist leaflets distributed for ad-vertising purposes and the guided tours through the missions. During the tours these guides, more and more, encourage the visitors to look at the heritage with critical eyes.

The farther from the tourist scene one gets, the more colorful and di-verse the views of the missions grow. It is possible to hear fishermen, peas-ants, and tradespeople saying that the Jesuits brought not only valuable scientific, artistic, and technical knowledge into Paraguay, but also a political and economic system that benefited the Europeans more than the Indigenous. In local testimonies, the violence exerted over the Native population was unwanted, of course, but inevitable: the country prior to the arrival of the Jesuits was a desert devoid of civilization.

This depiction of Paraguay's history is deeply rooted in local subjectivi-ties, and it is inseparable from how ethnic boundaries are drawn within the population. If the *criollos*, creoles, don't feel connected to the Guarani, it is not—or at any rate not mainly—for racial differences between them. The Paraguayans don't deny the blood ties they might have with the Gua-rani, and in fact they define themselves as *mestizos* (Potthast 2020). More important in the drawing of boundaries of identity are the cultural traits the creole Paraguayans attribute to the Guarani. The Indigenes, many say, keep to themselves and have never wanted to unite with the towns: they don't study, can't read, can't count, they don't know the value of their money. This sort of characterization marks out a social and cultural hier-archy. If the Guarani are savages, the creoles present themselves as civi-lized: *they* know how to read, they study, work, and have learned to manage their money properly. Above them, however, they place the tourists, whom they admire for living in evident comfort, having the wherewithal to travel for pleasure and to possess the necessary knowledge to appreciate the "value" of this local heritage. On the same level as the tourists they place the Jesuits, whom they portray as bearers of bodies of knowledge the Native population would never have been able to develop on their own. Knowledge is conceived in these parts almost always as some-thing injected, brought from outside, both today and in the colonial past. This sociocultural hierarchy is inseparable from a collective memory whose paramount feature is a sense of loss. "Our people was not always as poor as it is now," repeat the residents.

Related to these memories of loss are the stories of hidden treasures that spread so prolifically in these towns. In the local collective imagination, the riches, formerly abundant, have been wrested from the communities by outsiders: tourists, corrupt politicians, or gold-diggers from the city. Of the treasures Jesús, Trinidad, and San Cosme once had, there remain but a few saints carved in wood, fervently protected by the local populace. Some ten years ago the resistance of the inhabitants of San Cosme kept their religious images from being loaned out for an exhibition in France. The residents of Santa María, Santa Rosa, and Santiago have put up similar resistance. This attachment to the carvings is not to be explained solely by their artistic merit, or by their monetary value, of which most residents have no inkling. More important is their religious function in these majority Catholic towns. The saints' images are kept in the churches and figure every day in people's worship in them.

In addition to their religious value, the carvings represent in the local imagination the last vestiges of a vanished social order, a past of plenty, structured around values such as solidarity and equitable distribution of wealth and nourishment (von Thüngen 2021). The gold that abounded in the era of their forebears is represented by the inhabitants of San Cosme, Trinidad, and Jesús as a testimony to the splendor life had in the past. It is not associated with personal fortunes or with the hoarding of money by a few. Families humble and wealthy alike had access to it. In the past—I've often heard people say—everything was gilded: the cups, the dishes, the cutlery.

The insertion of the peasant economies into a capitalist market system in the last decades of the twentieth century transforms the meaning of gold in the popular local imagination. In the world of today it is no longer the symbol of a shared and general abundance, but rather of monetary wealth alone. In the face of this new sort of wealth, the peasants show mixed feelings. On the one hand, they need money to survive in an economic system based much more than before on monetary transactions. At the same time, this new form of wealth is associated with processes such as accumulation and inequality that are incompatible with the traditional peasant social order. That order, as I've mentioned, was based less on monetary transactions than on exchange. For this reason, gold as a new form of wealth involves social principles incompatible with those that until just a few years ago oriented the peasants' communities.

Conclusions

The Convention Concerning the Protection of the World Cultural and Natural Heritage signed by UNESCO in 1972 had a great influence on the design of policies for administrating and conserving cultural goods. It was then that the concept of "World Heritage" came into being and a list was drawn up of the sites that warranted that title. The administration of those goods, hitherto the exclusive responsibility of nation states, involved and engaged, much more than before, the whole of the international community. Their conservation was turned over to technicians and academics, professionals with specialized knowledge unknown to the rural settings in which the actual heritage objects often are located. In this sense, the recovery of the missions of Paraguay bears similarities with processes unfolding in many other parts of the world. Always at play here is a conception born at an international level that erupts into rustic imaginaries remote from the technical, aesthetic, and historical debates conducted by the experts in conservation, cultural management, and tourism.

In Paraguay the regulations and guidelines promoted by organizations like UNESCO entered later than in other South American countries. For that reason, the first actions taken to reclaim the Jesuit-Guarani heritage were founded on an image repertory closer to that of the Catholic Church than to that of UNESCO. The interventions of the Paracuaria Foundation were aimed at salvaging those goods for the communities themselves. Much in tune with the theological climate prevailing after the Second Vatican Council, it was felt that use of the structures and the exhibition of the wood carvings should lead to a religious, social, and economic advancement of the peasant sector in southern Paraguay.

Reclamation of the missions transforms their function in the day-to-day life of their towns. If in the past they were open spaces for common folk to use, today they are closed off with wire and are run as tourist attractions. The denizens for whom the reductions had always been parts not especially valued of their everyday life observed this transition with surprise. "We don't appreciate what we've got," they say again and again

as they see tourists from the world over visit the missions—words that exemplify this fundamental aspect of the heritage discourse, which is the
will to re-educate. Over time, spurred on by institutional intervention and
the growth of tourism, people start to incorporate into their own subjec-
tivity a repertory of values that was at first unfamiliar to them.

I have attempted to show that the assimilation of these new values is
inseparable from the economic processes that the rural world of Paraguay
has undergone over recent decades. Outstanding among those processes
is the crisis of the peasants' family farming. In the current context, the
economies of Jesús, San Cosme, and Trinidad are slowly being reshaped
around tourist activity, the only activity that is growing steadily. The Jesuit reductions stand in the local imaginaries as a promise of work and
economic development. People feel that to be able to take advantage of
this possibility, they must learn to appreciate the missions as their visitors do. The economic context, then, explains why the values that tourism and new conservation practices usher in have such power to take hold
as truths and to influence people's behavior. Resting on the promise of an
economic takeoff, those discourses seduce the local population not pro-
posing to them the return to an ideal past—as envisaged by the Catholic
Church—but guaranteeing them a place in a world presented as global and
interconnected. To learn to "value" the old edifices would enable local residents to belong to that new world they view as dynamic and laden with
possibilities.

The discourses developed outside of the towns are re-signified by the
townspeople confronted with them; they are then filtered out and molded
according to the local imaginaries. This is so because the locals take the
mission remains to be elements in their own history—a history that is not
necessarily the one they read of or learn in school, but rather another more
vital albeit less visible one, transmitted orally and horizontally among
them. We find an example of this in the legends of hidden treasures that
make the rounds here—stories that are not just a matter of tall talk or irrelevant fantasies, but part of a specific form of deciphering the past
and the present. The gold those narratives allude to should not be understood as monetary wealth, but rather as the expression of an ideal social
order in which the gold was abundant and within everyone's reach—
an order in which there was no social inequality, or poverty, or greed, or
scarcity, or need of money.

In the specific setting of the south of Paraguay, the symbolic and practical functions that the material remains of the Guaranis's reductions have fulfilled over the course of history are fundamental for understanding how people perceive and process the recovery activity that began around 1975. Entering into the formation of these representations are various social processes: the region's economic transformations over the last decades, the construction of memories of evangelization, or the formations of identity that pit Indigenous against non-Indigenous. This historical and social specificity determines just how, on the local plane, global practices and discourses linked to the protection of cultural heritage set in. In this contact between the local and the global, new representations are emerging of the Jesuit-Guarani past—they too destined for transformation.

References

Amaral, Blanca, and Margarita Durán. 1994. *San Cosme y San Damián: Testimonio vivo del pasado jesuítico.* Asunción: Universidad Católica.

Caravias, José Luis. 2019. "Zwischen Repression und Hoffnung: Interview mit Maximiliano von Thüngen." *Stimmen der Zeit* 7: 545–51.

Ciam (International Congress of Architects and Technicians of Historical Monuments). 1964. *The Venice Charter: International Charter for the Conservation and Restoration of Monuments and Sites.* Venice: Siam.

Frings, Paul, and Josef Übelmesser. 1982. *Paracuaria: Die kunstschätze des Jesuitenstaats in Paraguay/Tesoros artísticos de la República Jesuítica del Paraguay.* Mainz: Matthias-Grünewald-Verlag.

Galeano, Luis. 2010. "Los campesinos y la lucha por la tierra." In *Historia del Paraguay*, edited by Ignacio Telesca, 357–75. Asunción: Taurus.

Gasparini, Graziano. 1974. "Informe para la programación de la asesoría técnica y trabajos necesarios para llevar a cabo el proyecto de 'Restauración y puesta en valor de monumentos y obras de arte jesuíticos existentes en Paraguay.'" Unpublished report prepared for the Technical Unit for Cultural Heritage of the OAS. SENATUR Library, Jesús de Tavarangue.

Gutiérrez, Ricardo. 2003. *Historia urbana de las reducciones jesuíticas sudamericanas: Continuidad, rupturas y cambios (siglos XVIII–XX).* Madrid: Fundación Histórica Tavera.

Hall, Stuart. 1999. "Un-Settling 'Heritage,' Re-Imagining the Post-Nation: Whose Heritage?" In *The Politics of Heritage*, edited by Jo Littler and Roshi Naidoo, 37–47. New York: Routledge.

Page, Carlos. 2012. "El lento proceso de valoración del legado cultural de la provincia jesuítica del Paraguay." *Estudios del Patrimonio Cultural* 9: 9–30.

Pavone, Sabina. 2007. *Los jesuitas: Desde los orígenes hasta la supresión.* Buenos Aires: Libros de la Araucaria.

Perasso, José. 1992. *Historia y arqueología del pueblo de la Santísima Trinidad del Paraná.* Asunción: Instituto Paraguayo de Prehistoria.

Plá, Josefina. 2006. *El barroco hispano-Guarani.* Asunción: Universidad Católica.

Potthast, Bárbara. 2020. "Mestizaje and conviviality in Paraguay." Mecila Working Paper Series 22. São Paulo.

Riquelme, Quintín, and Elsy Vera. 2015. *Agricultura campesina, agronegocio y migración: El impacto de los modelos de producción en la dinámica de los territorios.* Asunción: Centro de Documentación y Estudios.

Smith, Laurajane. 2006. *Uses of Heritage.* New York: Routledge.

Sustersic, Bozidar. 1999. *Templos jesuítico-Guaranies.* Buenos Aires: Universidad de Buenos Aires.

Telesca, Ignacio. 2009. *Tras los expulsos: Cambios demográficos y territoriales en el Paraguay después de la expulsión de los jesuitas.* Asunción: Universidad Católica.

———. 2014. "La reinvención del Paraguay: La operación historiográfica de Blas Garay sobre las misiones jesuíticas." *Revista Paraguay desde las Ciencias Sociales* 5: 1–17.

UNESCO. 1972. *Convention Concerning the Protection of World Cultural and Natural Heritage.* Paris: UNESCO.

von Thüngen, Maximiliano. 2021. *Ruinas jesuíticas, paisajes de la memoria: El patrimonio cultural de los antiguos pueblos de Guaranies.* Buenos Aires: SB Editorial.

Wilde, Guillermo. 2008. *Religión y poder en las misiones de Guaranies.* Buenos Aires: SB Editorial.

Claiming the Missions
as Indigenous Spaces

LISBETH HAAS

When the Franciscans arrived to establish missions in the territories of Native people along the coast of California, they situated each mission on the ancestral and village lands of a particular tribe. They did not imagine that the land belonged to its inhabitants. Rather, the military took possession of it for the Spanish crown. Yet California was one of the most highly populated and diverse precolonial Indigenous spaces outside of central Mexico. If mapped, the borders of tribal lands would have consumed the entire area the Spanish claimed. Some of that land included shared resources and religious sites. Trade routes through tribal territories further defined California's Indigenous geography.

The Indigenous population of California in the precolonial era was second in size to that of central Mexico. Each tribe had precolonial territory that embraced different climatic zones, private and shared resource sites, and a ceremonial life that embraced specific other tribes. In leaving out the Indigenous history of the land and the missions, the institutions foreground old Spanish myths that tourists and settlers in California have propagated, even as the descendants of the missions have never been far away as living communities still marked by a violent colonial past.

Of the many tribes that went into the missions, built and labored in them, were born, died, and are buried within them, very rarely is an Indigenous tribe mentioned in mission displays and museums. Nor are the living descendants of those who built the missions even acknowledged. Yet each mission has the documents to be inclusive about the Indigenous histories that transpired therein; they simply have refused to offer a history that explains the tribal life of the missions. Instead, the church and the friars are still believed to have promoted civilization.

Narrative dispossession has meant the lack of accounting for Native societies and land. It has established a long legacy of absent stories about Indigenous people's experiences, leadership, and means of survival and endurance. At critical moments, such as in the 1820s, after Mexico gained its independence from Spain, the friars reported that Indians throughout the California mission system wanted their land returned and wanted to form the autonomous Indian communities that the governments of Spain and Mexico proposed at various moments, without enacting the law. In the 1850s, as American settlers settled California in huge numbers, violent dispossession became the norm.

The US government sent a treaty commission to California in 1850–51 to establish new boundaries for tribal lands. That treaty, signed by some of California's tribal leaders, never got out of the Senate. The Senate filed it away for fifty years and then failed to revive the agreements with those tribes. By the end of the nineteenth century, a few California tribes were granted federal recognition. By the 1930s, some tribes received state recognition without the acknowledgment of the federal government, but many California tribes remain unrecognized. Whether formally acknowledged or not, Indigenous people lived their lives during most of the twentieth century in a society that did not extend equality or human rights to them.

The Myth: Mission Indians

Typical is the display at Mission San Diego, where one sign gave the huge public that visits this tourist site daily and the congregation that calls the mission their own a single introduction to "Mission Indians" in three paragraphs. The sign begins by describing the term "Mission Indians" as a designation given to them by the federal government. In one sentence it identified the tribe as Kumeyaay, but then included a reference to the Yuma tribe, who were unrelated to the mission. "In the San Diego area these Indians—the Kumeyaay—are linguistically related to the Yuman Indians." Yuma is the language spoken by the Yuma tribe. It is from the Yuman language family. The sign offered incorrect information, brought in a curious interjection when it mentioned "Yuman," and did nothing to explain who the Kumeyaay were as a historical and contemporary group of different tribal groups. The paragraph ends by referring to the Kumeyaay as "Diegueños," to identify them through the mission.

The second paragraph offers the classic colonial imagery that focuses on what Indigenous people ate prior to the missions. Diet as a beginning point suggests people lived as animals, always in search of food, in this case acorn and seeds, and the sign mentioned a range of rodents and animals, with "berries, fruits, and vegetables where possible." It mentions two stone tools, and a final sentence described "the huts" they occupied. The information provides a sense of people living in search of scarce food without a social, cultural, political, or intellectual order. It does not identify the Indigenous geography of ancient territories. Nor did it record the many languages the Kumeyaay spoke.

The information prepared the reader for the explanation that the padres attracted the Kumeyaay with "food, clothing, blankets, and beads." Once they entered the mission they became "neophytes," new to the beliefs and skills they would be taught at the missions. It mentioned carpentry and blacksmithing, classic references to Western civilization. The plaque ends by noting that "they had many festivities during the mission period." Unmentioned are the histories each tribe carried and the burden of illness, labor, and death that hung heavily at the missions. The myth has been written and spoken against by historians and descendants of the missions, yet it persists. The announcement of the canonization of Junípero Serra generated renewed attempts to speak against the idea of the "Mission Indian" and to demand a truer picture of Indigenous society during the colonial era.

The Walk for the Ancestors

Caroline Ward, a tribal elder and leader of Fernandeño-Tataviam descent, attended a meeting organized by the American Indian Movement (AIM) against the canonization of Junípero Serra. She made a life-changing decision at the meeting to make a "walk for the ancestors" to commemorate all the Indigenous people who lived and died in the California missions. Caroline's father's family had lived for generations in a village that predated the Spanish conquest of the area that became known as Mission San Fernando, established in 1797. Caroline envisioned a Walk for the Ancestors that would acknowledge them at a time she felt they were being disrespected by Serra's canonization.

Caroline had been told by her Indian grandmother, years before, to save her shoes for the long walk she would have to make. She had forgotten her grandmother's advice until after that meeting. Caroline's tribal chairman, Rudy Ortega, gave his consent to her project. Caroline invited her son, Kagan Holland, then an art student in college, to join in the walk.

The two began on September 7, 2015, at Mission Sonoma, weeks before the canonization of Serra, which took place on September 23, 2015. When they approached each mission, Caroline would call on the elders and tribal chairs in that region. She introduced herself, Kagan, and their purpose in making the walk. She asked permission to pass through their tribal lands as she sought their blessing. She invited the leaders and their tribal members to join them at the mission. Each mission had been composed of many different tribes over time. Disease, the loss of territory and resources to the missions, and adverse conditions sent villagers into them at "a time of little choice," when it became too difficult to survive in their territories as before (see Milliken 2009).

As Caroline Ward moved between missions on the walk, she began to see the way Indigenous ancestors had built and structured the missions for the well-being of the people. When they gathered at each mission, local tribal leaders and elders told the histories of the missions their ancestors had built. Their stories allowed Caroline to see the missions from another perspective. She came to understand them as places in which the ancestors did things and built things to try to heal the mission populations who were often in severe distress from disease and their losses. She pointed out the stone church at Mission San Juan Capistrano where the ancestors had put obsidian and abalone to protect the Indian congregation. As she said, they built in "medicine for us." At each mission they created a prayer circle, and all joined in prayer, singing, and ceremony. People made speeches and played music, and ceremonial dancing took place. In one of her speeches about the walk, Caroline mentioned their desire to assure those who had passed in such difficult conditions. "We want our ancestors to know that we understand their suffering. And we're going to voice it, so people will know that it wasn't a posh life with the Catholics feeding you and protecting you." The truth she wanted to make clear was that life in the missions "was a horrible existence for them. It's really heart-wrenching, it's sickening." In that long walk Caroline argued that "we want to feel what they went through and try to let everyone else know what really happened. It's almost like bringing them to life through what we're doing."

They ended the walk two months later at Mission San Diego de Alcalá, the first mission founded in 1769 by Serra in Kumeyaay territory. Kumeyaay bird singers and flute players met the group outside the mission and proceeded onto the mission grounds together to form a large circle in a grassy area set aside for the gathering of about 300 people. What had begun as a walk to honor the ancestors had developed into something quite different as the walk came to an end, and a set of demands was formulated that expressed what they felt was a new consciousness about their relationship to the missions that had developed during the walk. The demands emerged out of the process of gathering and holding ceremony and reviewing the state of the missions.

They demanded that the missions include the Indigenous people who built and inhabited them in their displays and written material. They called for their lands and historic rights to the mission to be acknowledged. In a powerful vision, they called for their histories at the missions be taken back from those who currently claim possession of the missions. They wanted their ancestors' names to appear in the mission display and their tribal affiliations defined.

They called for the truth to be told, and that call would echo over and over, long after the walk ended. They wanted the truth to be told about the slavery, cruelty, and violence, including rape and lashings that left their backs marked forever, if they survived the punishment. They wanted the brutality of work and punishment at the missions to be acknowledged as unfair. They emphasized how the telling of this mission myth continued to produce deep cultural wounding.

They asked that Native people be present by using each mission's sacramental records and naming all of those who were baptized, married, and died at the missions. Many Native Californians have traced their ancestors through the records. But the mission displays do not make reference to individuals, tribal affiliation, or Indigenous village and territory of origin.

Though embedded in an Indigenous geography, the maps of the missions present them as if they are connected to each other along a fictive King's Highway instead of showing the actual situation of contending boundaries between missions and tribes. Tsim Schneider and Lee Panich work with soil and rock formations in dialogue with ethnohistory. In a piece on "Indigenous Landscapes and Spanish Missions," they offer material to understand the colonial landscape as made of "three spatial zones: colonial settlements as Native places; Native homelands/colonial hinterlands; and interior worlds and interspaces." This geography allows us to "critically assess how native people negotiated colonialism across the landscape" (see Panich and Schneider 2014; Panich and Schneider 2015). The missions did not stand alone, and they had only tentative control over a province where the Indigenous population predominated.

The Specificity of Historical Place in the Indigenous and Colonial Countryside

In the early building of the missions, the infringement on the autonomous political structures and lands of Indigenous villages and clans engendered responses (see Haas 2014; Hackel 2005). In the spring of 1775 around Mission San Diego, for example, the soldiers rode near Kumeyaay villages to the north, moving eastward through different territories. People continuously came out from their villages "to impede their pass and attack them." At a place called El Cajón de la Grulla, the village population "broke out and began to throw stones." The soldiers, riding on horses, had "very little gunpowder and only three bullets, so they returned to the Presidio without shooting," they said.[1] Lieutenant José Francisco Ortega reported to the governor that the lack of soldiers created a safety risk.

One hundred people had been baptized and lived at Mission San Diego in the six years between 1769 and the end of 1775, as tensions grew. Two missionaries, Frays Jayme and Fuster, initiated a campaign that brought in about 400 Indigenous people between July and September of 1775, including village leaders who came from some distance away from the mission. During this period, violence took place at the mission with the rape of women by soldiers and the destruction of village land by mission cattle. These are some of the violations that transpired. They may have been factors in the revolt (Carrico 2008, 32–33).

On November 5, 1775, shortly after midnight, warriors from at least fourteen villages attacked the mission. They shot Fray Jayme with a stone arrow and then beat him to death and killed José Arroyo, a carpenter from Guadalajara, and the blacksmith Ursalino from Tepic. Looting the church, they set fire to it and burned down the missionaries' house, the soldiers' barracks, and all the other rooms that had recently been constructed at the mission.[2]

The military estimated that between 600 and 1,000 people were directly involved in the attack. Only certain Tipai villages were invited to join the revolt, and some village leaders decided not to join the fight. Fourteen of the twenty-five villages that existed in twelve leagues or a thirty-six-mile area around the mission took part. These villages were connected through marriage and kinship relations, which followed the established pattern of forging alliances for war. As one historian emphasized, "Those rebel leaders recruited from their own ranks, relied upon traditional alliances, and sought redress for grievances experienced by their particular sib and clans" (Carrico 2008, 37).

The military governor sent every available soldier in the province to San Diego so that they could crush the leadership and end what they viewed as resistance to their legitimate presence.[3] A violent military reconnaissance ensued as soldiers roved through the villages of the entire region, entered in force, and singled out people they considered leaders of the attack.[4] The soldiers created terrifying conditions. Though the attack on the mission only involved specific villages, the entire Native population was treated as suspect.

Shortly after the San Diego revolt, another was planned in Lower California involving people from two missions—the Missions Santa Gertrudis (1751) and San Francisco de Borja (1762)—and two Indian villages named San Pablo and El Carmen. The missions claimed the villages, but the inhabitants disagreed (Jackson 2005, 58–59). The trial records are poignant with testimony about the injuries they suffered. Some rebels used the trial itself as an arena to express defiance.

Ramón Borjino, one of the rebels, explained that they wanted to kill the missionaries and set their quarters on fire because they made them work a lot without paying them. Miguel, the Indigenous blacksmith at Santa Gertrudis, stated that he wanted to kill the missionaries because they whipped him. Donato Aguilar, the chief of the village of San Rafael, wanted to kill them because they took his lands when he and his people ate some cattle from the mission herds. Aguilar defiantly explained that he permitted his people to do the killing, and he vividly described the vast quantities of meat they ate. He said he planned to kill the missionaries "with arrows in the night and burn their houses, and then steal all the cattle and other things in the mission." Agustín Casteh, an orphan, said that he wanted to kill them because they whipped him a lot for being a *cimarrón* (run-away) and that he didn't want to pray the Doctrine anymore.

Shortly after this revolt was planned, another was discovered at Mission San Juan Capistrano in 1777, to the north of Mission San Diego. Someone reported the plan to kill the missionary, all the soldiers, and one Indian from Baja California. All the people from the mountains and the villages along the coast planned to join in the attack. Their specific reasons for making the war had to do with the loss of seeds and grass and the humiliations that their leaders had suffered. They protested the loss of control over their territories.

Chief Siquinlo repeated the cause expressed by others: their anger stemmed from their inability to gather seeds after the arrival of the missionaries. People in the mission echoed this complaint: they wanted to kill the padres and the soldiers "who are devils and have come to destroy the seeds in their lands." The missionary reported, "In their songs they are clamoring that the padres and soldier are demons that have come to ruin their lands, that since they came it hadn't rained nor produced seeds."[5] In addition, people to the south of the mission wanted to take revenge against the soldiers because they had killed Indians in that area.

The attempts to expel the Spanish from California set limits on the area the Spanish controlled, and the center of the colonial population remained near the coast into the Mexican era, though alliances between the Chumash and Yokuts people allowed for a major revolt on February 21, 1824. Months earlier, the Chumash people at the Missions Santa Inés, La Purísima, and Santa Bárbara had carefully planned their action by sending people to villages in Yokuts territory to try to gain support. The population of 554 people at Mission Santa Inés became involved in a war planned by leaders at Missions Santa Inés, La Purísima, and Santa Bárbara.

The men took up bows, arrows, and rifles stolen from the soldiers' quarters. They set fire to the mission, destroyed the workrooms and the girls' dormitory, houses of the five guards and their families, and the Indian quarters. The toll in human life reflected the vulnerabilities of the entire population. Nineteen Chumash people from Santa Inés died in the insurrection and subsequent exile, the majority being fifteen women and children who died during the skirmishes. Four Chumash men burned to death in the fire, and one Mexican soldier died.[6]

The majority of the population fled to Mission La Purísima, where the 722 Indians at the mission had taken up arms. Their leaders gained control of the mission's firearms and killed José Dolores Sepulveda and three other settlers passing by La Purísima, seemingly by chance. The rebels welcomed the population from Santa Inés, who brought cannons, more arms, and bows and arrows.

As many as 1,270 Chumash participated in the occupation of Mission La Purísima for nearly a month. They kept the soldiers and their families at the occupied mission for three days. Some Indians sorted through their possessions and wore their things, flaunting in front of the soldiers and their families the clothing that had long connoted their elevated status of this frontier. When they left, they had to leave behind their goods, and sought compensation for them from the government a year later.[7]

The rebels sent along a message warning the soldiers who had returned to the ashes at Santa Inés that they would defend La Purísima by force. Fray Ordaz cautioned other officials against communication with Fray Rodríguez, who remained behind. Some of the rebels knew how to read and write, he warned, and they would intercept any message.[8]

In coordination, the Indigenous population at Santa Bárbara took up arms and fled the mission at dawn the next day. The women, children, and some of the men ran into the hills in the early morning hours. Others stayed to fight the presidio soldiers who arrived in force from their fort near the mission. As people fled, they drove livestock and carried other provisions and goods with them. The leaders needed to feed and shelter over 1,000 women, men, and children who moved into exile. They also used these things to gift the many allies they sought as they headed to the area around Buena Vista Lake in Yokuts territory.

Andrés Sagimomatsse, an *alcalde* at Mission Santa Bárbara and one of the leaders, chose three Yokuts men, all *cimarrones*, to be envoys for the group to get help from Yokuts villages. Hilarión Chaaj had been born at a Yokuts village on Buena Vista Lake, affiliated with the mission after he moved to Najalayegua, a large and politically important town on the upper Santa Inés River. He became one of 105 persons from that village who affiliated with Mission Santa Inés. Hilarión had fled the mission earlier. José Venadero came from Siguaya, a village on a stream in the higher mountains of the Santa Inés mountain range. His wife grew up in a village near the southern San Joaquin Valley, where the rebels headed. Luís Calala, the third messenger, had a brother who was the chief of Taxlipu, a Chumash village in San Emigdio Canyon, just south of Buena Vista Lake. Luis Calla and his wife had escaped Mission Santa Bárbara a few years earlier and lived in the southern valley in the region of Luis Calla's birth.[9]

In preparation for the war, the leaders had already sent beads to the Yokuts villages of Tachi, Telamni, Nutunutu, Wowol, and Suntaché and asked them to join. The people of Tachi and Telamni refused the beads. The village of Nutuoutu accepted them, but apparently did not join the war. The people of Wowol and Suntaché took the presents and headed for Mission La Purísima on the day that the war began.[10] During the four-month period it lasted, over 1,000 people from Mission Santa Bárbara would go into exile in Yokuts territory, in villages around Buena Vista Lake and beyond.

As the leaders moved toward Buena Vista Lake, Andrés Sagimomatsee sent messengers and gifts to Yokuts leaders and requested their presence at a meeting. At the village of the Pelones, for example, a messenger of Andrés arrived, inviting them to come and fight the troops. Half the people in Pelones said they would join the revolt; others refused. After a five-day walk, they reached Buena Vista Lake from where Andrés sent out additional envoys to each village in Yokuts territory. They held an initial meeting between Yokuts leaders and rebels and slaughtered twenty-five steers to divide up and feed the exiles and their Yokuts allies and send gifts back to the villages of their allies.[11]

The support of many Yokuts and other Indigenous people sustained the war. Within this larger geography defined by an emerging Apachería, maroon societies, and the elusive "Rio Colorado" and Mojave (Amajaba) groups, the revolt drew on interethnic and intertribal alliances.

The revolt thrived because of a unity between mission populations and independent tribes that the missionaries had long feared. The timing was important. The 1824 war took place about two years after official news arrived from Mexico about the country's independence from Spain. With it came pending changes, such as Indigenous legal equality. Those rights began to be discussed and debated in Indigenous communities. The alliances had a long history and yet involved careful negotiation and respect at each point to navigate the difficulties of the rebellion. When the war ended with a negotiated pardon for all involved, the Chumash peoples began to return to their missions.

They returned to their homelands having gained greater autonomy at their respective missions. Artisans rebuilt Santa Ines as an Indigenous space with painting and décor. The revolt remained an important history to the Chumash people.

Claiming the Missions

It is important, I think, to understand the missions as colonial and tribal places because both histories coincided as people reforged their communities, even as they still envisioned returning to their territories. This was clear when the missions began to be secularized. At Mission San Diego itself, in September of 1833, General Arguello, presiding over the Southern missions, brought together about one-fifth of the mission population, over 100 adults and their families. He said they were the people considered the "most civilized" and ready for self-governance by the padres. In this case he wanted to emancipate them from the mission to form an Indian pueblo at the place the missionaries called San Dieguito.

But when he announced this to the gathering, only those from the Indigenous territory of San Dieguito were willing to form a pueblo there. The others refused, even though the community had been very vocal about wanting what they called "their freedom" from the mission. One leader explained that good water and land existed in his territory, and he wanted to relocate there. But he only wanted his tribe to settle there. If they could not reinhabit the land, they wanted to stay at the mission. This attitude prevailed at Mission San Diego, one of many ways that one sees how memory and community stayed alive within the missions.

At Mission San Luis Rey the same thing happened in subsequent attempts to form Indian pueblos on particular Indigenous lands. General Argüello selected 449 people, almost half of the mission population, to form two pueblos at Santa Margarita and Las Flores.[12] He recounted his "surprise when an undercurrent of voices began to spread throughout the crowd and the interpreter said they wanted to speak to me." They told Argüello they did not want to leave their mission. One by one, they made it clear they wanted something different from the plan he announced: they wanted to return to their territories or be given possession of the mission proper.

The same Indigenous politics prevailed among this large group. Only four families, all born in Santa Margarita (or Topome), accepted emancipation to form a pueblo in that territory. One hundred families agreed to form a pueblo at Las Flores. They had either been born there or descended from people who claimed Las Flores as their ancestral land. The 138 adults who remained on the list had come from ten different villages surrounding the mission and had expressed the same ideas.

At San Juan Capistrano, in September 1833, the military officer Pablo Portillo called a similar meeting with those selected for emancipation and citizenship, and here he proposed to form an Indian pueblo at the mission's Rancho San Mateo. He thought this might work, as no one expressed overt resistance when they went with him to San Mateo so that he could show them where they would build their houses and the plots of land they would be given. He encouraged them to make their houses before the rains but said he could not yet supply them with horses, as they needed to be rounded up.[13]

Shortly thereafter, however, a group of Indigenous leaders came to Portillo, who had accompanied General Arguello, to express their opposition and propose that the mission itself be turned into a pueblo. Around the mission proper, they argued, "Everyone has their piece of land on which they raise crops, and they have an abundance of water, and already have their homes" and common land.[14] San Mateo, they argued, did not have the abundance of water that existed at the mission. In response, Portillo wrote Figueroa to see if this could be done, but Figueroa suspended the provisional emancipation before the distribution.[15] In the letter, Portillo also spoke up for the many who received their emancipation papers earlier but returned to the missions because they remained landless and without a means to sustain themselves. He insisted they too receive a portion of mission land, together with the rest of their compatriots at San Juan Capistrano, San Luis Rey, and San Diego.[16]

These histories of claiming possession of their ancestral lands and of the missions are not told in mission displays. Their lands and histories go unrecognized. The many ways that Native populations survived, and the burdens they lived with, are left out of a history that celebrates the institutions. Tribes whose ancestors formed part of the missions have continued to wrestle with this past and with different levels of involvement in local mission church communities.

The Persistence of Exclusion and the Myth

The myth has been attacked directly. Writer and scholar Deborah Miranda (Esselen) wrote a "tribal memoir" called *Bad Indians* that gave a non-heritage narrative of the missions, especially to establish the genealogy of violence that affected her fathers' family. Mission violence devastated the community and seemed to underline the persistently high degrees of violence against Indian women, she says (Miranda 2013, 27–30).[17] Miranda is working with the enormous archive of Isabel Meadows, who left records in Rumsien Ohlone and Esselen of their history and culture. During the last five years of her life, she lived in Washington, DC—far from home—to leave that record with the linguist J. P. Harrington.

But even as the myths prevail in many official displays, some of the tribes and people whose ancestors were associated with the missions began the slow process of reconciliation with the church. A few clergy became willing to recognize and apologize for the wrong committed by the missions against their ancestors. To acknowledge the disaster, Rev. Francis A. Quinn, bishop of the Diocese of Sacramento, apologized to the Miwok tribe during a mass he said on December 15, 2007, at Mission San Rafael. Miwok territory extended from the Golden Gate in San Francisco to northward of Bodega Bay. The Spanish founded Mission San Rafael in the middle of Miwok territory, effectively dispossessing bands and villages as the consequences of new forms of illness, labor, and confinement set in. Bishop Quinn made the unexpected apology for the atrocities committed against them to the Federated Indians of Graton Rancheria. Tribal chairman Greg Sarris accepted the apology.

The Amah Mutsun tribe, whose members descended from people on the mission roles at Missions Santa Cruz and San Juan Bautista, participated in a Mass of Reconciliation at Mission San Juan Bautista, where 19,000 Amah Mutsun people were buried during the course of the mission's existence. Bishop Richard Garcia offered a lengthy statement on December 22, 2012. He recognized the violations and asked the tribe for forgiveness for the acts committed against their ancestors. Tribal chairman Valentin Lopez accepted the apology for the Amah Mutsun tribe.

The canonization of Padre Junipero Serra in September of 2015, however, eroded the process of reconciliation for the Amah Mutsun. They
turned away from mission history toward a focus on stewardship of the
environment and developing a tribal healing practice. The Amah Mutsun
are a tribe whose ancestors were on the baptismal roles at Missions San
Juan Bautista and Santa Cruz. They decided to focus on acting as stewards of the land and sea, animal and plant life, and the well-being of the
marine world. The tribe received tens of thousands of acres of land for
their stewardship from different sources, both state and private, some land
on loan and other lands placed in the name of the tribe. Moving away from
any focus on the missions, the tribe is also placing their attention on well-
ness for each tribal member, instituting a program that involves monthly
meetings and access to mental health and other care in-between. The
Amah Mutsun program emphasizes Indigenous knowledge, environmental practices, health, and well-being.

Vincent Medina, a member of the Muwekma Ohlone tribe of the San
Francisco Bay Area, decided to join his uncle at Mission Dolores in his
role as historical curator at the mission.[18] Medina's great-great-great
-grandfather had been an *alcalde* during the mission era (Indigenous
leader and intermediary with the missionaries). Vincent decided to offer
tours through Mission Dolores that told the truth about the mission. He
took charge of the narrative and delivered it frequently to the mission's
constant parade of tour bus audiences.

But going over those painful memories of a place built on unceded
and unacknowledged land became too much for him. Vince Medina
stopped leading tours at the mission. Medina taught himself the Chochenyo language that had been spoken by their tribe and now speaks
and writes in the language, and he teaches the language to other tribal
members.

With partners, he formed Café Ohlone in Berkeley's gourmet ghetto,
where they use all foods that had been cultivated and eaten by Ohlone
peoples. It was a huge success as a space of Indigenous knowledge and
tastes—a celebratory cultural space that fosters the rethinking of foods
and critical approaches to the colonial legacies of eating and health.

I mention these movements that offer hope because, for many Indigenous people, the Heritage Mission continues to provoke traumatic memories of violence, loss, and unspeakable disrespect of Indigenous elders and

their loved ones. To change that, many descendants of the missions are engaged in the ongoing process of reclaiming their history and defining their rights. They want to form part of the narrative of the mission's pasts but encounter the difficulty of doing that when the missions, as Heritage spaces, have been claimed by so many others.

References

Carrico, Richard. 2008. *Strangers in a Stolen Land: American Indians in San Diego County from Prehistory to the New Deal*. San Diego: Sunbelt.

Haas, Lisbeth. 2014. *Saints and Citizens: Indigenous Histories of Colonial Missions and Mexican California*. Berkeley: University of California Press.

Hackel, Steven. 2005. *Children of Coyote, Missionaries of Saint Francis*. Durham, NC: Duke University Press.

Harrington, John, Elaine Mills, Ann Brickfield, and Louise Mills. 1981. *The Papers of John Peabody Harrington in the Smithsonian Institution 1907–1957: A Guide to the Field Notes*. Millwood, NY: Cross International.

Jackson, Robert. 2005. *Missions and the Frontiers of Spanish America*. Scottsdale, AZ: Pentacle Press.

Milliken, Randall. 2009. *A Time of Little Choice*. Banning, CA: Malki Museum Press.

Miranda, Deborah. 2013. *Bad Indians*. Berkeley, CA: Heyday Press.

Panich, Lee, and Tsim Schneider. 2015. "Expanding Mission Archaeology: A Landscape Approach to Indigenous Autonomy in Colonial California." *Journal of Anthropological Archaeology* 40: 48–58.

Panich, Lee, and Tsim Schneider, eds. 2014. *Indigenous Landscapes and Spanish Missions: New Perspectives from Archaeology and Ethnohistory*. Tucson: University of Arizona Press.

Notes

1. José Francisco Ortega to Rivera y Moncada, May 5, 1775, C-A 1: 162, Bancroft Library; hereafter BL.

2. Junípero Serra to Viceroy Antonio María Bucareli, December 15, 1775, San Carlos, JSC 589, Santa Bárbara Mission Archive and Library; hereafter SBMAL.

3. Teniente José Ortega, Informe "Complot de Indios para fugarse y destruir los," January 31, 1776, San Diego, C-A 1: 216–232, BL.

4. Fray Fermín Francisco Lasuén to Juan Prestamero, January 28, 1776, San Diego, JSC 616, SBMAL.

5. José Francisco de Ortega, Teniente y Comandante, Informe, May 1, 1778, San Diego, C-A 1: 289, BL.

6. Informe, December 31, 1824, Santa Inés, SBMAL.

7. July 15, l825, CA-18: 149–50, BL.

8. Fray Sarría a José Maríano Estrada, February 27, 1824, CMD 2579, SBMAL.

9. John Johnson, ms. on eleven villages of the Santa Barbara Backcountry, Santa Barbara (undated): 10.

10. Father Juan Cabot to Governor Argüello, February 28, 1824, Misión, C-A 1, BL.

11. Interrogatorio de los Indios, June 1–3, l824, Santa Bárbara, FAC 667, De la Guerra Collection, SBMAL.

12. [No date], "Lista de los Neófitos de la Misión de San Luis Rey que pueden salir de la neofía por ser emancipados según sus circunstancias," C-B 31, pt. 1: 123–26, Vallejo Collection, BL.

13. Pablo de la Portillo a José Figueroa, September 21, 1833 (dated October 12, 1833), C-B 31:128–29, Vallejo Collection, BL

14. Pablo de la Portillo a José Figueroa, October 12, 1833, C-B 31, pt. 1:130–31, Vallejo Collection, BL.

15. José Figueroa a Pablo Portillo, October 25, 1833, C-B 31, pt. 1: 132, Vallejo Collection, BL.

16. Pablo de la Portillo a José Figueroa, October 12, 1833, C-B 31, pt. 1: 113, Vallejo Collection, BL.

17. Miranda is currently writing a study of and poetic work about Meadows and others. To pursue these references, see Harrington et al. (1981).

18. "Q and A with Vincent Medina," by Mariko Conner, September 16, 2014, heydaybooks.com/qa, with Vincent Medina.

Reclaiming Cha'alayash through Applied Decolonization

Intervening and Indigenizing the Narrative in, around, and about California's Sites of Conscience

DEANA DARTT

The term "decolonization" has become a term widely associated with performative non-Native activities. While many Native scholars agree that decolonization is NOT a metaphor (Tuck and Yang 2014) (many others (Indigenous and non-Indigenous alike) have continued to discuss what the concept could mean in practice. Much of this dialogue around the theory of decolonization fails to identify actions needed to create lasting, systemic change, for fear of yet another perfunctory, box-checking endeavor that undermines Native leadership and lasting change. My research and consulting work has yielded a set of practical applications that can lead to a decolonizing intervention that serves to disrupt Western ideologies, reintegrate Native values, and anchor Native goals and leadership for lasting change. This chapter explores a multi-phase project—rooted in the principles of applied decolonization—called the Indigenous Coast Narrative Project (ICNP), which confronts the systemic erasure of Indian narratives by the California mission system and its legacy and presents a Native-driven effort to disrupt pervasive, corrosive, and false narratives with the anchoring of a Native one.

Missions: Sites of Teaching, Sites of Trauma

Mission sites in California continue to educate thousands of residents, tourists, and K-12 classes every year. These contested sites serve as event venues for weddings and parishioner gathering places and as backdrops for a variety of corporate gala fundraisers. Their museum spaces host tens of thousands of fourth-grade students every spring as teachers scramble to provide interesting supplemental content for their social studies curriculum, which mandates an introduction the colonization of the state by Spain and the Franciscan mission system. Mission museums offer programs designed to supplement the fulfillment of those educational standards, and public and private schools in turn provide museums with much-needed funding through entrance fees.

The curriculum standards, "California: A Changing State," requires early education about the *history* of local Indigenous populations; however, the mandate for information about those people into the present is not required. One result of this oversight is an absence of discussions about modern Indian people, both in the classroom and in many museums. My research over the past two decades reveals that in museums and missions along the Central Coast of California, representations of living Indians, or the lived experiences of those people, are almost completely absent. Furthermore, the realities of past generations of Indian people and their struggle to survive in their homelands are often glossed over. Brutal truths pertaining to treatment of Native people at the missions are missing, and the primary depictions of Native people are those of a romanticized precontact with Europeans and the mission experience.

The reality for the Native people who endured three subsequent colonial regimes, which included enslavement, destruction of language and culture, and constant policies of disenfranchisement from Native homelands, is missing in the public narrative. I have asserted elsewhere (see Dartt and Erlandson 2006, Dartt 2009) that this omission of the complicated and brutal truth is directly linked to the current disenfranchisement of coastal Californians in terms of federal acknowledgment. In areas where Native people lack status, they also struggle to assert themselves politically. Despite land, resources, and a political framework (a government-to-government relationship with federal, state, and local municipalities), Native coastal Californians have protested and saved sacred sites and cemeteries, revitalized aspects of traditional cultural practices and language, and fought for representation on advisory committees on environmental organizations. Still, landless, marginalized Natives are largely invisible in this landscape.

From north of San Francisco to San Diego County there are no federally recognized tribes, reservations, tribal museums, or visible Native presence.[1] The region, a 450-mile-long, approximately 100-mile-wide coastal plain, was one of the most densely populated areas in North America prior to European contact because of the abundance of terrestrial and maritime resources as well as the idyllic climate. Unfortunately for the Ohlone, Salinan, Chumash, and Tongva people of the area, these same qualities made it one of the most desirable regions in North America in terms of settlement and colonization. The area from Santa Barbara to Malibu remains today some of the most valuable real estate in the US. There are a multitude of causes for the absence of a visible Native presence, but I propose that a primary reason for the continued marginalization and ongoing lack of acknowledgment of the 250,000[2] non-federally recognized Native people occupying the Central Coast is the skewed public histories and continuing misrepresentations of Native life. While a complicated and multi-faceted issue, I assert that public representations of Native histories serve to further the notion of extinction in the minds of thousands of museum goers annually, undermining our efforts to reclaim our homelands and heritage in any sustained and supported effort. Also absent are examples of more recent activism and cultural revitalization efforts that include a Native language and cultural knowledge resurgence. Rarely reflected in the stories crafted by museums are examples of resistance, resilience, and the many facets of unprecedented revitalization among Native groups. This absence leads to a public memory about Native life that is radically different than the lived experiences of the local Indian community.

In addition to the analysis of absent or incomplete narrative, my research also exposed dominant narratives that lay the foundation of understanding about Native life in the Central Coast region and do this through the lens of Native community members' perceptions. The foundation of my research included a series of interviews and observations within Central Coast Indian / mixed heritage communities and the museums situated within those communities. This work (Dartt-Newton 2009) presented examples of the dominant messages that are observable in exhibits—the foundational forms of pedagogy in the museum—as well as insight into the perspectives of the docents and staff charged with interpreting them for the public. It then explored alternative narratives that are more closely tied to the lived experiences of Indian people through interviews and questionnaires, completing the first systematic analysis of Native perceptions of Native representations in museums ever conducted. The contrast of the two data sets ultimately revealed discontinuities between the dominant discourse of Indian-ness crafted from non-Indian historical and anthropological sources and the alternative histories and experiences of the people who live within those identities.

Of the twenty-one California missions, all but one, Mission San Rafael, has a museum or exhibit space devoted to the telling of mission history. All the missions have been restored to some extent. Some have been rebuilt or replicated almost entirely, and others remain in desperate need of foundational and architectural restoration as a result of years of decay. Most missions and their gardens were restored between the late 1920s and the early 1950s, some as part of the Civilian Conservation Corps program. More than half were restored and renovated between 1920 and 1935—not coincidentally between the end of WWI and the Progressive Era. This "booster era" during the early decades of the twentieth century saw many of the Franciscan missions restored as "historical" tourist sites. They stand now as pastiches of nineteenth-century missions (Kryder-Reid 2008) with adjoining shops selling postcards and gifts. The few reconstructed rooms with staged effects of mission life, open to public view, are cordoned off, a mission spectacle in the form of concealed space that one can examine from a distance. Unreconstructed or concealed are the forbidden places, like the *monjeríos* (women's dorms), where the neophyte (newly baptized) women were locked at night to keep them "safe" from extramarital sex and where the death rate of women and girls was 10 to 1 of others as a result of damp, unsanitary, and overcrowded conditions.

Anyone who has completed the fourth grade in a California school knows that the most memorable cultural icon of the state is the California mission. Whether they made a model of one of the missions with sugar cubes for a class assignment or visited one of the Franciscan foundations and completed a "mission fact sheet," students are familiar with the life of Junípero Serra and the Spanish influence on Alta California. In fact, images of these missions were a primary factor in attracting large numbers of Americans to California between 1890 and 1940 (Toomey 2001). They gave rise to their own modern architectural traditions in numerous railway stations, public buildings, and private homes, and in 1920 the City of Santa Barbara began to require that new development follow the Spanish model (DeLyser 2005; McWilliams 1946; Rios-Bustamante 1986).

Mission museums tell the history of colonization from the perspective of the Catholic Church and its adherents in seventeen of the twenty venues. Proud of the heritage of the church and somewhat blinded to its complicity in genocide, in most mission museums (all those still owned and operated by the local diocese) staff and docents perpetuate the benevolent and beneficial nature of the Spanish mission project. At the four sites owned and operated (at least partially) by the California State Parks system (La Purisima and Sonoma are state parks, Santa Cruz and San Juan Bautista are partially operated by California State Parks), interpretations are primarily derived from scholarly historical literature and offer a more accurate and balanced portrayal of colonization. While interpretation varies depending on the controlling entity, all the sites remain deeply problematic for many reasons. Elizabeth Kryder-Reid (2016, 37) encourages us to "see behind and beyond the simulacrum" to see the ways the discursive constructions are echoed in the mission museum, though most visitors are not able or invited to take that leap of critical analysis because the narratives are presented as "truth."

My research proposes that the portrayal of a genocidal history for the people who descend from survivors of that past causes new forms of trauma. As potential sites of healing and reconciliation, the missions' (and the road that connects them, El Camino Real) unwillingness to represent hard truths in favor of a Spanish fantasy narrative further harms California Indian people. Indeed, the entire road, lined with its booster-era bells—every five miles along Highway 101—is a constant reminder of the devastation brought by Spain's campaign to exploit the resources and the people along the coastline.

Virtually nonexistent in traditional tribal communities prior to European invasion (Yellow Horse Brave Heart 1998; Duran and Duran 1995; Poupart 2003; Duran 2006), American Indian communities now struggle with alcoholism and chemical addiction, suicide, and other forms of violence at rates double the averages for mainstream American society, according to the aforementioned scholars, who characterize these maladies as symptoms of historic trauma. Although my respondents were not asked to disclose traumatic events, the effects of historic trauma can be heard in many of their responses and are observable throughout the community.

Trauma in this community stems not only from impacts of denaturalization and lack of acknowledgment of the Indian people, but also from the artificial compartmentalization of the heritage and ethnicity for a person who descends from the local Indigenous population and the colonizing population. In essence, the mixed heritage nature of the "Indian" community is the embodiment of a painful and radically misrepresented history. Although many choose to identify solely with Indigenous roots, most are products of an era of ethnic mixing among members of the initial colonizing force—the "Californio" settler population—often characterized in mission representations as soldiers. Ethnic mixture manifests as erasure of Native communities. This history is a conscious memory for some in that their extended family members may identify solely with Chican@ aspects of their heritage, and family histories of life on "Californio" ranchos are part of their shared memories. But for others, the lack of knowledge of this history and its skewed portrayal also deny healing.

Theresa O'Nell's work on depression on the Flathead reservation found that communities of blended Indian and white ancestry were conflicted to some extent, and asserts,

> not only do some Indian families become fragmented with the critical bifurcation of the world into Indian and white, good and bad, but ultimately selves are fragmented for some as well . . . neither formal regulations nor informal definitions capture the fragmented and negotiated reality of contemporary Indian identity. (O'Nell 1996, 46)

In her research, O'Nell found that ethnic mixture led to identity conflicts and the unresolved histories of that mixture, exacerbated by the incidence of ongoing oppressive influences on and off the reservation, contributing to depression and deep loneliness. Similarly, in California, the continued inauthentic and bifurcated portrayals of Indians and Mexicans in museums likewise deny the actual history in favor of a simpler narrative.

In addition to the denial of ethnic mixing, dominant narratives ignore or gloss over traumatic historical truths, essentially eliminating the lived experiences of historic suffering. Scholar Cynthia Wesley-Esquimaux (2010) asserts that "it appears that the way people remember their past, and then interpret those events as individuals or groups can also contribute to continuing disease and individual and community health issues" (Wesley-Esquimaux 2010, 62). Esquimaux, who discussed the impacts that trauma has on the individual and community sense of self, suggests that trauma is an all-encompassing "legacy of hurt" that is a source of systemic disease in Native populations. Duran's (2006) work, too, building on the work of Maria Yellow Horse Brave Heart (2000, 2003), acknowledges the intergenerational nature of historic trauma. He states, "There is a process whereby unresolved trauma becomes more severe each time it is passed on to a subsequent generation" (Duran 2006, 16). Other scholars of historic trauma agree that for Native people, healing from psychological "illness" necessitates spiritual treatment above Western biomedical remedies (see Csordas 2000). Duran, who offers a pragmatic approach to Native community "soul healing," states explicitly that the first intervention that must occur in the historically traumatized individual or community is awareness of the *origin* of the spiritual wound. As sites of remembrance (Irwin-Zarecka 1994), mission museums commemorate fantasy histories and constructed pasts that deny historic truths. Mental, emotional, and sexual abuses were experienced by coast Native people at these exact locations—the origin sites of spiritual wounds—yet Native histories are suppressed there.

As sites for potential re-traumatization, mission museums have a crucial responsibility to the communities whose cultures they represent. Because museums are sites of education for California's third and fourth graders, Indian youth are also at risk of encountering insensitive portrayals and stereotyping that have potential psychological impacts.

The implication here is that museum sites are sources of ongoing trauma rather than sites of healing and reconciliation that they might otherwise be (Chandler and Lalonde 1998).

I do not suggest that it is the sole responsibility of museums to address past atrocities or current inequities, but to ignore these hard truths serves neither the descendant community nor the public, all of whom are desirous (and in need) of the truth. And while I also do not suggest that it is the job of the museum to address the results of historic trauma, I do think it is vital for the professional and scholarly communities to understand how and why it manifests. In my experience, two primary manifestations of historic trauma on the Central Coast are community division and internalized racism, both of which regularly create barriers to collaboration. Nonetheless, I would not recommend that a history museum tackle this topic without close work with the community. Rather, it is my goal to stress the importance of continued, deep involvement with the Native community in all exhibits and programs concerning them.

This rethinking of the mission narrative both within and separate from the actual historic sites builds upon notions expressed by scholars such as Gyatri Spivak (1996) and Jose Saldivar (1997), who discuss the unworkable assumptions about culture(s) as self-contained, bounded, homogeneous, and unchanging. I add that these assumptions of culture as static are then made public "knowledge" and codified as social truths when they are expressed through the art and materials of those cultures for the purpose of tourism, education, and infotainment (Hooper-Greenhill 1992). But as Spivak suggests, I have not sought to merely expose error, but to look into how these truths have been produced and follow this with the exposure of new, subaltern truths (Spivak 1996), which can then be used in the crafting of a Native discourse. This new inclusive narrative runs parallel to or, in the most hopeful scenario, replaces the dominant one.

While most museums conduct research to determine how best to serve their various "publics" (see, for example, Barker 1999; Chadwick and Stannett 1995; Edson 1997), the overall trend in California is to ignore an Indian public. Both in their visual representations of history and in their mission statements, institutions continue to overlook this component of the population—which inadvertently disregards the fact that a significant percentage of their constituency is living Indian people. In the Central Coast region there are over 100,000 people who identify as American Indian and another 150,000 that identify as American Indian / Mexican American. This population is a diverse one, comprised of Native people indigenous to the central and southern California region, but also families relocated from other areas of the country as part of assimilation laws of the 1950s that included relocation.[3] California's Native history is one of the most complex and interesting, yet the stories in museums are often uncomplicated and stereotypical. Many Californian institutions, it would seem, prefer that Indians remain sequestered in a romantic past, far from the modern reality.

Essentialized portrayals contribute to flawed notions of Indianness for the public and for Native people themselves, romanticized notions that are impossible to achieve as modern people. These codified narratives relegate alternatives, such as the lived experiences of local people, to obscurity. Indian people are expected to live within this fabricated Indian identity, constantly expected to play a role that conforms to an unrealistic expectation, rather than being allowed to be contemporary Indian people—rooted to place and culture, yet part of a modern world (see Cordero-Lamb 2002). Consequently, struggles to assert identity and stake claims to land and sovereignty (Strong and Van Winkle 1996) are thwarted by these representations.

In addition, a substantial underserved public, Native Californians are rarely considered even as their histories are being told daily to thousands of people by hundreds of institutions. In so doing, while ignoring or marginalizing modern descendant communities, museums also deny other public groups the opportunity to share in the exciting journey of revitalization that is currently underway in these communities.

Interviews with Central Coast Native people conducted for earlier research exposed perceptions of how their histories are delivered. These narratives were seen by the majority of respondents as conveying a message about Indian people as *primitive* and *animalistic*. These portrayals, they said, relegated Indians to a past, pre-contact state, leaving no room for adaptation and change. What's more, respondents noted that existing narratives rarely (if ever) portrayed living people. These portrayals, many feared, led to public assumptions about their extinction. Some expressed concern that Californios' history is also skewed and, when portrayed at all, they are depicted as wealthy Spaniards. This is not the history that they know. They discussed with me the impacts that the dominant discourse has had on their lives, including public expectations of essentialized Indianness. Some people complained about denial of access to Native materials held in collections for revitalization efforts, while others said that the miseducation of the public perpetuates stereotypes that promote racist attitudes in California. In all, the Native people I interviewed are dismayed at the portrayal of their cultures in Central Coast museums and missions.

Though the critiques of museum practices have led to wider involvement of Native people in the telling of their stories through tribal museums and the National Museum of the American Indian, mainstream museums continue to contribute to the invisibility of Indians in several ways—modes that I have spoken about here, but also in another, more subtle way. Indian communities today are delegitimated through the tokenization of one Indian person as the "representative" consultant. A current trend is to consult with individuals with Native ancestry to design exhibits and programs—a trend that gained steam during negotiations and since the passage of the Native American Graves Protection and Repatriation Act (NAGPRA). This 1990 law, which requires agencies and institutions receiving federal money to inventory and return Native American human remains to descendent communities, inadvertently legislated the creation of relationships between tribes and museums. In one of the museums in my research area an "advisory council" appointed during initial NAGPRA compliance is now expected to speak for their communities on other issues. This and other Native advisory committees are generally called together for museum interests, which are based in unrealistic assumptions about reconciling colonist legacies. The agenda of the museum in most cases neglects alternative paradigms of knowledge as non-Indian staff people assert their ideas and plans to committee members, in hopes of ascertaining Native support for them.

Intervention

Communities across the globe are finding new ways to reassert their presence in a colonized landscape through artistic engagement. In situations where colonial players maintain control of historic sites and commemoration of atrocities, artists and curators have enacted powerful interventions through the crafting of parallel narratives. This essay explores one such possible intervention in efforts to honor the Franciscan missions and the "Royal Road" that connected them. The California Mission Foundation, a group of non-Native historians and mission supporters, seeks UNESCO World Heritage designation without consultation with Southern and Central California tribal communities. Leaders of those communities have launched a counter-campaign to reassert a strong visual presence that underscores an Indigenous agenda—one that honors their histories and contemporary realities above glorifying the devastating mission project and the perpetuation of the Spanish fantasy narrative. In the last three years we have begun planning for a multi-phase, multi-faceted intervention in collaboration with tribal leaders, artists, and scholars from the Greater California Coast. This new narrative explores ideas of migration and movement among the Indigenous people whose trade route became the Camino and privileges relationships, social alliances, and the realities of interdependence within (Alta and Baja) California before, after, and beyond the mission system.

The intervention needs to extend beyond the mission museums, however, because the narrative is so pervasive and widespread. Throughout California, not only within the missions, are constant reminders of the genocide that occurred with the arrival of the Spanish. The history is celebrated not as a source of shame, but one of pride and regional identity. This fact has never been truer than at this moment in time when the California Missions Foundation seeks UNESCO World Heritage status for the missions and the El Camino Real. While Native leaders agree that the "road that connects us" should be acknowledged and celebrated, the goal to further amplify Spanish conquest through such an effort—led by white historians—is clearly problematic. The notion of a bi-national world heritage corridor is incredibly important as it recognizes our connections as Indigenous peoples along the Pacific Ocean borderlands. This coastline has always been our home, pre-mission, pre-federal recognition, pre-Camino pre-border. Resisting definitions that serve nation-states and neocolonial agendas, a new narrative reunites Native people along the road that has joined our communities for millennia: our road—no royal road, but our connection to each other.

Throughout the US, not solely in California, Native people, largely empowered by Black Lives Matter protests, have in greater numbers begun to remove symbols of oppression and to reclaim spaces as their own. At a moment when Indigenous peoples refuse to remain silent about monuments that celebrate genocide and actions in the form of protests, vandalism, and #landback (a movement throughout the US to restore ownership of public and privately held lands to Native Americans), the California Native community has mobilized, as well.

Toppling Junípero Serra statues at several mission sites and removing three El Camino Real bells in the city of Santa Cruz are some of the ways that Native people have individually and collectively mobilized in the past year to reclaim their narrative. From a speech given at the removal ceremony of three El Camino bells from three city of Santa Cruz sites, "To the Amah Mutsun and most California Indians, the El Camino Real represents the destruction and domination of California Indian culture, spirituality, environments and humanity," Valentin Lopez (Figure 17) said. "The El Camino Real represents the theft of our lands. The El Camino Real represents incarceration, slavery, brutality, torture, rape, fear, and terror. And the El Camino Real represents the deaths of nearly 100,000 California Indians along the coast."

FIGURE 17. Amah Mutsun Tribal Band Chairman Valentin Lopez addresses a gathering of more than 150 people at UC Santa Cruz on Friday (September 16, 2021). (Jessica A. York—Santa Cruz Sentinel)

Internal Mission Museum Intervention

One of the questions I posed to museum staff and docents in 2009–10 was, "Do you think it is the job of history museums to tell the stories of contemporary groups?" Seventy-five percent responded by asking, "If we don't, who will?" In many cases, museum directors and staff apologized for the state of their exhibits, and, in fact, the majority of them want to change the dominant message. Mission museums can work as advocates for social justice, and it does not require an enormous budget to do so. Exhibits can still inform public programs, even by using outdated exhibits to discuss stereotypes and commonly held misconceptions, as long as they are accompanied by a script that addresses the shortcomings of the exhibit copy. Rather than avoid such topics because their visual representations are outdated, I propose they incorporate the issues into the storyline of the ways people of color have been portrayed in the past, some of the impacts of such erasure, and how those ideas have changed and evolved over time. In this scenario, visitors are educated about the changing role of the museum, and docents become better informed. These changes can be done with little or no money. In addition, it could be extremely useful to staff and docents to visit tribal museums to see self-representations of Native and Californio histories and the social justice issues these facilities address.

Although mission museums need work, scholar Arturo Escobar (1995) asserts that discourses such as these trap people within them. "Third world" people's histories, in his description, are constructed and codified within realms outside of their control. Certain representations become dominant and shape indelibly the ways in which reality is imagined and acted upon, where a certain order of discourse produces permissible modes of being and thinking while disqualifying and even making others impossible. This reality makes efforts by the mission museum staff and people interested to internally shift the narrative complicated, but not impossible. I have addressed the grosser issues within the mission museums in a former essay (Dartt-Newton 2011) that provides step-by-step instructions for an internal redress of these issues. It will require that museum professionals remain cognizant of their expectations. The development of a counter narrative, however, is occurring *without* the involvement of the missions themselves and is, finally, completely free of their control and approval.

Methodology: Applied Decolonization

This strategy was developed out of a painful, multi-year realization that my presence alone—though hired as a "change maker"—was not enough to create lasting systemic change. Over the course of the last ten years, my work as a museums anthropology scholar and curator in mainstream art and cultural history museums has enabled me to develop a lens to see what is needed for intervention and lasting results. Multiple stages of action, coupled with a commitment on the part of the organization, could manifest in what I call "applied decolonization."

This strategy, now proven in my work as a private consultant, disrupts, reintegrates, and anchors change in policy—the three stages, each of which is necessary for the next to take root. The following project, which stems from my research in California museums, represents that intervention in a real and visible way.

The first tenet of the Principles of Applied Decolonization is *disruption*. It requires that the student acknowledge that one's current worldview is shaped and anchored in a reality that is largely absent of Native Americans. For many, I have witnessed sincere regret that the education system in this country has failed them in this way and shame that they have been complicit in the subsequent erasure—in their lifetime—of living Native people.

The second tenet is *reintegration* and the recognition that the worldview of Native people is not only missing but a valuable and necessary set of perspectives if we as a species are to heal intergenerational trauma, among all humans and the land.

And last, the third tenet is about *rooting or anchoring* this new (old) thinking and the values of Native cultures in policy for sustained practice. The following project, currently underway in Greater California, is an example of the Principles of Applied Decolonization in practice.

Indigenous Coast Narrative Project (ICNP)

The Indigenous Coast Narrative Project is a three-phase project designed to intentionally intervene in the existing story about California's coastal Native people. Through the process of *gathering and processing, sharing* and *stewarding* first-person stories through a variety of strategies, we will anchor new understandings about the histories and cultures of the Native peoples who continue to thrive in Coastal California. This intervention is a multi-year, multi-phase effort that will change the existing narrative about coastal California Indigenous histories impacted by missionization and colonization.

The project *celebrates the connections, resistances, and revitalization of the Indigenous peoples* of the Greater (Alta, Baja, Baja-Sur) California Coast through a series of multi-media interventions throughout California. From the Bay Area all the way to the tip of Baja California, the ICNP asserts a powerful new set of values and core stories about Native California and celebrates the connections, resistances, and revitalization of California's Indigenous peoples.

The primary purpose of this project is to provide the Native communities of the Californias ways to express themselves in first-person narrative about their histories in their languages, on their terms. The goal is to be heard and seen in a place where their histories have been erased and experiences invalidated by colonial imagined narrative, which shapes public perceptions, and to take authority back from colonial strongholds such as missions, presidios, and non-Native academic institutions. This project will honor the original stewards of this land, building compassion for our struggle and reestablishing a story that connects people to the land. We believe that this is an essential step in the healing of both the land and the People.

Phase One: Story Gathering/Remembering

The first tenet of Applied Decolonization in this example is the disruption of the Western way of conducting research and collecting data. This phase, completely grounded in Indigenous methodologies, ensures not only a democratic and iterative, skill-building and sharing, Native-informed process, but also the safety and usability of the materials gathered (data). A series of in-person and online workshops, interviews, and story-gathering sessions will enable the team to populate an archive of resources for building the new set of narratives. Stories held within families that disappear when elders pass on will be gathered and stored for future generations. These stories will be gathered using Indigenous methodologies such as digital storytelling workshops, community-centered and Native-conducted interviews, and story-gathering sessions. Using Oregon's award-winning *Confluence Project* as a model for gathering and dissemination of Native perspectives, the new narrative will be developed through deep and on-going story collection and the development of an archive to create a *living continuum of family and community* histories. In so doing, the Native community will *take control of the public representations of history* and how it has been shaped, structured, validated, and dominated by outsiders.

Through the application of *Indigenous methodologies and a system of community accountability,* the development of these resources will integrate systems that are useful from the Western academic approach but be shaped and informed by an Indigenous worldview. In contrast to the historically oppressive and dehumanizing processes by which existing narratives were generated and then validated (many processes that remain in practice today), the ICNP will be an internally informed, vibrant, and complex story of resilience that empowers Native people everywhere.

STORY GATHERING FOR A NEW NARRATIVE

Digital stories form the backbone of the multiple interventions and will be featured on the ICNP website and the exhibition at the Autry Museum and will be incorporated into story maps on the Terra Stories platform—

linked to Google Maps and other points of access. Visitors to Cha'alayash and other segments of the El Camino Road will be able to access a place-based audio (and video) tour. Some stories have been (and continue to be) created through workshops where Native participants learned iMovie skills and crafted their own short films in collaboration with other community members.

Another tool we are using is story gatherings. These events are aligned with the way Indigenous people have always come together, usually in the winter, to share stories and food. Made a little more formal with a video camera, several key community members are asked to share on a specific topic for ten minutes or so each, and then the rest of the participants are invited to share theirs. And, of course, one-on-one, conversational interviews with people who prefer a more intimate setting will also be used as a way to gather stories. Protections for the cultural and intellectual property of these people and their communities are of the utmost concern, and legal and ethical standards are being developed by advisors and our community legal team.

PHYSICAL ARCHIVE

In most, if not all, of the efforts to represent Native Americans in museums and other formal and informal learning environments, the activity of outreach to community members and "data" gathering in the form of visual, textual audio material is regularly the loss of control of that material. To ensure care, protection, and proper management of this invaluable cultural and intellectual property, the ICNP has established a Native-controlled and managed archive at the Wishtoyo Foundation (www .wishtoyofoundation.org).

Part of what occurs is that during the story collection, people come forward with materials to share: old photos, land grant information, genealogies, for instance, that they reference in their story. The ICNP will make the digitization of those materials an option. From experience as Native people and researchers, we know that these documents that relate to our community history are held individually. There is a great need, if we are to craft our own story, to make these records accessible to our fellow community members. To establish an archive that is controlled by our own people is to create something for our children and grandchildren that celebrates our experiences and generates a sense of pride, unity, and connection with the land and each other, across borders, and across false divisions.

The goal of the archive is to create simple, straightforward access to primary-source and community-held resources for a greater sense of community connection and shared history. With such an archive, Native people who wish to learn more about their heritage can learn from other Native people, and students of California Native history and culture have a first-person, Indigenous narrative within which to view the history and ethnic reality of California and its first peoples.

ONLINE ARCHIVE

To protect cultural and intellectual property rights, the archive will have limited access. For this purpose, the Mukurtu Content Management System is utilized as it is an open-source free platform for use by Indigenous groups. The ICNP will continue to work closely with their support team and other tribal groups to build our archive and its database in a way that protects intangible cultural heritage and property. The ICNP also intends to access research and collaborative tools through the Reciprocal Research Network (RRN). Through RRN, partner institutions can discuss, share knowledge, and research First Nations culture in ways that aren't possible on any one institution's website.

Phase Two: Reintegrating the New (Ancient) Narrative/Relationships

As Indigenous peoples whose voices have always been silenced and whose stories have been co-opted for the convenience of a fantasy Spanish heritage, this intervention claims the road that has always connected our communities, pre-Spain, pre-mission, and pre-border. Further, it reasserts Native presence on a landscape where colonial players maintain control of historic sites and commemoration of atrocities.

The power of collaboration is the strength of this project. Working across borders with tribal and mixed-heritage communities enables rich, multivocal, multinational dialogue, underscoring interdependence and connection to community, land, and culture. A six-member binational board, tribal organization involvement, and Native curators enable first-person interpretation and a new dimension of hidden histories.

In addition to established featured California artists, the exhibition will include an open call to artists indigenous to the Pacific Coastline and juried by the six-member advisory team.

A major exhibition hosted at the Autry Museum of the American West, called, "Reclaiming El Camino: Native Resistance in the Missions and Beyond," is a collaboration between tribal leaders, artists, and scholars from the Greater California Coast. The exhibit, slated to run from December 2023 to June 2025, explores ideas of migration and movement among the Indigenous people whose trade routes were used to dominate their ways of life and continue to erase their histories. For the first time, this exhibit privileges the story of relationships, social alliances, and the realities of interdependence within California *before* the mission system and gives voice to those at the apex of this fight to reclaim our place in this region. The exhibition aims to seize this moment to educate Los Angeles and its visitors about the deep, rich history of activism and the potency of Native life in the borderland's region. It repositions the El Camino Real as a pre-Spanish ancient and well-worn trade route for Native people long before the establishment of the Franciscan missions in Baja and Alta California. Extremely timely, as the wall at the US-Mexico border fills the news, this exhibition explores how the border has served to alienate the Indigenous people of the US and Mexico from one another and tear them from their homelands—people who are interrelated through family ties and cultural heritage, on a landscape that has always shaped their lives. The physical exhibition will have a companion web-based version that will enable teachers to access the alternative narrative to their students.

While the ICNP will benefit all people, the target audience is California residents, tourists, K-12 students and teachers, Native people, and other communities of color. Current California K-12 curriculum does not adequately reflect Native historical perspectives, and Indigenous voices have often been silenced in favor of colonial perspectives (Clifford 1988). Research conducted by ICNP project director concluded that only 5 percent of residents of the central coast of California know that Native people still currently exist outside of the Santa Ynez Chumash reservation. According to a national study conducted in 2019 by the First Nations Development Institute (Reclaiming Native Truth), people cannot support and therefore be allies to Native people if they don't know they exist. In 2019, the American Indian Alaska Native Tourism Association (AIANTA) recognized that the coast of California in the missions region is sorely lacking in sites that might be attractive to tourists interested in eco-cultural tourism. A set of stories that enables California's lush coastline to come alive with songs, language, traditional ecological knowledge, and deep storytelling about past and present peoples could engage visitors from the US and abroad.

Phase Three: Leveraging Our Stories/Rooting

In the model I have developed, the way to anchor a new set of values and goals is to ensure new ideals are rooted in policy. Therefore, to codify a Native-informed narrative, the ICNP is collaborating with several organizations throughout and beyond California. To reclaim and rename the road, our goal is to partner with the California Department of Transportation (CalTrans) to literally rename the road as we remove the bells from Highway 101. In their place will be our Native names for the Road that Connects Us. From San Luis Obispo to Malibu, that name is Cha'alayash—literally, the road that connects our people.

The ICNP team is prepared to initiate the establishment of the road that connects us as a UNESCO world heritage corridor, a binational, multilingual effort to recognize the road as a necessary means for the flourishing of Indigenous life and connectivity. An effort for World Heritage Corridor status was started in 2015 by the California Missions Foundation (CMF) and was met with resistance by tribal leaders because of the manner in which it was once again promoting Spanish conquest. The CMF effort was aborted at the point that the US was pulled out of UNESCO in 2016. The new petition, initiated by tribal leadership from Greater California Native communities, is pending. Recognizing that El Camino Real was a route stolen from Native people as a part of the genocide brought to the Californias by the Spanish mission system, the ICNP's final phase will be to petition the Coalition of International Sites of Conscience for status for the road itself as well as for all the missions and presidios along the road.

Conclusions

For too long the power and resources to tell and leverage Native stories has been in the hands of those who would erase us. The missions continue to portray the history of Spanish arrival on—and usurpation of—our road in a glorified and completely fabricated manner (Kryder-Reid 2008). We no longer wait for them to rewrite this narrative or expect them to admit the devastating role the missions had on our cultures and our connections to the land. With this effort, we take it back. Moving our efforts from the tactical to strategic, we claim the road on our terms.

Ultimately, decolonization is about restoring the relationship between humans and the land that sustains us. The necessity for our survival as a species of honoring those relationships after centuries of neglect has become abundantly clear. And true decolonization, according to this theory, can only happen through the rebalancing and reintegration of the first peoples with their homeplaces and healing the trauma of forced extraction and denaturalization of those people. Utilizing the tenets of Applied Decolonization allows us a way forward. In developing actions aligned with disruption, reintegration, and anchoring, we will move toward decolonizing the road that has connected us—through narrative, policy, and—eventually—our physical reconnection with the land and stewardship of it, as well as our reconnection with our Indigenous relatives along it.

The ICNP is just one example of how the three tenets of Applied Decolonization can be used in the process of restoring balance to the land and the people. Tenet one can be accomplished through research, trainings, and personal decolonization work among organizational staff and boards, challenging the workplace to go beyond a performative land acknowledgment and moving toward disrupting Western ideals and remembering Native ways of knowing this place and the way to care for it. Tenet two means to learn what specific harms happened to the people of the lands occupied while working to identify resources an individual or organization might use to leverage privilege derived from being non-Native in Native lands. And tenet three involves working for justice and making it a part of organizational structures by anchoring one's commitment in policy, strategic plans, and missions.

For us to move toward a reality outside of the Western narratives, ideals, and values that undermine the health of our shared world, we must be conscious of the genocide that occurred under our feet.

References

Barker, Emma. 1999. *Contemporary Cultures on Display*. New Haven: Yale University Press.

Chadwick, Alan, and Annette Stannett. 1995. *Museums and the Education of Adults*. Leicester: NIACE.

Chandler, Michael J., and Christopher Lalonde. 1998. "Cultural Continuity as a Hedge against Suicide in Canada's First Nations." *Transcultural Psychiatry* 35 (2): 191–219.

Clifford, James. 1988. *The Predicament of Culture: Twentieth-Century Ethnography, Literature, and Art*. Cambridge, MA: Harvard University Press.

Cordero-Lamb, Julianne. 2002. *The Gathering of Traditions: The Reciprocal Alliance of History, Ecology, Health, and Community among the Contemporary Chumash*. Santa Barbara: University of California Press.

Csordas, Thomas. 2000. "Ritual Healing in Navajo Society: The Navajo Healing Project." *Medical Anthropology Quarterly* 14 (4): 463–75.

Dartt-Newton, Deana. 2009. "Negotiating the Master Narrative: Museums and the Indian/Californio Community of California's Central Coast." PhD diss. Eugene: University of Oregon.

———. 2011. "California's Sites of Conscience: An Analysis of the State's Historic Mission Museums." *Museum Anthropology* 34 (2): 97–108.

Dartt-Newton, Deana, and Jon Erlandson. 2006. "Little Choice for the Chumash: Cattle, Colonialism and Coercion in Mission-Period California." *American Indian Quarterly* 30 (3–4): 416–30.

DeLyser, Dydia. 2005. *Ramona Memories: Tourism and the Shaping of Southern California*. Minneapolis: University of Minnesota Press.

Duran, Eduardo. 2006. *Healing the Soul Wound: Counseling with American Indians and Other Native Peoples*. New York: Teachers College Press.

Duran, Edward, and Bonnie Duran. 1995. *Native American Postcolonial Psychology*. Albany: State University of New York Press.

Edson, Gary. 1997. *Museum Ethics*. London: Routledge.

Escobar, Arturo. 1995. *Encountering Development: The Making and Unmaking of the Third World*. Princeton, NJ: Princeton University Press.

Hooper-Greenhill, Eileen. 1992. *Museums and the Shaping of Knowledge*. London: Routledge.

Irwin-Zarecka, Iwona. 1994. *Frames of Remembrance: The Dynamics of Collective Memory*. New Brunswick, NJ: Transaction.

Kryder-Ried, Elizabeth. 2008. "Sites of Power and the Power of Sight: Vision in the California Mission Landscapes." In *Sites Unseen: Landscape and Vision*, edited by Dianne Harris and Fairchild Ruggles, 181–212. Pittsburgh: University of Pittsburgh Press.

Kryder-Reid, Elizabeth. 2016. *California Mission Landscapes: Race, Memory, and the Politics of Heritage*. Minneapolis: University of Minnesota Press.

———. 1946. *Southern California Country: An Island on the Land*. New York: Duell, Sloan & Pearce.

O'Nell, Terry. 1996. *Disciplined Hearts: History, Identity, and Depression in an American Indian Community*. Berkeley: University of California Press.

Poupart, Lisa. 2003. "The Familiar Face of Genocide: Internalized Oppression among American Indians." *Hypatia* 18 (2): 86–100.

Rios-Bustamante, Antonio. 1986. *Illustrated History of Mexican Los Angeles, 1781–1985*. Los Angeles: University of California Press.

Saldivar, Jose. 1997. *Border Matters: Remapping American Cultural Studies*. Berkeley: University of California Press.

Spivak, Giyatri. 1996. "More on Power/Knowledge." In *The Spivak Reader*, edited by Donna Landry and Gerald Maclean, 141–74. New York: Routledge.

Strong, Pauline Turner, and Barrik Van Winkle. 1996. "'Indian Blood': Reflections on the Reckoning and Refiguring of Native North American Identity." *Cultural Anthropology* 11 (4): 547–76.

Toomey, Donald. 2001. *The Spell of California's Spanish Colonial Missions*. Santa Fe: Sunstone Press.

Tuck, Eve, and Wayne E. Yang. 2012. "Decolonization Is Not a Metaphor. *Decolonization: Indigeneity, Education & Society* 1 (1): 1–40.

Wesley-Esquimaux, Cynthia. 2010. "Narrative as Lived Experience." *First Peoples Child and Family Review* 5 (2): 53–65.

Yellow Horse Brave Heart, Mary. 1998. "The Return to the Sacred Path: Healing the Historical Trauma Response among the Lakota." *Smith College Studies in Social Work* 68 (3): 287–305.

———. 2000. "Wakiksuyapi: Carrying the Historical Trauma of the Lakota." *Tulane Studies in Social Welfare* 21–22: 245–66.

———. 2003. "The Historical Trauma Response among Natives and Its Relationship with Substance Abuse: A Lakota Illustration." *Journal of Psychoactive Drugs* 35: 7–13.

Notes

1. There is one small *inland* group, the Santa Ynez Chumash (comprising only 154 members), with a land base of 127 acres, located in Santa Barbara County.

2. According to 2015 census data, people in the eight-county region identify as American Indian. I am accounting for relocated individuals belonging to tribes from outside of California by subtracting 20 percent. However, I am not accounting for possible Indigenous origins of the 15 million people who identify as Hispanic.

3. The Indian Relocation Act of 1956 (also known as Public Law 959, or the Adult Vocational Training Program) was a United States law intended to encourage Native Americans in the United States to leave Indian reservations, acquire vocational skills, and assimilate into the general population.

Violence, Destruction, and Patrimonialization of the Missionary Past

The Tohono O'odham Heritage, the Silenced Voice of the Magical Town Magdalena de Kino

EDITH LLAMAS

After many years of looking for the remains of the Jesuit priest Eusebio Kino, researchers from the Mexican National History and Anthropology Institute (INAH) announced an important discovery in the words of General Rubén García:

> The human remains of . . . the missionary, architect, explorer, historian, and preacher, the Jesuit Eusebio Kino were discovered in the town of Magdalena, Sonora (formerly Pimeria Baja) on May 24th, 1966. . . . The discovery was 255 years after he passed away, beset by painful illnesses, such as arthritis and osteosclerosis, . . . were worsened by his privations and penances, alongside fasting." (Gral. de Div. García Rubén,[1] "El Eximio Civilizador Tirolés Eusebio Kino" *El Informador*, July 4, 1966, Hemeroteca Nacional de México)

The discovery of the human remains of Father Kino in the Mexican newspaper *El Informador* forms part of a series of initiatives that started in the colonial era that have sought to preserve the memory of the Jesuit missionary's work in the region of Sonora, Mexico. For example, Jesuit chronicles followed by academic historical texts from Eugene Bolton (1870–1953) in the 1930s (Bolton 1936) and other Jesuit scholars, such as Ernest J. Burrus, SJ (1907–91) and Charles W. Poltzer, SJ (1931–2003). In addition, a bronze sculpture was given to the National Sanctuary Hall in the Capitol in Washington, DC, USA, in the 1960s to commemorate Kino's life. Moreover, the Mexican Secretaría de Tourism (SECTUR, by its acronym in Spanish) labeled Magdalena de Kino as a Magical Town [Pueblo Mágico] in 2012. All these initiatives have assured Kino the first step on the path of canonization. He was declared "Venerable of God" by Pope Francis in August 2020 (Escobar 2020; León 2020).[2]

The Jesuit priest's remains are housed in the Kino mausoleum, which was inaugurated in 1967.[3] This place was built by presidential order in collaboration with the governor of Sonora, Faustino Félix Chávez, in the municipality of Magdalena. This building was one of the main religious attractions promoted by the town of Magdalena de Kino to achieve its hasty recognition as a Magical Town in 2012.[4] SECTUR defines Magical Town as follows: "A Pueblo Mágico is a locality that has symbolic attributes, legends, history, transcendental facts, everyday life, all of which constitute magic that emanates in every one of their socio-cultural manifestations and that present today a great opportunity for touristic development" (Secretaría de Turismo 2016). To avoid confusion, from now on I will adopt Pueblo Mágico to refer to Magical Town.

Kino's mausoleum is located at the Plaza Monumental (Figure 18) on the banks of the Magdalena River, along with other tourist attractions, celebrating the imposition of the Catholic faith upon the local Amerindian population.[5] This vision excludes the agency and negotiating

FIGURE 18. Aerial view of the Magdalena Plaza Monumental, Sonora, Mexico. (© Photo by Luis Gutiérrez Martínez. Norte Photo)

capacities of the Amerindian peoples and justifies the use of violence in Christianization.

Moving away from the static mausoleum and the other tourist attractions of the Pueblo Mágico, today's Amerindian groups in the region remember their colonial past and present Christianism throughout an annual pilgrimage to honor their ancestral entities and Saint Francis in early October. In this multiday journey, local and international Amerindian groups come together, dance, and sing with decorated sticks used in their previous journeys (Schermerhorn 2019).

This study attempts to show how the Pueblo Mágico campaign promotes tourism by using notions of heritage linked to colonialist narratives that exalt a harmonious view of the past and hide truths of violence, abuse, and forced conversion against the Indigenous population in the region. I will try to use Pueblo Mágico Magdalena de Kino as a case study. I will analyze how the destruction of the Mission of Buquivaba (known today as Temple of Maria Magdalena and founded by the Jesuit father Eusebio Kino in 1687) subverts the colonial discourse used in the town's designation as Pueblo Mágico in 2012. My work is based on the hypothesis that there are diverse ways in which we can connect to what we call heritage.

For the Amerindian groups of Sonora, Mexico, and Arizona, USA, the destruction of the mission in the colonial era and the present annual pilgrimage is one, whereas for the Mexican mestizo Catholics who promote Pueblo Mágico, the mission's destruction and the current pilgrimage are two separate events. The two groups relate to the same location and sacred and human figures, even though their views can be incompatible. The first reflects inconstancy, the fragility of the conversion process, but also a special relationship with the landscape and Saint Francis. The second reproduces and justifies the colonizing discourse through "love speech or peaceful conquest" embodied in the material and visual narrative whose epicenter is the Christian faith as the extraordinary civilizing work. So, for us, "the challenge is understanding love speech as a powerful mode of subjection and effective violence" (Rabasa 2000, 5).

This essay is structured into four sections. First, I will explore how Amerindian groups were affected by the arrival of the Jesuits while occupying a binational territory (both Arizona in the USA and Sonora, Mexico). Second, I will analyze how the construction of the Magical

Town narrative for Magdalena de Kino is centered on the architectural and religious labors of the Jesuits, shown through the various tourist attractions. In the third subsection, I focus on how local Indigenous communities negotiated the forced imposition of Christianity by conducting acts of destruction and violence against Jesuits. Finally, I will explore how the Indigenous pilgrimage walk strengthens the community's connection to their ancestral lands and human and nonhuman entities, such as the figure of Saint Francis. To develop these ideas, I will draw on the work of scholar José Rabasa. In particular, I will focus on the academic's discussion of the "love speech" discourse or "peaceful conquest" (Rabasa 2000, 6) because it demonstrates that behind subjection lies effective violence, even if we refer to it as "love or peaceful conquest." As Rabasa underpins, it is possible to find the nature of "peaceful conquest" in the acts of violence led by missionaries and colonial agents (Rabasa 2000, 5). The sixteenth-century legislation, Ordenanzas of 1526, proclaimed against the use of violence in the conquest of new territories. However, far from eliminating violence, these new laws led to ways of transforming and concealing it using the formula of "love speech." Therefore, the abusive and exploitative acts of colonialization were camouflaged behind the rhetoric of love, usually expressed as "Entradas" instead of conquest or pacification, and as friendship and obedience or as a desire of the Amerindian groups to be Christian. Father Eusebio Kino offers an excellent example of this narrative:

> With these many repeated entries and missions which I made everywhere without particular expense to the Royal Treasury, there are reduced to our friendship and the obedience of the Royal Crown and to the desire to receive our holy faith more than 30,000 souls in these parts, both in this Pima nation, which has more than 16,000 souls, and in the nearby lands of the Cocomaricopos, Yumas, Quiquimas, Cutganes, Bagiopas, and Hoabonomas. Hoabonomas, etc. (Kino 1985, 14)

I will also use the concept of *patrimonialization* in reference to how scholars Xavier Roigé and Joan Frigolé consider heritage as cultural production in the present: "The production of heritage also entails the production of the past" (Roigé and Frigolé 2010, 14). Heritage deals with material and symbolic features. In this perspective, Pueblo Mágico projects and idealizes the work of Jesuit missionaries in all its tourist attractions. This recontextualization is crucial to understanding how the value of magic is attributed to this historical period.

Inside the open doors of the tourist attractions and local religious customs of this Pueblo Mágico de Magdalena, the colonialist discourse is predominantly built through the figure of Father Eusebio Kino. Therefore, his human remains in the mausoleum are presented as evidence of a history that began with Christianizing the different local Amerindian communities.[6]

By contrast, for the O'odham of the Sonoran Desert and the Indian Reservation San Xavier del Bac, their history started thousands of years ago in a land now located in the State of Sonora and southern Arizona.[7] They have a close relation to the town because it lies on their ancestral lands, which fully belonged to these Indigenous populations before the arrival of the colonizers in 1540 and the Jesuits in 1687. Nowadays, they make an annual pilgrimage in honor of Saint Francis, which they call "the walk" or *himdag* in *Odham* (Schermerhorn 2019). Through the pilgrimage to the town of Magdalena and the practice of singing and walking, the Tohono O'odham populations reaffirm their relationships with powerful entities.

Christianity has brought about violence and destruction for the Tohono O'odham culture. Nevertheless, this population has also learned how to survive by incorporating and adapting to certain Christian practices: the pilgrimage to the Pueblo Mágico de Magdalena de Kino, ritual knowledge soundscapes, and placemaking acts, walking through their sacred lands to strengthen their relationships with them and visiting Saint Francis housed in the recent chapel especially built for him, next to the Church Santa María Magdalena in the Pueblo Mágico, Sonora (Enríquez, Hernández, and León 2015; Erickson 1994; Quesada 1989; Schermerhorn 2019; Zepeda 2019).

The acts of violence perpetrated by colonial agents and missionaries in the early colonial era that forced the Tohono O'odham to settle in the Jesuit mission and convert to Christianity are echoed by the abuses of patrimonialization. In the Pueblo Mágico, Amerindians are shown only in terms of their subordination to Christianity.[8] The analyses show what part of history should be displayed, protected, and legitimized as heritage. Notions of heritage constructed around narratives of colonial power assume a symmetric view of religious memory based on the desires of present-day consumers, displacing other possible pasts and presents (Kaltmeier and Rufer 2017).

The rose-tinted narrative of Pueblo Mágico does not address the colonial violence and punishment faced by the Tohono O'odham. This colonial discourse is strengthened through the glorification of relics in the Kino mausoleum and religious and civil tourist attractions that, in the postcolonial context, convey and validate the "oxymoron of peaceful conquest" (Rabasa 2000). The paradox of historical memory constructed by the Pueblo Mágico invalidates violence through a single discourse of religious love.

In contrast, the Tohono O'odham resisted and rejected Christian and colonial order authorities by rebelling, killing several Jesuit fathers and destroying sacred images. The only chosen forms of accommodating Christianity involved appropriating religious figures and enacting practices such as a pilgrimage to Magdalena de Kino, Sonora. Thus, the colonial missionary past is linked to many economic, social, and cultural changes, but most importantly, the adoption and adaptation of Christianity. This is present even today and in different collective practices that can be considered as different forms of interpreting and relating with heritage.

A Brief History of the O'odham

It is the land that possesses people. Its influence, in time, shapes their bodies, their languages, even their religion.

—Ruth Underhill, *Papago woman*

The current largest population of the Tohono O'odham resides in the Tohono O'odham Indian Reservation, and this community is officially recognized as a nation by the US government. The community is scattered throughout the Sells District, San Xavier or Mission of San Xavier del Bac, the Gila community, and the San Lucy District.

When the Jesuits arrived in what is known today as Sonora, Mexico, and Arizona in the southwestern United States in 1687, many Native American groups had already lived in the lands for a thousand years (Ortega 2010). Many of these Indigenous groups self-identify as O'odham. The O'odham in Sonora are known as Papagos or "Desert people"; the Akimel O'odham "river people or Pima"; Hi Ced O'Odham "Sand Papagos";

and as Tohono O'odham in the United States (Alvarado 2007; Nolasco 1965; Radding 1995). Their land, known as "Papaguería" or Pimería, extends in a large expanse from Sonora to central Arizona, from the Gulf of California to the San Pedro River.

After Mexican independence in 1821, the Mexican government ruled the O'odham. However, their land was divided with the United States three decades later as a result of the Gadsen Purchase or the Treaty of Mesilla in 1853, when the Mexican government of Santa Anna agreed to sell more than 29,000 square miles of land (Acosta 2001; Servicio de Alimentación Agroalimentaria y Pesquera 2021; Ehrenberg 1854). Despite this division, the O'odham were free to cross the border to visit their relatives and their ancestral and religious places.[9]

The binational region of the O'odham encompasses the enormous desert of Sonora, whose barrenness contrasts with the surrounding forest. The seasonal rains in the highest parts compensate for the dry weather. In the words of the informants of anthropologist Gary Nabhan (2002, 5), "The desert smells like rain." Besides rain, this complex ecological landscape has groundwater, potholes, and rivers. There are also huge sahuaros that can live as long as 200 years, reaching fifty feet in height and weighing over ten tons. This cactus bears white blossoms and delicious reddish fruit that the Tohono O'odham have harvested for their rituals and subsistence for centuries (National Park Service 2015).

This region is also home to coyotes, small mammals, lizards, desert turtles, jackrabbits, and rats, all of which play a central role in the life of the Tohono O'odham. In their Mexican territory, where the O'odham are frequently called "Papago," they share their land with seven other Indigenous groups. They inhabit different *municipios* (municipalities) in Sonora, including Caborca, Saric, Puerto Peñasco, and Magdalena (Acosta 2001).

Like most Native American peoples in the territory of Mexico and the US, the Tohono O'odham in Sonora have suffered from violence since the arrival of the explorers, Jesuits, and colonizers in the colonial era and later in the hands of the Mexican government. The Spanish colonization was framed by the arrival of Jesuit Father Eusebio Kino and the influence of his religious order, which lasted until 1767, when members of the Company of Jesus were removed. The Indigenous peoples were later subjected to the colonial system with the arrival of the Franciscans.

The takeover of the Franciscan order in the Mexican territory took place after the expulsion of the Jesuits and lasted until 1850, when the last *doctrinas* [doctrines] were officially handed over to the secular clergy (Radding 1997, 3–5). During this period, the Feast of San Francisco Xavier on the 3rd of December was changed to the 4th of October to celebrate San Francisco de Assisi. According to Schermerhorn's ethnographic work, some O'odham "used to hate Franciscan Fathers" because they did not recognize them or the Feast of Saint Francis and their way to be Christians (Schermerhorn 2019, 166). This means that in the eyes of the Jesuits and later of the Franciscans, the O'odham assimilated a wrong kind of Christianity (Schermerhorn 2019, 12).

Kino and the *Pueblo Mágico*

Eusebio Kino was born in Segno, Italy, in 1645. He became a part of the Company of Jesus in 1665 in Landsberg (Bavaria) and aimed to travel to China as a missionary. After several unsuccessful attempts, he ended up in New Spain in 1681. In 1687, Alferez Juan Mateo Mange and Kino reached the Pimería Alta (which in the eighteenth century included the provinces of Sinaloa and Sonora and what is today known as southern Arizona).

This territory was inhabited by several Indigenous nations, including the Tohono O'odham (Pápagos), Comca'ac (Seris), Pimas o'oba, Ópatas (Tegüimas), Jácomes, Janos, Yumas, and Apaches. Eusebio Kino is accountable for founding twenty missions in the Pimería Alta, among them Nuestra Señora de los Dolores (Sonora, Mexico), San Ignacio de Cabórica (Sonora, Mexico), Santa María de Magdalena (Sonora, Mexico), San José de Ímuris (Sonora, Mexico), San Pedro y San Pablo de Tubutama (Sonora, Mexico), Purísima Concepción de Nuestra Señora de Caborca (Sonora), San Gertrudis del Sáric (Sonora), and San Xavier del Bac (Arizona, USA).

In a travelogue from one of their visits to Northern Sonora, after visiting the Mission of Dolores, Juan Mateo Mange writes:

> We followed a plain with a brook, with good pastures and water grounds for 12 walking leagues, until we came to the town of Saint Mary Magdalene [Santa María Magdalena] de Buquivaba, which lies alongside the river San Ignacio, with good agricultural lands and a thick cope of trees that adorn and protect it. . . . (Mange 1985 [1720], 28; my translation)

Kino christened this town Saint Mary Magdalen [Santa María Magdalena] de Buquivaba, uniting the Catholic name of the Virgin Mary Magdalen and a Spanish version of a presumably O'odham name. The history of the Pueblo Mágico Magdalena de Kino is extensive and includes several instances of destruction and preservation of what we conceive of as heritage. Today, the "magic of the town" resides in several civilian and religious attractions. The latter are, however, the ones with the most impact on the history of Magdalena, besides being the most exciting and complex. Most tourists and visitors come to the town because of the celebrations and festivities dedicated to its patron saint. However, these religious spaces were built upon the silencing of other histories, such as the attacks and destructions suffered by the town, both during and after the life of Eusebio Kino.

The "magic of the town" overshadows the significance of the civilian attractions in Magdalena (Enríquez, Lúgigo, and Valenzuela 2017, 510). However, the Palacio Municipal [Municipal Palace] of Magdalena contains murals decorated with a series about the missionary work of Eusebio Kino (Figure 19).[10] In the lower center of the wall a stained-glass window depicts the Jesuit priest on horseback. These prominent stained-glass windows are known as "the mounted priest" and decorate the main stairwell of the Palace[11] (Lorini 2017). The artist is Hugo Cesaretti Petinary. Kino appears as a founder of the Christian mission, accompanied by the figure of a church and the Spanish fleet in the central upper section of the work. It is not difficult to recognize the direct link between the Spanish conquest and the arrival of the missionaries, who founded the first church in the location. Cesaretti Petinary, who worked as a chief tourism promoter of Sonora for several years, learned which narrative elements would be most attractive to his target audience, the tourists. Both the mural and the stained-glass window utilize historical religious discourse as a touristic attraction. Therefore, missionary history is reformulated to glorify Father Kino and to achieve the coveted canonization.

The other religious tourist attractions of the Pueblo Mágico de Magdalena de Kino complement this narrative: the mausoleum of Padre Kino, the temple of Saint Mary Magdalen, and the chapel of Saint Francis.

In 1967, a year after the identification of the remains of the Jesuit priest, the mausoleum of Kino was built. The importance of recovering the body of the missionary and displaying it publicly was promoted by a coalition

FIGURE 19. Murals and stained-glass windows on the stairway of the Municipal Palace of Magdalena. (© Photo by Luis Gutiérrez Martínez. Norte Photo)

of the archbishops of Phoenix, US, Hermosillo, Mexico, and Trento, Italy. Following the big event, "Father Kino Week in America," on February 14, 1965, the governors of Arizona and Sonora presented the statue of Eusebio Kino by the sculptor Suzanne Silvercruys in Washington, DC, as part of the National Statuary Hall Collection in 1965 (Kino Historical Society n.d.). These celebrations only increased the urgency of finding the mortal remains of this Jesuit priest.

Following the study by forensic anthropologist Patricia Hernández on May 23, 1966, several researchers of INAH[12] made public the identification of the bodily remains of Father Eusebio Kino (Hernández 2016). However, this finding responded to a "presidential order" by Gustavo Díaz[13] to the Ministry of Education and from that office to the archaeologists Wigberto Jiménez and Arturo Romano Pacheco and to the historian Jorge Olvera.

After an arduous search, the archaeologists found two burials with human remains in Santa María de Magdalena: one was marked by its military attire, the other by a rusty cross placed above the skeleton. Hernández (2016, 269–72) writes that the morphometry of the skull of the "purported Jesuit priest" was incomplete, making its identification more difficult. She also points out that the remains "could belong to any other missionary," since we know no portrait or engraving of Kino, nor does he have any descendants that could be used to identify the remains. The few documents that existed about Kino were destroyed by a fire in the parochial archive in 1906. The forensic anthropologist blames irregularities in the identification process on the hastiness and the limited time frame that was given. They also point out how little evidence there is to claim that the bones truly belonged to the Jesuit priest. This has not dissuaded the many visitors the mausoleum has received to this date.

The supposed discovery of Father Kino, following Zambrano and Gnecco's (2000) reflections on the relations between memory and history, is an example of how the voice of the past is called upon from the point of view of Western hegemony as "love speech" in a new configuration: the Pueblo Mágico, which capitalizes on the history of colonization and religious conversion for touristic consumption.

This historical "recovery" constructs a homogeneous view of history and consecrates the religious past within the public sphere. These practices of "showing and exhibiting" objects/material history in the local realm are linked to constructing patrimony (Kaltmeier and Rufer 2017). The local also acquires a global dimension through the romanticizing of the universal power of religion.

The commemoration of the "discovery" of the remains of Kino and their exhibition in the mausoleum operate as a demonstration and a certification of the authenticity of this "glorious" colonial past. Local agents, such as tourism promoters and politicians, heavily rely on the discourse of love promoted by the Catholic Church. Patrimony is, therefore, rooted in the spaces, meanings, and authority of this discourse.

The Temple of Saint Mary Magdalen [Santa Maria Magdalena]: Space of Destruction, Violence, and Negotiation

The case of the temple of Saint Mary Magdalen and the image of Saint Francis tells different versions of histories regarding how the Tohono O'odham, Pimas, and Seris negotiated their Christianization (Erickson 1994; Llamas 2011; Mirafuentes 1994). These stories allow us to go beyond the discourse that preserves, reproduces, and justifies the colonizing narrative, centered on the imposition of the Catholic faith as a civilizing action, embodied in the images and remains of the Jesuit father, and premised on the erasure of Indigenous voices, as poet and scholar Deborah A. Miranda has pointed out. The mission, town, and municipality now called the Pueblo Mágico de Magdalena de Kino were marked by acts of violence and destruction through the centuries that were often attempts of negotiation made by the Amerindians. The acts were in response to severe punishments by the Spanish military and the priests (Erickson 1994, 25).

The material destruction of the Jesuit mission, the killing of priests, and the desecration of the liturgical objects carried out by several Indigenous groups during the Jesuit period (1687–1767) were a part of an agenda of resistance and adaptation and made visible the tensions and negotiation between the parties. They were also acts of self-affirmation. As the Mexican artist Eduardo Abaroa (2017) has noted, the destruction of a building or object means a rejection of what dominant powers consider relevant, which, in this case, was the church, the ornaments, and the image of San Francis.

The dispersal of the missions and the rebellions were also frequent during the Franciscan periods, both before the arrival of the Jesuits in Sonora and after their expulsion. In the post-revolutionary period in 1934, Magdalena was the site of a series of iconoclastic actions directed against its temple. As a corollary of the shadows of violence that haunt this town, Magdalena was the birthplace of Luis Donaldo Colosio, the candidate of the ruling PRI party murdered in Tijuana in 1994.[14] These events are absent from the harmonious touristic narrative.

In the seventeenth century, small Spanish settler towns, villages, missions, and military camps (*presidios*) in Sonora were surrounded by Indigenous nations who were primarily hunter-gatherers and itinerant cultivators. They migrated following seasonal cycles around vast areas of the desert in what is now northern Mexico and the Southwest of the USA. According to several Jesuits, the nations they found were groups with "an antinatural behavior" who wandered from place to place in search of food, trying to hide for fear of being confined to the missions they had already experienced.

In April 1690, General Marcos Fernández de Castañeda notified the governor of Nueva Vizcaya, Don Juan Isidro de Pardiñas, that the "Tarahumares and Conchos" had rebelled, killing Father Diego Ortiz de la

Foronda. General Fernández de Castañeda affirmed that the Indigenous governors had "declared that nine priests should be killed all at once" (González 1977, 202). He also pointed out that the Indigenous Pimas had joined the rebellion. According to research by the historian Luis González, ten missions were burned in Sonora by the rebel Pimas, Janos, Sumas Jácomes, and Ópatas, who had been "tlatoleados" Nahuatlism, which meant being persuaded through words by the Tarahumara. Several missions suffered more than one attack (González 1977).

This rebellion was the first of many through the years. Another example is the killing of the Jesuit Francisco Xavier Saeta, close to the San Ignacio River, on April 2, 1695, of which little has been found. However, the Company of Jesus strived to perpetuate the memory of those they regarded as the martyred members of the order. Therefore, they sought to exalt Saeta's name in several chronicles, stressing his faith, bravery, love, and dedication to the missional endeavor.

In a document written by Father Kino and later published in 1961 by scholar Ernest Burrus, *Life of Father Francisco Javier Saeta: Missionary Blood in Sonora*, we can observe the love speech:

> At the end of January 1695, the venerable Father Francisco Javier Saeta returned from his pilgrimage to Nuestra Señora de los Dolores . . . with affection and with his heart, had never been absent from it . . . it seems manifested his apostolic zeal, love, and very great charity for not only his dear children but also his great love for them. (Kino 1961 [1695], 68).

In this case, the narrative of love serves to warn and justify the use of violence at the hands of the militia in the eyes of the fathers of the Society of Jesus:

> While the Governor of Nuestra Señora de los Dolores grabbed the main offender by the hair, saying to the camp's captain, Antonio Solís: "This is one of the murderers"; and the captain then cut off his head with a knife; and all the others, good and bad, were so frightened and excited that they fled. Moreover, a closed order had been given that whoever let any of them go would have to take their place and die, having mixed good and bad, guilty and innocent, in an instant, between the soldiers and neighbors and Tepoquis Indians, who, for that purpose, were already with their weapons, they killed 48 Pima natives: the 18 who, as

criminals, had been left aside; and the 30 who, although innocent, because of their misfortune, having been told not to mix, were mixed in the uproar with the other 18. (Kino 1961 [1695], 126)

Eusebio Kino also narrated these conflicts in the Pimería Alta in his work *Favores Celestiales*. In the text describes the uprising that followed the death of Father Saeta:

They burnt down the house and chapel of San Ignacio, San José de los Himeris, [Sain Mary Magdalene] *Santa María Magdalena*, and the Concepción, which they had not burnt during the killing of VP. They desecrated the ornaments and destroyed all the food, livestock, and horses. (Kino 1985, 32)

The mission of Magdalena and its chapel were destroyed, and the Christian ornaments were desecrated. We can assume that after these violent actions, the people who dwelled in the missions fled from them. This may be why Alferez Juan Bautista Escalante, a military man and explorer who had traveled with Kino in 1695, is credited with the new foundation of Magdalena in 1700. Bautista Escalante belonged to Sonora's Roving Company and followed the orders of the Alcalde mayor of Jironza. He was famous for his cruelty in the "pacifications" of the Seris, whom he imprisoned and lynched.

Eleven years after the re-foundation of the town of Magdalena by Bautista Escalante, the construction of the chapel in honor of Saint Francis Xavier [*San Francisco Javier*] was finished, as indicated in the diary of Alferez Juan Mateo Mange, who accompanied Kino in the Pimería and tells us that the Jesuit himself consecrated it, and passed away in that place, where he was laid to rest.[15] The connection between the remains of Kino and the religious space was not regarded as necessary for centuries until historians like Bolton and his followers started to reconstruct the history of the Jesuit priest. This led to the presidential order commanding the search for his mortal remains. This historical evidence proved key for finding the purported coffin of the Jesuit:

He died in the house of the priest, where he had come to consecrate the chapel . . . in the town of [Saint Magdalene] Santa Magdalena, dedicated to San Francisco Xavier [*San Francisco Javier*], shown dead in a whole-body image of remarkable quality and his golden urn[16] . . . by being buried in his chapel he would accompany the dead statue since he had been an imitator of the original in his apostolic endeavors, so he could accompany him in Glory, as we believe. (Mange 1985 [1720], 145)

Nevertheless, the historian Julia Ulloa (1958) argues that the missions of the Pimería were almost totally abandoned and others were lost in the first half of the seventeenth century. This led to a new request to open new missions by the viceroy of New Spain in 1730. In the second half of that century there were other Indigenous rebellions:

Around the first half of 1751, the strange rumor announcing the imminent end of the world circulated in several missions of the Pimera Alta. This rumor reached the mission of Sonoitac, where the Indians asked their missionary whether it was true. (Mirafuentes 1988, 147)

For Luis de Saric, the Indigenous leader of the uprising of 1751, the end of the world meant getting rid of the yoke of Catholic and Spanish domination. It was the end of the European world. The rebel Pimas killed two Jesuits: Tomás Tello, a missionary in Caborca (today also a Pueblo Mágico), and Enrique Ruhen. Besides, several houses and churches were ransacked and burnt down. Both livestock and crops were severely damaged. The Jesuits were beaten to death with sticks. As Luis de Saric confessed years later, their deaths were payback for his continued mistreatment and scolding at the hands of the priests. Jesuit accounts describe frequent corporal punishment of Indigenous "converts."

The hostility of the allied rebels also reached the missions of Pitic, Saric, Sonoitac, Caborca, San Javier del Bac, and Tubutama, where Jesuit priests were also killed and Christian symbols were desecrated:

They used the recipient for the Holy Oils to carry their cigars and tobacco and the silver chains of the incensories to bridle their horses. Some rebels were seen tying their hair with cingulum and others drinking from chalices, but they mostly loved wearing the jewelry from the church in their bodies and clothing (Mirafuentes 1988, 149).

This uprising included the Tohono O'odham from [Saint Magdalene] *Santa Maria Magdalena*, according to Julia Ulloa (1958). This Indigenous nation rejected the life in the mission, the authority of the Jesuits, and that of the Spanish colonizers. This represents a far cry from the image of love presented in the mural "Kino's worldview" in the Palacio de Ayuntamiento of the Pueblo Mágico de Magdalena.

The news of this uprising soon reached the military captains and other Jesuit priests. Luis de Saric, also known as Luis Oacpicagua, the leader of the rebellion, originated from the mission of Saric, founded by Kino in the 1698s, in the Valley of Altar. That mission did not have a permanent missionary until 1750, which means that for thirty years, Indigenous authorities supervised it, and it was only visited sporadically by ministers from the region. For instance, in 1749 Jacobo Sedelmayr, who was in charge of the Mission of Tubutama since 1736, asserted that he could not look after the 4,000 souls in the missions of Tubutama and Caborca. Therefore, he involved Luis de Saric in running the mission, first as an *alcalde* and then as a governor. Luis familiarized himself with the colonial networks and with the different Indigenous groups. He established and benefited from trade routes with neighboring missions. Saric also helped the Spaniards in the military campaigns against the Apaches. When the missionaries were away, he tolerated all kinds of practices that the missionaries rejected, like dancing, drinking, and soothsaying. Most important, however, was his largesse in distributing food stock and material goods. Spaniards agreed that he "was very well regarded, loved and feared by his people because of his affability, bravery and behavior" (Mirafuentes 1988, 156–57). Thus, the fame of Saric transcended the confines of the missions, and he established a vast regional network of relations, with many followers.

In 1750, Governor Diego Ortiz Padilla granted him a personal escort because he was the one who came through every time the colonizers needed a contingent of Indian auxiliaries (Mirafuentes 1988). Taking all this into account, it is easy to understand how and why Saric was able to assemble a coalition of many different Indigenous groups throughout such a vast territory and why he promised to bring about the end of the world. The Jesuits and the Spaniards had become obstacles to Saric's agenda and his followers; thus, they decided to eliminate them.

The situation did not change much after the expulsion of the Jesuits in 1767 and the arrival of Franciscan missionaries. In November 1776, Santa María de Magdalena would again be the target of destruction and violence:

> At eight in the morning, the Seris and some piatos and Apaches fell upon the town of María Magdalena with the most ferocious assault. They set it on fire and almost demolished it in the first attempt . . . the enemies were forty and the defenders four, and that is why they took

everything without finding resistance . . . an apostate Indian called Juan Cocinero . . . was led by his infernal rage to ransack the Church, break down the door, and do the same with a box of Ornaments, they took them all away, with the Holy Chalice, and spilled on the ground the Sacred Oils, they took the vases. They destroyed the Baptismal Pile, the Chandeliers, and all that served for the liturgy; they tore the clothes and Images and took that of San Francisco Xavier out of its urn, and they broke it and threw it on the ground. (Arricivita 1792, 486)

According to the Franciscan friar Juan Domingo de Arricivita (1792), they burned the livestock and the houses of some Indians. However, it is also relevant for our analysis that the image of Saint Francis Xavier was thrown to the ground and desecrated.

The sculpture of Saint Francis found in the Chapel of Saint Francis is the central religious and tourist attraction of the Pueblo Mágico, and it holds a special meaning for the Tohono O'odham pilgrims from Arizona and Mexico who annually arrive at the Patron Saint festivities on October 3. Therefore, the saint holds different values in Indigenous and non-Indigenous contexts.

The Memories of Saint Francis and the O'odham in Motion

Magdalena de Kino is the home of Saint Francis, patron of the Tohono O'odham of San Xavier del Bac and the Papagos in Sonora (Acosta 2001, 10). Moving away from the view of the mission as a space of destruction and negotiation and toward the O'odham's relationship with Saint Francis and the pilgrimage to Pueblo Mágico Magdalena Kino, I would like to focus on how the Tohono O'odham walk and move through the landscape of the desert landscape and build on their relationships with other human and nonhuman entities.

Today's Tohono O'odham, "the walking"—what they use to refer to pilgrimage—is the major journey of the year in which they evoke their memories (Schermerhorn 2019). In this multiday journey on foot, several days before the feast in honor of Saint Francis on October 4, they sing, ask for favors, and pay their debts. When they arrive at Magdalena de Kino, they get together with the O'odham from Sonora and dance around the Temple of Maria Magdalena (Schermerhorn 2019).

For the Tohono O'odham of Arizona, the image of Saint Francis in the Church of Saint Magdalene is a replacement for the original one, as indicated by Mary Narcho:

> I do not know if it is true or not that this [Saint Francis at San Xavier] is the real one that they have here because he has no legs anymore. They just made him artificial legs, and he is very old and falling apart, and we tied him together all over the place. However, he is just half of a statue, and we just tie him up. He has got artificial legs and feet and everything. I do not know if it is true that this is the real one, but they say that they have got a new one over there. (Schermerhorn 2019, 8)

Mary Narcho's description of the contemporary image appears to reference the sculpture of the saint brought to the region by Eusebio Kino. However, the inhabitants of the mission of San Xavier del Bac assert Kino was merely an intermediary between them and the sculpture. Kino was supposed to bring the image of San Francis to the mission in San Xavier del Bac, but he could not accomplish this task because he died on the way to the mission of Saint Mary Magdalene [María Magdalena]. Because of this, the image of Saint Francis had to walk on his own from the town of Magdalena. As a result of the long journey, his legs were worn out. This is the reason the Tohono O'odham in San Xavier del Bac built artificial ones for it.

During the O'odham acts of violence and destruction of 1776, as we have seen, Frey Arricivita asserts that the image of San Francis was thrown down on the floor and broken. Therefore, we can assume that a new image of Saint Francis was manufactured. Though we cannot know for sure what happened with the image of Saint Francis between 1776 and 1934, we know that it was destroyed once more in that year, with the context of the Cristero War. The Cristero War was a confrontation between armed groups of Catholics and secular militias provoked by the policy of religious intolerance inaugurated by Plutarco Elías Calles (1877–1945), who served as president of Mexico from 1924 to 1928.

In his quest for modernizing society, the government defined the Catholic Church and its religious practices as an obstacle, and popular cults and religious images were considered idolatrous (Cejudo 2019; Guerra 2007). Because of this confrontation, in 1934, governors Tomás Garrido and Rodolfo Elías Calles in Sonora started two iconoclastic movements, recruiting young men as *camisas rojas* [red shirts] (in charge of destroying all the religious images in the temples). In large public rituals in which all the members of the community were made to participate, hundreds of images were hacked to pieces and then doused with flammable liquids and set on fire. This was the ideal ending to these ceremonies of desecration (Bantjes 1998; Cejudo 2019; Moreno 2011). Not all Catholic images had the same fate: the one of Saint Francis found inside the Church of Magdalena was taken out of its ornamental wooden coffin in 1934 and transported to the capital city of Hermosillo, where it was incinerated in the furnaces of the Sonora brewery, alongside other images (Bantjes 1998; Cejudo 2019).

This means that the sculpture of Saint Francis that can be seen today in the Pueblo Mágico (Figure 20) was manufactured in Puebla forty years ago. We cannot be sure that Eusebio Kino brought along an image of Saint Francis and intended to carry it to San Xavier del Bac. However, what stands out in Narcho's interview is the link between San Xavier del Bac and Magdalena de Kino. The community's relationship with the saint is constant.

FIGURE 20. Sculpture of Saint Francis. (© Photo by Luis Gutiérrez Martínez. Norte Photo)

For the O'odham, Saint Francis is one of the many heralded saints, as Mary Narcho asserts when she recounts how she prays for her dead husband. For this community, death is considered a transformation into a new form of life. The dead live in tiny house altars and in desert spots. In the desert landscape, saints (that is, dead relatives) are found alongside other entities known as "devils." However, their strength is not diabolical, since they are associated with the mighty mountains, the coyotes, and the giant sahuaros.

The path through the desert is a ritual procession involving small altars with the house of Saint Francis in Magdalena as the destination. Thus, the desert is not regarded as a fixed stage but rather as a continuum of movement linking the kinesthetic narrative of the bodies that move through the landscape with the memories of the life stages of the O'odham. This movement facilitates building relationships with other communities and with Christian and non-Christian "saints" and "devils," such as Narcho's dead husband (Kozak and López 1999) and other kinds of beings through songs, ritual walking sticks, and stories (Schermerhorn 2019).

This way of conceiving the pilgrimage goes beyond the classical interpretations of these rituals, which followed Turner's ideas (Turner and Turner 2011), and which regarded the point of destination as the most essential element and underestimated the importance of moving and walking as ways of establishing networks of beings and relations (Sallnow 1987; Schermerhorn 2019). Following Sallnow's and Schermerhorn's analyses, we can say that the pilgrimage to the Magdalena landscape is built through songs. The echoes of the songs accompany the walkers in a sequence. The songs are also a narrative of previous pilgrimages to Magdalena. The sound of singing recalls the landscape in the past, evoking other pilgrimages and other pilgrims, and narrates their stories. As the pilgrims move along, they encounter their saints, their devils, and other beings. Thus, the pilgrimage not only consists of walking toward Magdalena but also of singing, dancing, drinking, and eating, as well as reuniting with the past.

During this pilgrimage, each night, the walking sticks are buried together to form a movable altar, which is surrounded by the small saints and rosaries carried by the pilgrims. This arrangement echoes the one made in each house after returning from the pilgrimage. The sticks are related to Christian practices. Some of them also work as calendrical records. Their owners make marks on them and sing with a sound that recalls that of rain and wind, in the words of Frances Manuel.

Once the walkers arrive at the Magical Town of Magdalena Kino, the Tohono O'odham join other groups of Papagos, Yaquis, and Mexicans. There they all prepare to visit Saint Francis and stand in the long line waiting their turn. Upon entering the chapel, some come to ask for a favor or to pay a *manda* [promise made to the saint in return of a penance]. According to scholar Quesada's interviews with pilgrims, the saint has the ability to cure difficult illnesses and to intercede in conflicts and calamities (Quesada 1989).

The pilgrims lift the head of San Francisco from the pillow where it reposes. If it weighs too much it means that the favor will be challenging to fulfill, therefore, the payment through penance will have to be greater. If the head is light, the command will be less onerous. Interviewees refer to Saint Francis as a "very punishing saint," meaning that if the payment is not fulfilled, the saint will send a punishment. A similar ritual is performed by the O'odham of San Xavier del Bac in their church.

For their part, the Tohono O'odham of San Xavier del Bac evoke the powers of Saint Francis all through their long walk to Magdalena de Kino. Upon arrival, they place their staffs with colored ribbons, which, like transportable altars, are charged with the power of Saint Francis. While they ask the saint to intercede in their petitions, the staffs show their scrapings, which encode the memory of each walk, the memory of the roads traveled, the dead relatives, and the maintenance of the ecological forces.

With this, I can say that the Fiesta of San Francisco in the first days in the Pueblo Mágico, far from the static memory suggested by the narrative of the Pueblo Mágico, remains a space of negotiation. And that the memory that the O'odham maintain with this place remains alive through the chanting on their walks, in their staffs with ribbons, and in their continuous displacements.

Final Thoughts

Recent literature on Indigenous conversion has shifted our interpretations of how Indigenous people adopt Christianity (McNally 2000). Mexican colonial historians still pay little attention to how these groups relate directly to Catholic saints. Clearly, for the Tohono O'odham, their Catholic images have potent entities that can cry, laugh, cause diseases, provide acts of service, and walk on their own, as seen in the case of Saint Francis at San Xavier Indian Reservation and Mary Narcho's testimony.

The significance of the landscape, songs, sticks, and Saint Francis contributes to the complexity of the pilgrimage. It also gives us the possibility to think that this saint holds a different purpose and value in San Xavier del Bac and in Magdalena. The coexistence of two saints suggests that the pilgrimage is a form of memory made in movement and a mesh of ancestral practices, a missionary past, and a Christian present that has never been labeled as heritage.

Since the popularization of road travel in México, many nationals have visited nearby locations that are attractive because of their history, charming architecture, use of color, markets, handicrafts, and festivals. This form of tourism is known as *pueblear* (Fernández 2016). If we add "magic" to this mixture, the cultural tourist experience aims to not only entertain the visitors but also to transform them magically and mysteriously.

"Magic" is a word usually employed in contraposition to reason. It is frequently associated with the living traditions of *pueblos*, particularly ones with Indigenous roots. In the case of Magdalena, it is associated with the cultural value of its missionary past. Therefore, the use of "magic" in this context excludes the historical memories of the marginalized, and these actors struggle with violence and negotiation. Instead, the magical tourist campaign merely propagates a narrative of love centered on the religious magic of the miraculous acts of the fathers of the Company of Jesus in their missionary endeavors.

Archives

Hemeroteca Nacional de México (HNM), UNAM, *El Informador*, July 4, 1966.
HNM, UNAM, *El Nacional*, May 25, 1966.

References

Abaroa, Eduardo. 2017. *Total Destruction of the National Museum of Anthropology*. Mexico: Athénée Press.
Acosta, Gabriela. 2001. *Pápagos de Sonora (O'odham): Perfiles Indígenas de México*. Mexico: Documento de trabajo.
Alvarado, Neyra Patricia. 2007. *Pápagos*. Mexico: CDI.

Arricivita, Juan Domingo. 1792. *Crónica seráfica y apostólica del Colegio de Propaganda Fide de la Santa Cruz de Querétaro en la Nueva España, dedicada al Santísimo Patriarca el Señor San Joseph.* Mexico: Don Felipe de Zúñiga y Ontiveros.

Bantjes, Adrian. 1998. *As If Jesus Walked on Earth: Cardenismo, Sonora, and the Mexican Revolution.* Wilmington, DE: SR Books.

Bolton, Eugene. 1936. *Rim of Christendom: A Biography of Eusebio Francisco Kino, Pacific Coast Pioneer.* New York: Macmillan.

Cejudo, Elizabeth. 2019. "Ciudadanas y católicas: Mujeres laicas organizadas contra la campaña desfanatizadora de Sonora (1932–1939)." PhD diss. Mexico: Universidad Nacional Autónoma de México.

Ehrenberg, Herman. 1854. Map of the Gadsden Purchase: Sonora and Portions of New Mexico, Chihuahua and California. Scale 1: 2.210.000. n/p. Paper lithography. http://bdmx.mx/documento/map-gadsden-purchase-sonora -new-mexico-chihuahua-california.

Enríquez, Jesús, Hermes Hernández, and Cristina León. 2015. "Peregrinación y devoción a San Francisco: Percepciones sociales del patrimonio cultural y el turismo religioso en Magdalena de Kino, Sonora." *Revista de Estudios Urbanos y Ciencias Sociales* 5 (2): 27–48.

Enríquez, Jesús, Manuela Lúgigo, and Blanca Valenzuela. 2017. "Magdalena de Kino Sonora: Turismo Religioso en un pueblo mágico del noroeste mexicano." In *Pueblos Mágicos,* vol. 3, *Una visión interdisciplinaria,* 509–32. México: UAM/UNAM.

Erickson, Winston. 1994. *Sharing the Desert: The Tohono O'odham in History.* Tucson: University of Arizona Press.

Escobar, Amalia. 2020. "Celebran en Sonora declaración del Papa de Venerable al Padre Kino." *El Universal,* August 9, 2020.

Fernández, Ana María. 2016. "Una revisión del programa Pueblos Mágicos." *Revista de Cultura y Turismo* 10 (1): 3–34.

Gómez, Gabriel. 2013. "Historia e importancia de un proyecto sobre Eusebio Kino, SJ." *Espiral* 20 (58): 215–45.

González, Rocío. n.d. 1993. "Rubén García." Accessed December 16, 2021. http://www.elem.mx/autor/datos/129390.

González, Luis. 1977. *Etnología y misión en la Pimería Alta, 1715–1740: Informes y relaciones misioneras de Luis Xavier Velarde, Giuseppe Maria Genovese, Daniel Januske, José Agustín de Campos y Cristóbal de Cañas.* Mexico: UNAM.

Guerra, Enrique. 2007. "La salvación de las almas: Estado e Iglesia en la pugna por las masas, 1920–1940." *Argumentos* 20 (55): 121–53.

Hernández, Patricia. 2016. "El proceso de identificación en el caso de material ósea histórico: Reflexiones para la antropología forense." In *Anales de Antropología 50,* edited by Instituto de Investigaciones Antropológicas UNAM, 266–87. Hermosillo: Centro INAH Sonora.

INEGI. 2012. Censo de Población y Vivienda 2010. inegi.org.mx. Access July 2022.

Kaltmeier, Olaf, and Mario Rufer, eds. 2017. *Entangled Heritages: Postcolonial Perspectives on the Uses of the Past in Latin America.* London: Routledge.

Kino Historical Society. n.d. "Dedication of Arizona's Kino Statue: Rotunda of the U.S. Capitol." Arizona Mission Day—February 14, 1965. U.S. Capitol Statue. Accessed September 18, 2021. http://padrekino.com/kino-s-legacy/us -capitol-statue/.

Kino, Eusebio Francisco. 1961 [1695]. *Vida del P. Francisco J. Saeta, S. J.: Sangre misionera en Sonora.* Mexico: Editorial Jus.

———. 1985. *Crónica de la Primería Alta: Favores celestiales.* Hermosillo: Gobierno del Estado de Sonora.

Kozak, David, and David López. 1999. *Devil Sickness and Devil Songs: Tohono O'odham Poetics.* Washington, DC: Smithsonian Institution.

León, Judith. 2020. "Misiones del padre Kino serán patrimonio cultural de Sonora." *El Sol de Hermosillo,* August 9.

Llamas, Edith. 2011. "Los nuevos gobernadores pimas: Negociadores intercul-turales en las misiones jesuitas de Sonora." In *Los pueblos amerindios más allá del Estado,* edited by Berenice Alcántara and Federico Navarrete, 95–116. Mexico: UNAM.

Lorini, Alessandra. 2017. "The Pageant of Father Kino." *Southern California Quartely* 99 (4): 395–424.

Mange, Juan Mateo. 1985 [1720]. *Diario de las exploraciones en Sonora: Luz de tierra incógnita.* Hermosillo: Gobierno del Estado de Sonora.

McNally, Michael. 2000. *Ojibwe Singers: Hymns, Grief and a Native Culture in Motion.* Oxford: Oxford University Press.

México Desconocido. n.d. "Magdalena de Kino: Palacio Municipal" Access January 5, 2022. https://pueblosmagicos.mexicodesconocido.com.mx /sonora/magdalena-de-kino-sonora/atractivo/palacio-municipal-2.

Mirafuentes, José Luis. 1988. *El enemigo de las casas de adobe: Luis del Sáric y la rebelión de los pimas altos en 1751.* Hermosillo: Instituto de Investigaciones Históricas.

———. 1994. "Estructuras de poder político, fuerzas sociales y rebeliones indígenas en Sonora (S.XVIII)." *Estudios de Historia Novohispana* 14 (14): 117–43.

Moreno, José Alberto. 2011. "Quemando santos para iluminar conciencias: Desfanatización y resistencia al proyecto cultural garridista (1924–1935)." *Estudios de Historia Moderna y Contemporánea de México* 42: 37–74.

Nabhan, Gary. 2002. *The Desert Smells Like Rain.* Tucson: University of Arizona Press.

National Park Service. 2015. "Saguaro fruit: a traditional harvest." *Experience Your America.* www.nps.gov/sagu/learn/historyculture/upload/Saguaro-Fruit -A-Traditional-Harvest-Brief.pdf. Accessed July 2021.

Nolasco, Margarita. 1965. "Los pápagos, habitantes del desierto." In *Los Anales del Instituto Nacional de Antropología e Historia*, edited by Museo Nacional de México, 375–448. Mexico: Imprenta del Museo Nacional.

Ortega, Sergio. 2010. "Crecimiento y crisis del sistema misional: 1686–1767." In *Tres siglos de historia sonorense, 1530–1830*, edited by Sergio Noriega and Ignacio del Río, 135–84. Mexico: UNAM.

Osterhammel, Jürgen. 1997. *Colonialism: A Theoretical Overview*. Cambridge: Cambridge University Press.

Padilla, Gabriel. 2005. *Kino: ¿Frustrado alguacil y mal misionero?: Informe de Francisco Xavier de Mora, S.J., al Provincial Juan de Palacios, Arizpe, 28 de Mayo de 1698*. Guadalajara, México: Universidad de Guadalajara.

Quesada, Sergio. 1989. "La fiesta de San Francisco en Magdalena de Kino, Sonora: La influencia de Kino en un día ajeno a él." *Relaciones del Colegio de Michoacán* 10 (38): 5–28.

Rabasa, José. 2000. *Writing Violence on the Northern Frontier*. Durham, NC: Duke University Press.

Radding, Cynthia. 1995. *Entre el desierto y la sierra: Las naciones o'odham y teguima de Sonora, 1530–1840*. Mexico: CIESAS-INI.

———. 1997. *Wandering Peoples: Colonialism, Ethnic Spaces, and Ecological Frontiers in Northwestern Mexico, 1700–1850*. Durham, NC: Duke University Press.

Roigé, Xavier, and Joan Frigolé. 2010. "Patrimonialitzation and the Mercantilization of the Authentic: Two Fundamental Strategies in a Tertiary Economy." In *Constructing Cultural and Natural Heritage: Parks, Museums and Rural Heritage*, edited by Xavier Roigé Ventura and Joan Frigolé, 27–54. Girona: Institut Catalá de Recerca en Patrimoni Cultural.

Sallnow, Michael. 1987. *Pilgrims of the Andes: Regional Cults in Cusco*. Washington, DC: Smithsonian Institution.

San Xavier del Bac Mission. n.d. Tohono O'odham Nation. Accessed January 5, 2022. https://sanxaviermission.org/tohono-oodham-nation.

Santana, Agustín. 2003. "Turismo cultural, culturas turísticas." *Horizontes Antropológicos* 9 (20): 31–57.

Schermerhorn, Seth. 2019. *Walking to Magdalena: Place and Person in Tohono O'odham Songs, Sticks, and Stories*. Tempe: Arizona State University.

Secretaría de Turismo. 2016. Programa Pueblos Mágicos. Accessed January 5, 2022. https://www.gob.mx/sectur/acciones-y-programas/programa-pueblos -magicos.

———. 2019. "Magdalena de Kino, Sonora." Accessed January 5, 2022. https:// www.gob.mx/sectur/articulos/magdalena-de-kino-sonora.

———. n.d. "Pueblos Mágicos: Reglas de operación." Accessed January 5, 2022. https://transparencia.info.jalisco.gob.mx/sites/default/files/Reglas%20 de%20Operación%20Programa%20Pueblos%20Mágicos.pdf.

Senado. 2020. "Gaceta del Senado." Accessed December 16, 2021. https://www
.senado.gob.mx/64/gaceta_del_senado/documento/113680.

Servicio de Alimentación Agroalimentaria y Pesquera. 2021. "Tratado de La
Mesilla." Blog. Accessed January 5, 2022. https://www.gob.mx/siap/es
/articulos/firma-del-tratado-de-la-mesilla?idiom=es.

Tohono O'odham Nation. n.d. Official Web Site of the Tohono O'odham
Nation. Accessed October 9, 2021. http://www.tonation-nsn.gov/.

Turner, Victor, and Edith Turner. 2011. *Image and Pilgrimage in Christian
Culture.* New York: Columbia University Press.

Ulloa, Julia. 1958. "La sublevación de Luis de Saric en la Pimeria Alta." *Revista
Española de Antropología Americana* 2 (4): 167–76.

Zambrano, Marta, and Cristóbal Gnecco. 2000. "El pasado como política de la
historia." In *Memorias hegemónicas, memorias disidentes: El pasado como
política de la historia*, edited by Cristóbal Gnecco and Marta Zambrano,
11–22. Bogotá-Popayán: ICANH-Universidad del Cauca.

Zárate, José Luis. 2016. "Grupos étnicos de Sonora: Territorios y condiciones
actuales de vida y rezago." *Región y Sociedad* 28 (65): 5–44.

Zepeda, Ofelia. 2019. *When It Rains: Tohono O'odham and Pima Poetry.* Tucson:
University of Arizona Press.

Notes

1. General Ruben García was a prominent Mexican military that partici-
pated with the Constitutionalist Army (1913–20) and was director of the
National Archive of Mexico. He also collaborated with articles in different
Mexican newspapers and magazines. See (González 1993).

2. This Mexican newspaper recognized the pronouncement of the leader of
the Roman Catholic Church of the Jesuit Order, Pope Francisco (Jorge Mario
Bergoglio), who was born in Buenos Aires in 1936. Canonization involves
several steps: Servant of God, Venerable, Blessed, and Saint. In another
Mexican local newspaper of the capital of the State of Sonora (Hermosillo) on
the headlines, it is possible to see the declaration of the mission as a heritage.

3. Charles W. S. J. Polzer devotes a section of his book *Eusebio Kino Padre
de la Pimeria Alta* (Sonora, México: Gobierno del Estado de Sonora, 1984),
117–34, explaining how different groups of archaeologists, anthropologists, and
historians searched for years for the remains of Father Kino until their final
success in 1966.

4. This government project was part of the National Plan for Touristic
Development from 2000: It aimed to "extract value, consolidating and/or
reinforcing the attractive of localities with touristic potential and attractive-
ness"; Secretaría de Turismo 2016, 4, https://www.sectur.gob.mx/wp-content
/uploads/2018/10/Memoria-Documental-MRPM.pdf; consulted August 22,

2023. The program included the transference of public resources for their operation. It was directed to small towns and municipalities with a population of less than 20,000 to achieve sustainable tourism development. Once a town is selected, it must be evaluated yearly to continue in the program and to keep receiving federal funds. According to a document from the Mexican Senate from March 19, 2019, there was an increase in funds to 1571 million Mexican pesos for funding 121 Pueblos Mágicos (Senado 2020).

5. Eugene Bolton led the historical studies of the Northwestern colonial era and was a strong influence among Mexican and North American historians. Gabriel Gómez (2013) has analyzed in detail the work of Eusebio Kino in Mexican archives and other countries. He also worked with Charles W. Polzer in the analysis of Documentary Relations of the Southwest (DRSW), whose original idea came from Ernest J. Burrus, to decentralize documents from the Archives of Company of Jesus (ARSI) in Rome.

6. Colonial discourse is a perspective and epistemic tradition that still requires critique. In the eyes of Critical Heritage (Manifest of 2012); all studies need to rebuild away from colonialism because it involves relations of power and imperialism. Heritage studies emerged from Western triumphalism, excluding other actors by class, ethnicity, and religion. In the case of Pueblo Mágico Magdalena de Kino, there is a hegemonic and Eurocentric narrative centered on one interpretation, "the Divine Plan of salvation of the pagans," as Jurgen Osterhammel (1997) has underpinned.

7. According to Schermerhorn, "O'odham" is a term used as a "pluralization" of Odham. (It includes Tohono O'odham, Akimel O'odham, and Hi-ced O'odham). Also, "O'odham" is a Uto-Azteca family language, accepted by linguistics since the 1900s and commonly spoken by Pima Papago; see Schermerhorn 2019. Also, see San Xavier del Bac Mission (n.d.).

8. Marta Zambrano and Cristóbal Gnecco (2000) question how social memory is constructed and legitimized. There is a fine line between memory and history.

9. INEGI (Instituto Nacional and de Estadística y Geografía, by its acronym in Spanish). This institution is in charge of capturing and disseminating information regarding territory, resources, and population. According to the Mexican 2010 census, the *Tohono O'odham*, who live in Mexico, are 11,211; INEGI 2012, quoted in Zárate 2016, 9. Most *Odham* population lives in Arizona in 11 districts, with a total enrollment of 17,000; Tohono O'odham Nation, n.d.

10. See Secretaría de Turismo (2019); México Desconocido (n.d.).

11. Alessandra Lorini (2017) has studied the representation of Father Kino on three identical equestrian statues (Hermosillo-Sonora, Tucson-USA and Segno-Italy). The idea of presenting a Jesuit on horseback is to exalt the role of the missionaries in the colonization of North America. Lorini underpins how

the historian Herbert Bolton perpetuated and enhanced the image of the missionary and the Spanish heritage in the 1890s. This usable past had an echo during the twentieth and twenty-first centuries, especially in the states of northwest Mexico, where a multifaceted memory emerged in public places, streets, festivals, and churches.

12. INAH is the institution charged with preserving, protecting, and promoting heritage in Mexico.

13. Díaz was a member of PRI (Institutional Revolutionary Party) and served as president of Mexico from 1964 to 1970.

14. PRI (Partido Revolucionario Institucional) by its acronym in Spanish is a political Mexican party.

15. As we can see in the quotation, the chapel during the period of Father Kino was built in honor of Saint Francis Xavier. However, the devotion to this saint changed to San Francisco de Assis after the expulsion of the Jesuits and the arrival of the Franciscans in 1767. Nowadays, however, devotees refer to this place as the Chapel of San Francis. Perhaps in this way the saint who lies there could be either St. Francis Xavier or St. Francis of Assisi.

16. In this quotation, I translated from Spanish "*urna*" into English "urn," trying to respect the original Spanish text. The 1739 *Dictionary of Authorities* defines "urn" as follows: "URNA. n. a. Caxa regularly in the form of a small chest of marble, silver, gold, or other materials, in which the ashes of the corpses were placed, and deposited in the olden days, to be placed in the magnificent sepulchers . . . the large ones are called assi, in which the corpses of Kings, and persons of authority are buried." From now on, when the word "urn" appears, it is the same case, unless specified.

Conclusion

The Missions as Heritage

CRISTÓBAL GNECCO

The most salient issue of this book is the comparative perspective that it delivers. Why bring together scholars from all over the Americas to discuss the missions and their heritage meanings? Isn't it more worthwhile to restrict such a discussion to particular areas, as is normally the case, hardening long-blessed academic traditions (not only among disciplines, but also among geopolitical configurations)? Well, the comparative perspective provides an invaluable ethnographic fodder, especially when it brings to the fore issues that otherwise would not be seen. This is especially true when the comparison is made between quite different trajectories— be they historical, disciplinary, even ontological. In such cases, it is frequent to spot oddities in several fields, oddities that ask to be researched. I take that to be one of the demands and, at the same time, one of the virtues of ethnographic inquiries. When Adriana Dias and I started our ethnographic research on the heritage meanings of the Jesuit-Guarani missions in Brazil, we also got our hands on the literature on the topic produced in Argentina and Paraguay. When I asked Adriana what research there was comparing the issue in the three countries, I was astonished to learn that there was none. That is why we extended our work to the other two countries. Soon after, oddities began to appear. One of them, which is the subject of my essay in this book, concerns the uneven presence of contemporary Guarani in the missionary story, past and present. Others, to name just three more, are the disparate opinions about the Jesuit legacy; the divergent routes taken by national narratives regarding what counts in them as heritage; and the relationships (sometimes problematic, sometimes peaceful) between things religious and things secular regarding the missions. Oddities, of course, are not immanent or transcendent to anything; they are just discursive objects to be accounted for.

A comparative perspective not only reveals oddities; it also reveals coherent archival regularities, which, to a certain extent, and given the modernity-coloniality of the institutions and discourses involved, are to be expected. The more telling regularities concern the work of the disciplines and their relation to the narrative of modernity-coloniality. Disciplinary interventions operate within the arrow of modern-colonial time, which implies a single direction and a single point of arrival—however one chooses to call it: civilization, progress, development, or just the "idea," as Joseph Conrad (2016 [1899]) called it in *The Heart of Darkness*, that dreadful novel through which colonialism still speaks—that hierarchizes, marks, values. These regularities form a leading part of the scaffolding of the racial story, the most enduring and brutal narrative existing in the social architecture of our countries. The following are a few of those regularities that crisscross the essays reunited in this book.

First, the narrative of the missions as that of Indigenous birth (into civilization) and then of Indigenous death and disappearance (into the past) as the missions collapsed, turning them into disciplinary objects (of archaeology, heritage, museums). That twofold aspect of the narrative is responsible for the current division between Indigenous peoples subjected to the missions (targets of historical inquiry, whether archaeology, museums, or heritage) and contemporary ones (targets of anthropological interventions). Modern master narratives—such as that of the missions—had at their core a baptismal operation: the birth of savages into civilization. History and the Letter inaugurated their existence in modernity, not in their own terms but by being recounted by an already encrypted story that banished them from the present. The entry requirement imposed upon them into that existence was their denial. The ontology of Indigenous people in the discourse of the moderns is a long negative: they are not, they do not exist. They inhabit that discourse only as absence (what they lack) and as possibility (what they can acquire). They do not inhabit it for what they are, but for what they must cease to be. Baptism creates something new and eliminates something old. The baptized are reborn. The Indians are not only born into civilization, but what they were die in it. That is the long story of indigenism (of which the missions were the beachhead), whose ultimate meaning is redemption—a secular story as religious-laden as that of the missions. The heritage meanings of the missions describe societies that were ceasing to be—or, at least, that was what was expected of them, that they shed their vernacular atavisms—and celebrate the tragedy of their disappearance.

Such a violent act has enacted the separation of memory and history ever since: while memories speak of resilience, existence, futurity, history speaks of a secluded and bygone past. The coming of age of Indigenous societies into the historical transit was then signed as one of tutelage, imposed silence, foreclosure. They were not allowed to speak; they were told about. That is why the strong Indigenous voice that has positioned itself against the hegemonic mission story is so destabilizing for the disciplinary solidity and for the ontology of the moderns: it undermines the narrative monopoly of the lettered, takes the expression into its own hands, and occupies a sounding place in the spaces of history that previously excluded it.

As for Indigenous death, the mission narrative partakes, and not unimportantly, of the centuries-old tropes modernity built to deal with its others: the tropes of catastrophes, disappearances, collapses, all of which ended up hardening what Johannes Fabian (1983) called allochronism, the denial of coevality, which produced an all-embracing rhetoric of discontinuity. Archaeologists and heritage "experts" interpreted—and still interpret—the "archaeological record" and heritage as a set of traces of the past and as a reflection of extinct societies, the relationship of which to contemporary societies is merely anecdotical, if not entirely instrumental. In such a rhetoric the past assumes an ontological condition that is independent of the present and the future, making it possible to burn the bridges of meaning that Native communities world over have with their forebears. Archaeology and heritage continued the colonial process of "extirpation of idolatries," whereby Native religious practices were crushed; this time the disciplines sought to extirpate non-modern temporalities through the catastrophism that alluded to their contemporary annihilation.

This brutal rhetoric claimed precolonial alterity as the basis for national projects, while the contemporary other was marginalized as long as it did not dissolve into the thick and problematic sea of national unification. Indigenism and the tandem archaeology-museums-heritage provided the disciplinary input the national discourse needed to push forward its monological script. The situation in this regard has not changed much in current multicultural times. The missions as heritage are nowadays cases of the extension and exercise of the sovereignty of the multicultural state. They mean control and dominance. If the presence of the state has diminished in most aspects of social and political life, it has increased in realms it had previously unattended or taken for granted, such as things cultural and, especially, things historical. In this regard, the heritage boom of which the missions participate is an expression of the presence of the state, of the way it handles (through its controlled promotion) the diversity implied in multiculturalism.

Second, the celebration of civilization brought about by the missions is not confined to the past, of times already gone. It survives, and it is well and alive, through heritage and disciplinary practices and the way they objectify, send into the past, and write off Indigenous populations from history. The horrors of modernity-coloniality, such as the racial story, are at the root of all societies in the Americas. Yet, most contemporary accounts of the missions' legacy treat it as something good that happened to the Indians, in spite of its acknowledged evils—rather minor, the story goes, as compared to the benefits it provided. The mission story is thus surely about the present. The question to be tackled is what that story seeks to legitimate, in centuries past, but especially nowadays. What is the purpose of hiding the disruptions the missions brought about? What is the purpose of their utter naturalization, as if what happened in the past was inevitable, something to be praised (and celebrated, of course, in the heritage mood), and whose devastating consequences (dispossession, sheer violence, ethnocide) were considered mere side effects, fully unintended? The materiality of the missions—but also their representation, and the modern-colonial memories they trigger—continues to shape the understanding of mission history and underscores the ongoing power dynamics of colonialism and white/mestizo supremacy.

Third, the racial war that was started over two centuries ago by the enlightened elites that created the nation-states in the Americas was also staged in the missions—and still looms large. In this part of the world the historical temporality enacted by the modern-colonial order was a deliberate intervention in the racial scene, the place of the production of a modern-colonial mark (the national/white/mestizo history) that participated, with force, in what Michel Foucault called the "war of races," a war based on the principles of "elimination, segregation and, finally, the normalization of society" (Foucault 2000, 64–66). (That was the task of historical discourses: the normalization of temporality in the racial war.) In the meantime, the battles, the wounds, and the consequences of the war, such as racism, were hidden. (That was the task of the ideology of a unique, superior, and triumphant race, whether the white or the mestizo.) The triumphant race was deracialized from the beginning of the racial war. In their unrestricted participation in the construction of nationalism (a deracialized racist war) historical discourses underestimated, despised, or ignored nonmodern temporalities. Their racism was not only expressed in the rupture of the historical continuity of the nonmodern or in the use of typologies that devalued and subalternized their cultures. Their racism, more insidiously, took shape in the making of a racialized temporality—civilizing, teleological, progressive: the temporality that history created for the whites and the mestizos and that allowed them to have a privileged place in racial battles—and in the displacement of other temporalities. This demarcation of identities and differences is historical. Understanding historical operations, such those enacted by heritage, from the perspective of what Stuart Hall (1995, 21) called the "grammar of race" frees us from liberal and positivistic ideas about disciplinary innocence. It also frees us from the aseptic script of the mission story. Such is the task to which the essays in this book are devoted.

Fourth, archaeology and heritage are paramount participants in the theater of national and post-national production: they forge a particular temporality (teleological and past-concerned) and contribute to elevate critical symbols—things, places, sequences—to the national and post-national imagination, in which the birth to civilization played the master role. Archaeology and heritage in the Americas were carried out by and for the whites and the mestizos; they were tools for glorifying and cementing the national unity from where minorities—or majorities, as in Bolivia—were utterly banished; they provided the new temporality that bridged pre-European civilizations with the civilized, modern world implanted by the bourgeois logic while leaping over condemned colonial times. They also built a homogeneous history: fracture-less, cumulative, fluid, continuous. The archaeological and heritage eulogy of a glorious past, such as that represented by the Jesuits and the missions, is bucolic and aesthetical; it silences the tragedy of modernity-coloniality and the brutal disruption it brought on Indigenous societies. The past was emptied of conflict, of the power of power. A double operation was set in place: one pasteurized the past and the other severed Indigenous historical continuity. The national and post-national appropriation of heritage severed its connection with contemporary Indigenous societies, implying that only the whites and the mestizos (the so-called national society, without a hint of irony) were the worthy heirs of its splendor, the ones in charge of its custody and promotion, and the only ones authorized to recount its story and to stage its exhibition. The missions were a part, an important part indeed, of such a dispossession.

Finally, Native resistance and activism do not just disrupt the story of the missions as icons of civilization but also disrupt the modern-colonial order. That is, the challenge they pose is not epistemological, as if it were a matter of a different interpretation of the same heritage, but ontological, because it is a matter of different conceptions of different worlds, of different realities. In such a challenge heritage enters the field of ontological politics. Alternative curricula, critical heritage studies, new narratives, post-heritage, all are expressions of this emerging conflictive arena. The crucial and transformative issue, then, is not to write the Indigenes *into* the mission story but to *undo* that story. The issue is about deconstruction, suspension, crossing-out. Instead of eliminating the mission story, the move is to tell it differently as a way to understand and oppose the politicized heritage intentions built into it. Not a struggle around heritage (a modern concept, anyway) but the positioning of different conceptions of time, ancestors, life. The missions are thus contested not as modern referents whose narrative, property, or control are disputed to be appropriated otherwise, but as constructed (and construed) object-signs whose ontological significance is challenged.

The Indigenous voice against the hegemonic heritage meaning of the missions is very vocal in California and much less in the other two regions. There is a wealth of publications by Indigenous activists dealing with the missions as heritage in California, ranging from memoirs (Miranda 2013), to history (Chilcote 2017; Schneider 2019; Schneider, Schneider, and Panich 2020), to anthropology and archaeology (Panich and Schneider 2014; Panich and Schneider 2015), to art history (Chavez 2017, 2023; Cordero 2020). The seminal book on this regard is a collection of essays edited by Rupert and Jeannette Costo (1987) that labeled the missions as genocidal— with the disruptive force and provocation implied in the word. They have not only read differently the missions' legacy but have also positioned themselves against the heritagization of the Camino Real, the physical trail that used to link the missions. In the same frame of contestation, the iconic statue of Junípero Serra in Ventura, California, was turned down in 2020. In South America there is scant literature of Indigenous activism on the matter (de Souza et al. 2012; de Souza and Morinico 2009, 2012) but quite another story emerges when considering audiovisual media from Guarani filmmakers who have been active in putting forward an alternative vision of the missions as heritage; theirs are not complementary versions of the canonical mission story, but entirely different interpretations in their own right.

The Missions as Heritage Object-Signs

The essays in this book come from different regions and brand different approaches, but all are critical of the mission heritage intention. They all engage the missions as object-signs—that is, they don't engage them as just objects (the utter monumentality of whatever remains of them) but as signs, as something that is in the place of something else, a place where a different meaning appears, other than that overtly conveyed by the objects and the heritage discourses that surround them. The missions are much more than just merchandise that circulates in the networks of the heritage industry. Those object-signs articulate a world of uneven developments, a modern-colonial world from where their heritage meaning is uttered alongside not-so-modern worlds from where that meaning is disputed. As object-signs, the missions play quite complex roles. They are brands and emblems; icons of identity; heterotopic and heterochronic; nostalgia and authenticity.

The missions as brand and emblem of the modern—and (post)modern—states exist as if they were the exclusive property of the heritage apparatus and circulate as a logo. The existence of the brand, of the logo, of the image, is a characteristic of the nation-state (but also of the post-national state), of what Benedict Anderson (1983) called "print capitalism," thanks to which "a sort of pictorial census of the state's heritage becomes available" and a "reproducibility made technically possible by print and photography, but politico-culturally by the disbelief of the rulers themselves in the real sacredness of local sites" (Anderson 1983, 182). Thus, a general domain of the logo is achieved through this desacralization, expressed in photos, posters, stamps, coffee-table books. The conversion into a logo operates at a more comprehensive level that is not limited to the production of goods for tourist consumption. Its effect is more profound. The strength of the missions as heritage is not their mere existence in (sometimes) secluded and bucolic places, but their ubiquitous appearance as an emblem and as a logo everywhere. Their strength lies in the general reproducibility of their imagery (in souvenirs, documentaries, curricula, what have you). Their emblematic character places them at the forefront of historical wars.

The missions are icons of identity. The hegemonic narrative of the missions portrays them as embodying identity (regional and national, secular or religious), no matter that the forms of engagement of local and not-so-local populations with them greatly vary and that the identity promoted from above is highly contested. Further, the emphasis on identity trivializes other functions of the missions as heritage, the most significant of which is the hardening, if not advance, of the ontological frontier of modernity-coloniality. This trivialization is a decoy because it diverts the gaze (and the emotions) from where they can be focused more productively: on what the heritage value of the missions means nowadays beyond the truths promoted and circulated by their heritage agents. Identity, thus, plays a quite complacent role; it loses its former prominent role in the machinery of national construction to become just a wildcard in the positional movements in which postmodern history indulges.

The missions are heterotopic. The heterotopias are counterpoints to utopias (places without place, prone to be called unreal by the realists) and are thus "real places—places that do exist and that are formed in the very founding of society—which are somehow like counter-sites, a kind of effectively enacted utopia in which the real sites, all the other real sites that can be found within the culture, are simultaneously represented, contested, and inverted" (Foucault 1986, 25). The experience of the missions (as ruins, but even as living sites) is of a terrifying timelessness: it is a current experience in current object-signs, but their emotional meaning (and their heritage value) is tied to the past and to their civilizational glory. This timelessness is deliberately acted out in the heritage scene, sustained and fed by the market and by a powerful institutional apparatus (in which academic discourses play fundamental roles). The missions dramatize the past in contemporary settings full of controlled, promoted, and marketed heritage meanings. That timelessness is an index of the epoch, no longer concerned with time as much as with space. The missions are places, even though their appeal, their calling, are, pretend to be, temporal. The missions are heterotopic places, and as such they are absolutely real, so much so that the experience of visiting them, the intimate phenomenological relationship established while doing so, defines their heritage value. They are also absolutely unreal because the time they summon, the time that defines them, that gives them value, is gone by, but it is also another time, with all the denial of coevalness that one can imagine, and a time of others, in which case we are already talking about appropriation and dispossession. The missions as heterotopias juxtapose in a single "real" place many places, many incompatible places, and they are linked to various time segments; hence, they are also heterochronic. In spite of their presentation as past, they are fully (post)modern because they speak of a time lost, but one that collapses (without a sense of direction) in one place a wide range of temporal experiences. The rediscovery of a heterotopic place, warned Foucault (1986, 26), has the ability to abolish time. But the missions (ruined or otherwise), of course, were not heterotopic when they were simply missions and not heritage. That is why they are not discovered (or rediscovered, for that matter) but created as heterotopic and heterochronic, as places where the abolition of time is decreed.

The missions are a target for the market of nostalgia. They evoke the nostalgia of a vanished grandeur, in which the church and its narrative of salvation occupy the prominent place; a vanished time in which the civilizational thrust was realized without an excess of physical violence; a vanished time in which the Lascasian dream of a desired peaceful, seductive, and compassionate conquest found its best expression. Nostalgia sells well and, within the framework of the colonial relationship, turns the missions into a commoditized herald. In a paradox that can only be (post)modern the missions—abandoned, ruined, forgotten, transformed by national histories—are now valued as part of discourses of continuity and even sacredness, alternative to the brutal de-historization of the past. Nostalgia is the negation of the ruinous effects of time.

Nostalgia would be nothing without the company, not uncomfortable, of authenticity. Since a ruin (as in the case of the Sonoran and South American missions) is a product of modernity-coloniality and not a phenomenon emerging from a deep premodern past, its authenticity is a difficult balance between what remains and what is desired. The modern-colonial enactment of the ruins wants them to be authentic, opposing the abstract concept of authenticity to their concrete character. The missions at large, not just their ruins, are places for the deployment of authenticity. Their authenticity is tantamount to what Walter Benjamin called aura: its originality and singularity, its here and now. The aura is a "unique phenomenon of a distance however close it may be" (Benjamin 1968, 222). It is an unrepeatable manifestation, of course, but the heritage industry makes a titanic effort for it to be credibly close, if not anxiously repeatable; much of that task rests in its phenomenological sense, which explains the need of the visitors *to be there*, touching, seeing, feeling, seeking a repetition that is imagined possible, yet it is unattainable. But the access to the aura of the missions does not actually happen through its reproduction, but through what the heritage industry calls "valorization" (a staging, in every sense) that appeals to the sense of the authentic. The missions, whether in ruins or not, must represent an age (or an era, in a broader and emblematic sense), but its place in the (post)modern imaginary demands its aestheticization: their wrinkles cannot be seen, although they are the origin of its value. The valorization seeks to beautify the traces of the past, to facilitate their access and to put them to circulate in the market—like iconic places of the relation of the subjects (visitors, if not pilgrims) with a time gone, but desired and exoticized. Yet, the missions routinely attend to what Jameson (1991, 6, 19) called simulacrum, "a consequent weakening of historicity" that lives out of an "omnipresent, omnivorous, and well-nigh libidinal historicism." This is the nostalgia that dominates the experience of the missions as heritage and does not place the past, as Jameson would say, "beyond all but aesthetic retrieval" but, precisely, within the exclusive limits of that aesthetic retrieval—if by that we understand a retrieval that deliberately avoids the world of politics as transformation. Because the power of heritagization is its ability to neutralize (if not eliminate) the *real* historical meanings of the thing turned heritage at the same time that it delivers it to consumption as a cultural good in a space emptied of historicity—and I put *real* in italics not to refer to the modern naturalization of the real but to its meaning prior to the heritage action. That is why heritagization is capable of taking the missions out of their contested and conflictive history and placing them in an aseptic and harmless space where heritage consumers attend as unprepared and innocent as at a Sunday party.

The missions are simulacra, a weakening of historicity—the highest point of which is the social forgetting of their constitutive violence. The past as "referent" is gradually fenced off and finally erased, after which only current object-signs remain, whose meaning is vigorously filled by the pervasive and lingering civilizational project. Now the missions appear as texts whose reading is already predetermined—merchandising has a role here, but also, as in the case of the California missions, do school curricula and the widespread recreation of history.

References

Anderson, Benedict. 1983. *Imagined Communities*. London: Verso.

Benjamin, Walter. 1968. *Illuminations*. New York: Schocken.

Chavez, Yve. 2017. "Indigenous Artists, Ingenuity, and Resistance at the California Missions after 1769." PhD diss. Los Angeles: University of California.

———. 2023. "Decolonizing California Mission Art and Architecture Studies." In *The Routledge Companion to Decolonizing Art History*, edited by Tatiana Flores, Florencia San Martín, and Charlene Villaseñor Black. London: Routledge.

Chilcote, Olivia. 2017. "What the "California Dream" Means to Indigenous Peoples." *Conversation*. https://theconversation.com/what-the-california -dream-means-to-indigenous-peoples-79889#:~:text=The%20California%20 Dream%20is%20a,place%20decolonization%20at%20its%20core.

Conrad, Joseph. 2016 [1899]. *The Heart of Darkness*. New York: Norton.

Cordero, Jonathan. 2020. "Concluding Thoughts: On Decolonizing the Study of Mission Art." *Latin American & Latinx Visual Culture* 2 (3): 109–11.

Costo, Rupert and Jeannette Costo, eds. 1987. *The Missions of California: A Legacy of Genocide*. San Francisco: Indian Historian Press.

de Souza, José Otávio Catafesto, Carlos Eduardo Neves de Moraes, Daniele de Menezes Pires, José Cirilo Pires Morinico, and Mónica de Andrade Arnt. 2012. *Tava miri São Miguel Arcanjo, sagrada aldeia de pedra: Os Mbyá-Guarani nas missões*. Porto Alegre: IPHAN.

de Souza, José Otávio Catafesto, and José Cirilo Pires Morinico. 2009. "Fantasmas das brenhas ressurgem nas ruínas: Mbyá-Guaranis relatam sua versão sobre as missões e depois delas." In *História geral do Rio Grande do Sul*, vol. 5, *Povos indígenas*, edited by Arno Kern, Cristina dos Santos, and Tau Golin, 301–30. Passo Fundo: Méritos.

———. 2012. "Táanga tava mirí: São Miguel (RS, Brasil) enquanto espectro da morada dos deuses aos Mbyá-Guarani." In *Missões, militancia indigenista e protagonismo indígena*, edited by Protasio Langer and Gabriela Chamorro, 339–57. São Bernardo do Campo: Nhanduti Editora.

Fabian, Johannes. 1983. *Time and the Other*. New York: Columbia University Press.

Foucault, Michel. 1986. "Des espaces autres" (Of other Spaces: Utopias and Heterotopias). *Diacritics* 16 (1): 22–27.

———. 2000. *Defender la sociedad*. Mexico: Fondo de Cultura Económica.

Haas, Lisbeth. 2014. *Saints and Citizens: Indigenous Histories of Colonial Missions and Mexican California*. Berkeley: University of California Press.

Hall, Stuart. 1995. "The Whites of Their Eyes: Racist Ideologies and the Media." In *Gender, Race, and Class in Media: A Text-Reader*, edited by Gail Dines and Jean Humez, 18–22. London: Sage.

Jameson, Fredric. 1991. *Postmodernism or, the Cultural Logic of Late Capitalism*. London: Verso.

Miranda, Deborah. 2013. *Bad Indians: A Tribal Memoir*. Berkeley, CA: Heydey.

Panich, Lee, and Tsim D. Schneider, eds. 2014. *Indigenous Landscapes and Spanish Missions: New Perspectives from Archaeology and Ethnohistory*. Tucson: University of Arizona Press.

———. 2015. "Expanding Mission Archaeology: A Landscape Approach to Indigenous Autonomy in Colonial California." *Journal of Anthropological Archaeology* 40: 48–58.

Schneider, Tsim. 2019. "Heritage In-Between: Seeing Native Histories in Colonial California." *Public Historian* 41 (1): 51–63.

Schneider, Tsim, Khal Schneider, and Lee M. Panich. 2020. "Scaling Invisible Walls: Reasserting Indigenous Persistence in Mission-Era California." *Public Historian* 42 (4): 97–120.

Editors' Acknowledgments

We owe our thanks and recognition to several people who made this book possible. The pun in the title is a bright idea of our dear friend Tammy Bray, who was also instrumental in the acceptance by Dumbarton Oaks of the symposium in which the book originated. At Dumbarton Oaks we thank Frauke Sachse, Director of Pre-Columbian Studies, and Adrianne Varitimidis, Program Coordinator, for their kindness and their assistance in putting the symposium together; the start of the Covid pandemic prevented its in-person holding, but its virtual realization in December 2020 was successful in all regards and made it feasible for many people to attend. It was Barbara Mundy who first suggested to us to think about editing a book with the papers presented at the symposium; she also suggested sending the manuscript to Fordham University Press. As it is now evident, we took Barbara's suggestion seriously! At Fordham University Press Fredric Nachbaur, Director, and John Garza, Acquisitions Editor, guided us through the editorial process; we thank them for their encouragement, support, and patience. The two reviewers— one remains anonymous, the other, Mario Rufer, asked his name to be disclosed—made extraordinary suggestions that translated into the overall improvement of the book. Above all, we thank our colleagues, the contributors to the book; we want them to know that we are amazed and grateful at the level of their scholarship. It is an honor to have them in these pages. We hope that the readers can benefit, as we do, from the breath, depth, and scope of the arguments they put forward.

Contributors

DEANA DARTT is Coastal Chumash and Mestiza, descending from the Indigenous people of the Californias. Her scholarly and professional work strives to address the incongruities between public understanding, representation, and true acknowledgment of Native peoples, their cultures, histories, and contemporary lives. She earned her MA and PhD from the University of Oregon and has held curatorial positions at the Burke Museum of Natural and Cultural History and the Portland Art Museum, as well as teaching appointments at the University of Oregon, University of Washington, and Northwest Indian College. She recently completed a writing fellowship at the School for Advanced Research, where she revised her book manuscript for publication titled, *Subverting the Master Narrative: Museums, Power and Native Life in California.*

ADRIANA SCHMIDT DIAS holds an MA in History from the Catholic University of Rio Grande do Sul and a PhD in Archeology from the University of São Paulo. She is professor in the Department and in the Graduate Program in History at the Federal University of Rio Grande do Sul and professor in the Graduate Program in Social and Cultural Anthropology and Archeology at the Federal University of Pelotas. She has carried out research and published on Brazilian precolonial archaeology; theory and method in archaeology; Indigenous history; and cultural heritage.

CRISTÓBAL GNECCO is professor in the Department of Anthropology at the Universidad del Cauca and chair of its Anthropology Program, where he works on the political economy of archaeology, geopolitics of knowledge, discourses on alterity, and ethnographies of heritage.

LISBETH HAAS is a Professor Emeritus and Research Professor in history at the University of California, Santa Cruz. She has written three books on Indigenous California, all of which place Native knowledge and political ideas to the foreground of colonial history. Her first book, *Conquests and Historical Identities in California* (1995), examined the Spanish, Mexican, and American eras in two places and how Indigenous, Mexican, Anglo, and European immigrants defined their histories and sets of rights through conflict and settlement. More recently, in *Pablo Tac, Indigenous Scholar writing on Luiseño History and Grammar* (2011), she examines the history of Pablo Tac, born at Mission San Luis Rey in 1821, on the land of his father's tribe, and the manuscript he wrote in Rome; Tac's writing reveals how Luiseños understood and survived a drastic colonization. Her book *Saints and Citizens* (2014) similarly works from Native sources and colonial and national archives to render the significance of tribal history in California under Spain, Mexico, and the United States. She is currently co-editing the book *Indigenous Archives* (University of Nebraska Press) and cooperating with tribal Chair Valentin Lopez on his book concerning Amah Mutsun history.

ELIZABETH KRYDER-REID is Chancellor's Professor of Anthropology and Museum Studies in the Indiana University School of Liberal Arts at IUPUI, Director of the Cultural Heritage Research Center, and former Director of the IUPUI Museum Studies Program (1998–2013, 2017–20). With a background in archaeology, art history, and public history, her research investigates how humans appropriate the tangible and intangible remnants of the past and mobilize them in the constitution of social relationships. Her particular focus is the intersections of landscape and power and how materiality, whether the built environment or other forms of material culture, is deployed in the contestation of social inequalities across boundaries such as gender, race, class, ethnicity, and religion. She has disseminated this work in a variety of scholarly formats, including peer-reviewed publications and publicly accessible exhibits, forums, and online platforms. Her research focuses on landscape history and the production of public memory, particularly in the Chesapeake, the Midwest, and California. Her work on the California missions has explored their landscape history, place in public memory, and significance in settler colonial context of contemporary US cultural narratives. She has published this work in architecture history, heritage studies, and archaeology literature and in the award-winning monograph *California Mission Landscapes: Race, Memory, and the Politics of Heritage* (University of Minnesota Press, 2016). Her current research investigates toxic heritage and the ways in which places of environmental harm are mobilized and marginalized in contemporary memory practices.

EDITH LLAMAS teaches at the Universidad Nacional Autónoma de México. She has published *Esquimales, Kwakiutl, y Hurones: Los indígenas de Canadá, Alaska y Groenlandia* (Nostra, México, 2014); "Jesuitas que sufren plantas que alivian: Poderes ocultos contra la religión cristiana en las misiones del Noroeste Mexicano" (in *De la circulación del conocimiento a la inducción de la ignorancia: Culturas médicas trasatlánticas, siglos XVI y XVII*, ed. Angélica Morales, José Pardo-Tomás, and Mauricio Sánchez(México: UNAM, 2017); with Tania Ariza, "Piedras bezoares entre dos mundo: De talismán a remedio en el septentrión novohispano, siglos XVI–XVIII" (*Historia Crítica* 73 [2019]: 43–64); "Los nuevos gobernadores pimas: Negociadores interculturales en las misiones jesuitas de Sonora," in *Los pueblos amerindios más allá del Estado*, ed. Berenice Alcántara and Federico Navarrete (México: IIH-UNAM, 2011).

CHARLENE NIJMEH is the Chairwoman of the Muwekma Ohlone Tribe of the San Francisco Bay Area. Her ancestors are the direct descendants of Native people brought into the California mission system Missions Santa Clara, San José, and San Francisco de Asís. As Chairwoman, she represents over 600 tribal members who comprise the ten lineages of the previously recognized, never terminated Verona Band of Alameda County. She also chairs the board of the Ohlone Family Consulting Services, a corporation devoted to the preservation of the material and cultural heritage of the Muwekma Ohlone Tribe.

LEE M. PANICH is an Associate Professor of Anthropology at Santa Clara University. His research employs a combination of archaeological, ethnographic, and archival data to examine the long-term entanglements between California's Indigenous societies and colonial institutions, particularly the Spanish mission system. He has conducted collaborative investigations of Indigenous life at Mission Santa Clara de Asís and Mission San José in Alta California, as well as at Mission Santa Catalina in Baja California, Mexico. Panich is the co-editor of *Indigenous Landscapes and Spanish Missions: New Perspectives from Archaeology and Ethnohistory* (University of Arizona Press, 2014) and the author of *Narratives of Persistence: Indigenous Negotiations of Colonialism in Alta and Baja California* (University of Arizona Press, 2020).

MAXIMILIANO VON THÜNGEN holds a PhD in History from the University of Cologne (Germany) and a master's degree in social Anthropology from the Latin American Faculty of Social Sciences (FLACSO). Currently he works as a researcher at the Ibero-Amerikanisches Institut in Berlin. His academic research explores the meanings and uses of cultural heritage in Latin America. He is the author of *Ruinas jesuíticas, paisajes de la memoria* (Buenos Aires, 2021), in which he analyzes the restoration of the Jesuit cultural heritage of Paraguay.

GUILLERMO WILDE is researcher at the National Scientific Council and professor at National University of San Martin (Buenos Aires). Author of the book *Religion y poder en las misiones Guaranies* (2009) awarded the Latin American Association Studies Premio Iberoamericano Book Award (Toronto, 2010), the collection *Saberes de la conversión* (2011), and several articles on Indigenous history, colonial art and music, Iberian borderlands, Catholic missions of colonial Latin America, and religious conversion in comparative perspective. He has been fellow of the Wenner-Gren Foundation for Anthropological Research, the Alexander von Humboldt Foundation, the National Museum of Ethnology (Japan), and the Fulbright Commission. He has also been visiting professor at the École des Hautes Études en Sciences Sociales and the University of Paris-Sorbonne.

Index

trauma, 17, 78, 169, 173–175, 182, 188
traumatic histories/memories, 17, 78, 166, 174–175
Trinidad mission, 31–32, 47–48, 131, 134, 136–138, 140, 144, 146, 148, 150
Trouillot, Michel-Rolph, 4
Tukano, 54
Tupi-Guarani language, 54

UNESCO, 12–14, 16, 31–32, 48, 50–51, 53, 60, 89, 107, 113, 116, 133, 137, 140, 143, 149, 178–179, 187
United States, 1, 8–9, 14–15, 67, 88–89, 91, 93, 97, 191, 197–198

Uribe, Rafael, 9
Uruguay, 28, 54
Uruguay river, 13, 55
utopia(n), 5, 16, 25, 50–51, 59, 61, 116, 125–126, 228

War of the Triple Alliance, 11, 28
Ward, Caroline, 155–156
World Heritage, 12–13, 15–16, 48, 50, 60, 89, 107, 113, 116, 137, 140, 144, 149, 178–179, 187

Yaquis, 212
Yokuts, 91, 160–162
Yuma, 154–155, 199

CATHOLIC PRACTICE IN THE AMERICAS

www.ingramcontent.com/pod-product-compliance
Lightning Source LLC
Jackson TN
JSHW021934250125
77758JS00006B/39